# Offerings

A
Daily Collection
*of*
Wit *and* Wisdom
wrapped in an
Attitude *of* Gratitude

## JIM MUIR

Deep*River*
B O O K S

*Offerings: A daily collection of wit and wisdom wrapped in an attitude of gratitude*
© 2019 by Jim Muir

Published by Deep River Books
Sisters, Oregon
www.deepriverbooks.com

Printed in the United States of America

ISBN – 13: 9781632694928
LOC: 2019935645

Printed in the USA
2019—First Edition
28 27 26 25 24 23 22 21 20 19      10 9 8 7 6 5 4 3 2 1

# INTRODUCTION

There are 1,440 minutes in each day—I'm asking for three of them! Just three minutes!

That's the approximate reading time of each of the daily "offerings" that are contained in the book you hold in your hand. And if you will give me the three minutes I'm asking for, I will make you a promise: I promise that you will be challenged, motivated, and that each of these "offerings" will give you something to think about and to serve as a daily reminder that every single day contains another chance, a new opportunity, a fresh slate, and a clean page to be the absolute best person you can be.

I want readers to look at *Offerings* as a guide, a playbook, and a template to help you when you go through those rough patches that come along, when the road of life gets bumpy and visibility is poor.

Most authors devote a portion of their book to detailing the extensive and exhaustive research they conducted to come up with the words of wisdom contained within the pages of their book. I want to stress that the research I conducted for *Offerings* was to "live life." I made mistakes, and hopefully learned from them. I got knocked down and I got back up. I've enjoyed success and never let it go to my head—and have learned to deal with failures and never let them get to my heart. I've dealt with and learned from contrary and negative people, and most importantly I finally came around to accept something I've known all along—that our relationship with God through his son Jesus Christ is the single most important decision we can ever make.

I want to emphasize that there is no condemnation—zero, nada, zilch—within the pages of this book. After all, how could I possibly condemn somebody else when I'm using myself as an example for the mistakes, problems, and failures we all encounter from time to time? There is an old, often-used common expression that states: "Experience is the best teacher." Well, you hold the absolute truth of that statement in your hands right now!

I truly believe that every single person can relate to the examples and illustrations I've used in this book, and I am supremely confident that applying the simple principle of developing an attitude of gratitude detailed in the pages that follow can be a life-changing experience. I know firsthand—they changed my life!

Again . . . three minutes a day, just three minutes . . . that's all I'm asking you to give.

God's blessings to you!

*Jim Muir*

**January 1—***Today be thankful and think how rich you are. Your family is priceless, your time is gold and your health is wealth.* **—Zig Ziglar**

Since this is January 1, the start of a new year, there are many catchy phrases that could be used. However, when I tried to wrap my mind around what I wanted to say, a very familiar verse kept coming to mind: "This is the day the LORD has made. We will rejoice and be glad in it" (Psalm 118:24). I decided it would be a great one to share to start a brand-spanking new year. The powerful fact that God made this day especially for us truly is a reason to "rejoice and be glad in it."

This verse—only two short sentences and sixteen words—says so much that I could literally share it every morning for the next 364 days, and that should provide more than enough motivation for us to jump on each day with an attitude of gratitude, joy, excitement, and optimism. Think about that, wrap your mind around it, and let it sink in . . . a day the Lord has made just for us!

As we flip the calendar over to a fresh set of 365 days, let me remind you once again that a good life is when you assume nothing, trust in God, do more, need less, trust in God, smile often, dream big, trust in God, cherish small joys, laugh a lot, trust in God, and realize every single day how blessed you are for what you have.

God's blessings to you on this day that is especially for you! Have a blessed day!

**January 2—***It's not what you are that is holding you back, it's what you think you're not.***—Bob Proctor**

Today is the day for many when "resolutions" turn into "reality." It's the day when planning for life changes requires us to do more than talk or resolve to change. And regardless of what type of a resolution you've made, it is a certainty that it will require us to either start a new action or end a harmful one, period. However, the biggest problem many people will face can be found in a familiar old saying: The devil is in the details.

How many times have you had a positive thought about embarking on a new journey in life, a new direction, and immediately doubt and fear took over and your ideas and dreams were tossed to the side? If you're like most people, me included, this has happened often. When I read today's quote I thought of a phrase I had heard recently: Make sure your own worst enemy doesn't live between your ears.

Because it's that voice in your head that says you're not good enough, smart enough, gifted enough, talented enough—you fill in the word in front of "enough"—that keeps all of us from being the best person we can be. That voice keeps people from reaching out to God and it keeps people in dead-end jobs, harmful relationships, and dozens of other life-traps. Doubt and fear are the two culprits behind the statistic that shows that 75-80 percent of all New Year's resolutions fail!

Be strong, don't let doubt and fear set up residence between your ears . . . because just like today's gem states: It's not what you are that is holding you back, it's what you think you're not.

As you begin a new year, tackle a resolution or begin a new journey in your life my prayer is that you stay strong, move forward and tell the voice that says 'you can't' to be quiet.

God's blessings to you on this day! Have a blessed day!

**January 3**—*No one can go back and make a brand-new start, but everyone has the opportunity to start from this day—in fact this very minute—and make a brand-new ending.*—**Carl Bard**

I have a large desk calendar that I use to keep track of important dates, appointments, meetings, ballgames, etc. It's eighteen by twenty-four inches and at the end of each month I tear off the top sheet, which by month's end is covered with marks, doodles, phone numbers, and notes.

The outside edges are always frayed and ragged. When I pull off the old month, underneath is a bright, white month with no marks and no ragged edges. I always like the feeling of tearing the old month off and seeing a new month in front of me.

But, the beauty of today's quote is that in real life, we don't have to wait until the end of the month to see a clean slate in front of us or the start of a new year to make a resolution to change. We have the opportunity and the ability any second of any day to make a new ending. And I would be remiss if I didn't point out that making Jesus Christ a priority in your life is a great start in making that new ending.

As we continue through this first week of a new year—regardless of your start—my prayer is that you find your path to create a brand-new, meaningful, hopeful ending.

God's blessings to you on this day! Have a blessed day!

## January 4—Strength—*A river cuts through rock not because of power but because of persistence.*—Jim Watkins

If you asked one hundred people to define the word "strength," more than likely you would hear words like "powerful," "forceful," and "mighty" . . . but I doubt you would hear the word "persistence."

I've learned through the years, while traveling down a few bumpy roads, that persistence is a wonderful and much-needed quality. I'm convinced that any strength developed in life, both physical and mental, comes from persistence.

In a nutshell, persistence means you never, ever give in and you never, ever give up, regardless what you're facing. Persistence means that if you get knocked down seven times . . . you persistently get up eight. I believe with God's help, persistence is one of the greatest virtues any person can have or develop. Persistence can help ordinary people achieve extraordinary things.

As we roll along in the first week of the new year—and maybe those resolutions aren't off to a great start—remember the power of persistence and keep in mind that small, incremental steps now can lead to huge strides later. My prayer is that we can all roll along like that river, cutting through obstacles in our path—not by power, but by being persistent.

God's blessings to you on this day! Have a blessed day!

### January 5—*Where there's a will there's a way . . . sometimes.* —common expression

This old saying is one that most people have heard and said many, many times. Simply stated, it means that with "will" we can find a "way" to correct or make it through any situation or problem.

But in today's offering, I've added a single word behind the familiar old quote, because sometimes putting the will and the way together to fight through one of the many obstacles life can throw our way is not quite as easy as this little proverb states.

I have traveled so many different roads in my life—and some of them were full of potholes and quite a bumpy ride—that I understand more than most that it's very difficult sometimes to put the will and the way together. There are those who have the will but are so far off track they can't find their way, and then there are others that know the way but can't muster up the will to get back on course.

Sometimes it's not as easy as putting mind over matter and correcting a problem or "fixing" our lives. Sometimes the will and the way are miles and miles apart. So, my humble prayer today is that God would pour out an extra special blessing of strength and courage and direction to all those who have lost their will, and also provide a clear and straight path for those who can't find their way. With God's grace, strength, and help . . . "where there's a will . . . there really is a way." Not sometimes, but all the time!

God's blessings to you on this day! Have a blessed day!

**January 6—*Where there is no struggle, there is no strength.***
**—Oprah Winfrey**

The older I get and the more I observe, I'm convinced that life's struggles do one of two things: They either defeat us, or strengthen us. How many times have you seen a person go through a bad experience and then let that particular event defeat them and become their reason to frown and have a bitter, sour attitude about every aspect of life?

On the other hand, we also see people who go through the same struggles and use a difficult experience for motivation to become stronger, better people, to help others, and to achieve their goals. In short, they turn an obstacle into an opportunity and become the victor instead of the victim. Many times, failing or losing reveals much more character about a person than winning. Nobody goes through life without some adversity—some seem to have more than their share—but to me it's how you handle the adversity that reveals your character. Some people simply hunker down and quit, while others say "watch this" and pull themselves back up by the bootstraps, square their shoulders, hold their head up, and fight on.

My prayer today is that you take any obstacle in your life and turn it into an opportunity to help yourself and others and that you also use the struggles in your life as motivation to become a stronger person.

God's blessings to you on this day! Have a blessed day!

**January 7—*Give thanks, regardless of your circumstances, regardless of obstacles, regardless of temporary defeats and setbacks, give thanks anyway!*—anonymous**

When I read this quote, I recalled a story I heard many years ago about a man who continued to work hard despite many setbacks. Despite his problems, he continued to trust and thank God daily. One day this man was toiling at his meager job and he came in contact with a wealthy man, a man very much full of himself. With sweat dripping off the end of his nose he proceeded to tell the wealthy man how thankful he was for his many blessings and how much God had blessed him and his family.

The reply by the wealthy man: "Thankful? You're standing here with nothing, with sweat running off you, scratching out a living, and you tell me you're thankful. You're just too stubborn to give up and quit."

The working man's reply was a classic and one I've always remembered: "Thanks for reminding me of two more things to be thankful for—I'm thankful to God for the sweat, and for the stubborn streak that keeps me pushing forward."

Just as today's offering states: Give thanks, regardless of your circumstances, regardless of obstacles, regardless of temporary defeats and setbacks, give thanks anyway! And that includes giving thanks for even sweat and stubbornness.

God's blessings to you on this day! Have a blessed day!

### January 8—*Knowledge is knowing what to say. Wisdom is knowing when to say it.*—common expression

We all cross paths with people daily who, for whatever reason, are looking for a confrontation or an argument. Some are chance encounters, while others are at work—and oftentimes it's people we know. A fact that a lot of people don't know or haven't learned yet is that you are in control, and how you react to these people is entirely up to you.

I heard a speaker recently say that getting in an exchange with a person, particularly a person looking for an argument, is giving up your power to control your own attitude. It took me a lot of years to learn that most times, in that situation, no comment is the absolute best and strongest comment you can make, or as the saying goes: "Silence is a powerful voice." In fact, by not making a comment you control both your attitude and the situation at the same time—and you do so by never uttering a single word.

As my late mother often told me, "God gave you a mouth that closes and two ears that don't . . . that should tell you something." My prayer today is that we all learn to recognize that knowledge is important but wisdom is even more important.

God's blessings to you on this day! Have a blessed day!

**January 9**—*Your true character is most accurately measured by how you treat those who can do nothing for you.*—**Mother Teresa**

There is an old phrase that says: "You scratch my back, and I'll scratch yours." Of course, this phrase is just a catchy analogy that means if I do something for you, then I am expecting you to do something in return for me. Many people spend their entire life on this give-and-take merry-go-round, treating people a particular way simply because they want something in return.

But, what about the people we cross paths with who can do nothing for us, who can't scratch our backs? How do we treat them? While this quote might mean something totally different to somebody else, to me it starts—it certainly doesn't end here, but it starts—with the little things we can do in the course of any day—things that might seem insignificant on the surface like being kind to every person we come in contact with, smiling at people, opening a door for someone, or even something as simple as asking someone how they're doing or initiating a short conversation. All these things might seem trivial or inconsequential, but keep in mind that it could be the only positive interaction that person has all day, maybe all week.

I believe our true character really is most accurately measured by how we treat those who can do nothing for us, so that means today's offering requires a little soul-searching for all of us. How would you measure your true character? Only you can answer that question!

God's blessings to you on this day! Have a blessed day!

## January 10—*Gratitude helps us see what is there instead of what isn't.*—Annette Bridges

What are you thankful and grateful for today? Wait—before you give me the standard answers, think about the question and let it roll around in your mind. Then start from the moment you opened your eyes this morning, to the ability to think about what your plans are today (probably while you were still in bed), to your feet hitting the floor, to taking a first step, to a cup of coffee, to the quietness and beauty of God giving you another day . . . another opportunity . . . another clean slate . . . another chance. And don't forget that caffeine that gave you a little kickstart this morning!

What are you thankful and grateful for today? You might want to grab a pen and notebook, because if you answer honestly about all the little things we all take for granted and then add in family, friends, freedom, beauty, wonders, excitement, and the physical and mental ability that make up your life, it will take you a while. If we all wrapped our mind around "gratitude" to help us see what is there, we could all probably spend the rest of the day compiling our thankfulness list.

In these daily offerings, I share a lot of quotes and write about the importance of attitude. I have often pointed out that our attitude is the one thing we are in control of every single day. I am convinced that an attitude of gratitude is the most important and by far the most life-changing thing we can acquire. I want to point out again that an attitude of gratitude does not change the scenery; it merely cleans the glass you look through daily, so you can see the bright colors you've been missing. Or, as today's offering says: Gratitude helps us see what is there instead of what isn't.

God's blessings to you on this day! Have a blessed day!

## January 11—*Something to be thankful for is that you're here to be thankful.*—common expression

Every single day I thank God for the many blessings in my life, and then I quickly follow that sentence with another prayer of thanks that I have the knowledge to recognize where those blessings come from. I understand that the blessings in my life—and they are many—have nothing to do with me and everything to do with God's mercy and grace. I want to say unequivocally that I have not earned, nor do I deserve, the goodness that God has shown me! I am blessed beyond measure, period!

Let me pose a question to you, and I want you to pause and give it some thought before you give your answer. It's a simple question: What are you thankful for?

Before you answer that question, I want you to go back to the moment you opened your eyes this morning and think of all the things that had to happen for you just to navigate from Point A to Point B as the day progressed. From the time you open your eyes in the morning until you close them at night, God's countless blessings are there—even in our everyday life. You just have to open your eyes and your heart—particularly your heart—and recognize them.

When you really focus, really home in on your blessings, the list is endless. And the word "endless" is certainly not an exaggeration. All you have to do is just take a close look at your life!

God's blessings to you on this day! Have a blessed day!

## January 12—*What lies behind us and what lies before us are tiny matters . . . compared to what lies within us.*—Ralph Waldo Emerson

This one-sentence quote deals with three important things that make up every person's life—the past, the future, and what lies within us. It's important to point out that two out of three of those don't matter.

The past is the past, and what lies behind us is exactly where it should stay—behind us. Remember, there is no way to start a new chapter of your life if you keep rereading the last one. It's OK to glance back, but that's not the direction you're going and not the direction you should be looking. As far as the future and what lies before us, that chapter has not been written yet, so it does absolutely no good to worry and fret about what might happen. Worrying about the future is like carrying an umbrella with you on a sunny day on the chance that it might rain.

The beauty of this quote comes in the last six words: "compared to what lies within us." Because what lies within us is the ability to do whatever we set our mind to do, to dream big, strive for an attitude of gratitude, work hard to be better person every day, be a positive influence, reach for the stars, and choose the exact direction we want to take our lives.

God's blessings to you on this day! Have a blessed day!

### January 13—*Always be a work in progress.*—Emily Lillian

How many times have you heard a person make the comment: "I'm still a work in progress"? Usually that phrase is used after a mistake, a misstep, or a failure. It's a phrase that's often used almost as a built-in excuse.

But today's simple little six-word quote puts a different spin on that phrase, encouraging us to always be a work in progress. In other words, never be too content, never be too satisfied, and never be too comfortable with where we are in life. Always be a work in progress. Always strive to be a better person; always strive for a closer relationship with God; always strive to be healthier; work hard to be a better friend, a better co-worker, a more caring person, a more compassionate person, a more understanding person—the list is endless.

I think this offering is so important to so many people. You see, life is like riding a bicycle: If you stop moving, you'll lose your balance. So, whether you're twenty-three or ninety-three, set goals, trust God, dream dreams, trust God more, and keep your balance by moving forward. Always be a work in progress! And most importantly, keep on trusting God!

My prayer, to go along with today's offering, is that, regardless if you're trying to achieve great things or accomplish small things, we will all have the strength, stamina, and determination to take that difficult first step . . . and then keep on high-stepping and always be a work in progress!

God's blessings to you on this day! Have a blessed day!

## January 14—*It's not what you gather, but what you scatter that tells what kind of life you lived.*—Helen Walton

We hear the word "legacy" mentioned a lot these days, and certainly our legacy can be measured in many different ways. Many folks only consider what they accomplish and what they accumulate when thinking of their legacy. This one-sentence quote certainly puts that in a different perspective and speaks volumes about the legacy that we pass on. Two words in today's offering—"gather" and "scatter"—define the legacy that we all pass along.

You might be saying: "I don't have anything to scatter." My answer to that would be: "Sure you do!" You have a smile, a kind word, a message to everyone that God loves them, a pat on the back, or a word of encouragement. You can buy lunch for a stranger, pay for the person behind you in the drive-through, and the list goes on and on. Perhaps the greatest thing we can scatter is to simply stop for a moment and talk—or maybe more importantly, listen —to what those we cross paths with have to say. You never know—your contact with someone might be the only kind word that person hears on any given day.

I often remember things my parents said, and I still recall my dad saying: "We came into this world with nothing and we're leaving the same way." When you look at life through those eyes, what we gather sort of pales in comparison to what we scatter, doesn't it? So, what are you waiting for? Get out there and start scattering!

God's blessings to you on this day! Have a blessed day!

**January 15—***Faith is the bridge between where I am and where God is taking me.***—common expression**

Faith is an easy thing to talk about, but sometimes a difficult thing to grasp—particularly in trying and uncertain times.

In writing, a metaphor is used to tie a word or phrase to an object. In this quote, the words "faith is the bridge" immediately puts an image into my mind. I can see that bridge in front of me and it's a strong, sturdy bridge, wide and safe. And even though I can't see what's on the other side, I know that God is taking me there.

We all have varying levels of faith, but this one-sentence gem puts all that in perspective. Examples of mustard seed and childlike faith are wonderful, but the steadfast knowledge and unwavering belief of knowing without question that God is daily directing our path across that "bridge" is the ultimate testament of faith.

There might be those who question and say, "How do you know? How can you be sure?" To those I would simply say, "I know, that I know, that I know." Or, as that old familiar quote states: "Faith is not knowing what the future holds, but knowing who holds the future." Again, I know!

God's blessings to you on this day! Have a blessed day!

**January 16—***Never say never, because limits, like fears, are often just an illusion.***—Michael Jordan**

Nobody is born being afraid, scared, fearful. It's a flaw we all acquire at some point in life. And be assured that regardless of a person's rough, tough exterior, everybody has fears. Let me say it again: Everybody. Has. Fears.

The key point in today's offering is that fear crushes ideas and dreams, limits life experiences, and at its worst can cripple a person's mind. But, it's how we handle those fears that define us. I am a big believer that many times in life we must face our fears to overcome them, but I also believe that we also need God's help. And today's offering certainly puts fear in perspective. The fears we don't face become our limits, and those fears are often unfounded, an illusion in our mind.

One of my favorite verses says: "Fear not, for I am with you" (Isaiah 41:10). Did you know that more than one hundred times in the Bible, we're told to "Fear not"? Think about that—a constant reminder from God that he will provide strength and courage to help us face our fears. My prayer today is that you have a day, a week, a month . . . a life . . . where your faith in God overcomes and conquers any fear.

God's blessings to you on this day! Have a blessed day!

**January 17—*You can't start the next chapter of your life if you keep rereading the last one.*—common expression**

I read the quote above, and it reminded me of a question I heard a minister ask one time.

The minister asked if anybody knew why the windshield on a car is so big, while the rearview mirror is so small. The answer, he said, is because while we are driving, we should spend almost all our time looking forward at the big window in front of us, with only an occasional glance back. Think what would happen, he said, if we were driving down the interstate and locked our eyes on the rearview mirror and never looked forward. He then noted that the same holds true for life—it's OK to look back once in a while, but we should keep our eyes focused on what's in front of us. And just like the quote says, you can't start a new chapter—a new job, a new goal, a new relationship, a new anything—if you continue to stay stuck reading the last chapter over and over again. And really, isn't every single day a new chapter?

My prayer today is that you stay focused on your new chapter with your eyes firmly locked in on the big picture in front of you.

God's blessings to you on this day! Have a blessed day!

**January 18—*A moment of patience in a moment of anger can save you a thousand moments of regret.*—Ali Talib**

Since the key word in today's quote is "moment," I'm going to suggest you take an extra moment today and read that quote again . . . slowly. Wrap your mind around it, and let it sink in and register. Think about it and then try to imagine how much different life would be for everybody—how many bad situations would have been averted, how many hearts would not have been broken, how many dreams wouldn't have been shattered, how many injuries would not have happened, and how many lives would have been spared—if we all just exercised that one moment of patience?

You know, I've learned (far too late in life) that I don't have to reply to everything that is said or done to me. In fact, I've found that most of the time, the very best response when someone is looking for a confrontation is no response at all. The loudest answer is silence. Many people have the belief that you can reply in anger and get even with another person. I've learned that it's much, much better in life to try and get even with those who helped you, and to happily ignore those who harmed you. My prayer today is that we tuck this simple one-sentence gem away and that we all exercise that moment of patience and possibly save a thousand moments of regret.

God's blessings to you on this day! Have a blessed day!

**January 19—*To me . . . and through me . . . should be our daily prayer.*—Jim Muir**

I recently heard a speaker deliver a message that really stayed with me. The speaker said that many people begin the day with a defeatist attitude, a black cloud over their head, expecting something bad or negative to happen. She said we should all begin every day with a prayer and the belief that "something good is going to happen to me" that very day. The fact that we are breathing, speaking, can see, can put our feet on the floor (and so on and so on) is an answered prayer every single day.

But it was the second part of her message that really caught my attention. She said we should also begin every day with the prayer and belief that "something good is going to happen through me" that very day. Say that again and think about how powerful that statement is—"something good is going to happen through me." What if we all, every single person, began each day with the belief that "through me," something good is going to happen? Maybe it's just a smile or a kind word to a stranger or a pat on the back or a call to an old friend or any number of countless things, but we all have the potential to be a "through me" person every day. In reality, "through me" is much more important than "to me." And because life is an endless echo when you become a "through-me" person, your positive actions will reverberate over and over and over again. What you send out will certainly come back!

"To me . . . and through me"—keep those little words in mind every morning, because they hold the potential to be that one, small, positive thought that can change your day.

God's blessings to you on this day! Have a blessed day!

**January 20—***We can complain because rose bushes have thorns . . . or we can rejoice because thorn bushes have roses.***—Abraham Lincoln**

This quote sums up exactly the way that many people look at life. There are those who totally miss the beauty of the rose simply because they are focused on the thorn, while others have the ability to do just the opposite.

For some folks life is the exact same way; they completely overlook the countless blessings in life (roses), and instead home in on a few problems (thorns) that most of the time they have no control over anyway. Sadly, some people would rather see and focus on the thorn than the beauty of the rose.

I believe if we're not careful, we all have a tendency to zero in and focus on the thorns (the problem) while totally missing the good things. We talk about the thorns, we write about the thorns, we worry ourselves sick about the thorns, we fix our attention on the thorns, and we obsess about the thorns . . . while those beautiful roses—the countless blessings from God—are staring us right in the face and are ignored.

While Ol' Abe was way ahead of his time with this quote, in recent years we've been reminded in song to "stop and smell the roses." Either way, both provide a wonderful reminder and a great life lesson.

My prayer today is that we all learn to overlook and completely ignore the thorns we sometimes encounter in life, and instead focus all our energy on an attitude of gratitude and on the beauty of the rose.

God's blessings to you on this day! Have a blessed day!

**January 21—***When you're struggling with something, take a look around you and realize that every single person is also struggling with something in their life, and to them it's just as hard as what you are going through.***—Nicholas Sparks**

When I read this quote, I was reminded of a short video I watched a while back that showed people walking through a busy office building—people moving up and down an escalator, getting on and off an elevator, entering and leaving the building. There was no sound, but as each person walked along a caption appeared. One man's caption said, "Just lost his job." Another woman's said, "Just diagnosed with breast cancer." Others said: "Son committed suicide last year." "Has a child battling an addiction." "Mounting financial problems." "Just went through a nasty divorce." And on and on it went—dozens of people and dozens of unique problems.

The point of that video, just like today's offering, is a reminder that everybody—and I mean every single person—faces unique challenges and deals with problems and obstacles. Some of these are small, some large, and some monumental. Keep in mind as you go about your daily travels that the people you deal with who might seem irritable, short-tempered, or distracted could be facing one of those life-altering or life-threatening situations.

Since we can't look into each other's hearts, maybe the solution is to always strive to treat each other with much more kindness and respect.

God's blessings to you on this day! Have a blessed day!

**January 22**—*Today will never come again. Be a blessing. Be a friend. Be kind. Encourage someone. Take time to care. Let your words heal and not wound.*—anonymous

While every short sentence in today's quote is meaningful, the very first sentence is the most important. Today will never, ever come again. We get one chance at it on this day—just one chance, that's it. And the plain fact that today will never come again puts even more importance and significance upon this meaningful quote.

Think about the many people you will come in contact with today. Think about the many different situations you will encounter today and then, again, apply the sentences in this offering in some way—something as simple as reaching out to an old friend, saying a pleasant "good morning" to a stranger, or holding a door for somebody you don't know might be the only positive interaction that person has on this day—a day that will never come again.

Remember, it was Mother Teresa who said, "Kind words can be easy to speak but their echoes are truly endless."

God's blessing to you on this day—a day that will not come again. Have a blessed day!

**January 23**—*It is the set of the sails, not the direction of the wind that determines which way we go.*—Jim Rohn

In one short sentence, this quote sums up life in general. There are going to be troubling and difficult winds that blow in life in the form of mistakes, missteps, sickness, hardships, and problems. That's just a given, and for some it seems those ill winds howl more often.

It's how we navigate those "winds" that will make us or break us. But the key to today's offering can be found in the first seven words —"It is the set of the sails. . . ."

Many people experience a failure (or failures) in life, and then use that as a standby excuse to never try again. It's been said that hardships and failure often prepare ordinary people for an extraordinary destiny. I truly believe that because it seems that a constant rule for people who have enjoyed success is that they simply refuse to give up. Somehow these people use setbacks, failures, obstacles, the doubts and negativity of others and the word "no" as motivation to reach their goals. They learn that you cannot stop the winds in life . . . you simply learn to adjust your sail.

Proverbs 3:6 says: "In all your ways acknowledge Him, and He shall direct your paths." Based on today's quote, we could certainly paraphrase it to say: "In all your ways acknowledge him and he will 'set your sails.'" We can't direct the wind, but we can trust in God to direct us through rough waters and to adjust our sail!

God's blessings to you on this day! Have a blessed day!

## January 24—*A grateful heart is one that finds the countless blessings of God in the seemingly mundane everyday life.*—anonymous

The key word in this quote to me is "mundane." We all know (sort of) what "mundane" means, but I thought it would be interesting to see what was offered in the way of an exact definition. "Mundane" is defined by dictionary.com as "lacking interest or excitement; dull; routine; ordinary."

It's easy to say "I'm blessed" when a job promotion, new child, or grandbaby comes along. But you might be asking, where are the countless blessings in a dull, ordinary day? Well, let me reel off eight or ten quick blessings and you can take it from there. Many of these blessings happen before you every put your feet on the floor. Blessing one, you woke up this morning . . . then in no particular order—the bed you slept in, the roof over your head, you put your feet on the floor, electricity, coffee or caffeine, the smile of a friend or loved one, a job to go to or rest from, sunshine or rain because both are good, and so you see, our blessing list really is countless. From the time you open your eyes in the morning until you close them at night . . . God's countless blessings are everywhere . . . even in our mundane, everyday life. You just have to open your eyes and your heart—particularly your heart — and recognize them.

God's "countless blessings" to you on this day! Have a blessed day!

**January 25—*Talking about our problems is our greatest addiction. Break the habit. Talk about your joys.*—Rita Schiana**

Today's offering is one of those quotes that should make us pause and examine the words we use daily—the topics we focus on the most. I know it certainly was an eye-opener for me. It's easy—and I'm as guilty as anyone—to focus on a problem while ignoring countless joys all around us. And just like this quote states, it's an addiction for many people to talk about problems, to concentrate on the negative, when there is joy all around them. Perhaps that's why bad news travels so much faster than good news. The age-old quote by Mark Twain goes well here: "A lie and bad news can travel half way around the world before the truth and good news can get its shoes on."

The key in today's offering can be found in the little three-word sentence: "Break the habit." There is a powerful single sentence by the Persian poet Hafiz, "The words you speak become the house you live in." I thought of this when I read today's quote. Just like the clothes we choose every single morning, we also have the ability every day to choose our vocabulary, what we say, and what topic of conversation becomes our addiction. Will it be the problems in our life or the many joys and blessings? The answer to that question—and the house you live in—lies solely with you.

Today's quote begs two questions: "What words will be your addiction?" and "What house will you live in?"

God's blessings to you on this day! Have a blessed day!

**January 26**—*A bend in the road is not the end of the road . . . unless you fail to make the turn.*—**Helen Keller**

Every person, and I mean every single person, has faced the proverbial "bend in the road." We've all been there, cruising along the straight highway of life, and then out of nowhere comes the bend in the road—that sharp curve that is difficult and seemingly impossible to navigate. It could involve family, a relationship, finances, loss of employment, health issues, and the list goes on and on.

As I get older, I realize that it's not the times when we're cruising down the wide open road with great visibility that defines us. Instead, it's those sharp curves and hairpin turns, when the road is slippery and it's really difficult to see, that shapes our character. Sometimes you have to slow down to a crawl to navigate these rough patches of life's highway, and sometimes you have to stop completely to get your bearings.

Other times, when you can't stop and you have to keep moving, you have to turn loose of the steering wheel completely—let go and let God!

One of my favorite Bible verses states: "Trust in the LORD with all your heart, and lean not on your own understanding; in all your ways acknowledge Him, and He shall direct your paths" (Proverbs 3:5–6). Let me paraphrase that last sentence: "In all your ways acknowledge him and he shall direct your paths . . . particularly when there's a bend in the road. Remember, it's not the end of the road!"

God's blessings to you on this day! Have a blessed day!

**January 27**—*You will never reach your destination if you stop and throw rocks at every dog that barks.*—**Winston Churchill**

Any person who has ever tried to do better, be better, achieve more, accomplish more, stand up for an injustice, or make a life change understands that there are a lot of barking dogs along the way.

Of course, the phrase "every dog that barks" is a clever metaphor for the naysayers, detractors, pessimists, and Chicken Littles who love to bring rain and dark clouds to a sunny day. These barking dogs love to dampen your enthusiasm, hand out a heaping helping of negativity and criticism, and then move on to their next victim.

The key point in today's offering is that you cannot, under any circumstances, stop and throw rocks at these barking dogs. Keep your faith strong, keep moving forward, keep your eyes on your goal, and protect your spirit from contamination by limiting your time with people barking out negativity.

And in the event that you are cornered by one of these barking dogs and can't escape . . . keep a muzzle handy, and remember that you don't have to participate in every negative conversation that you're invited to.

God's blessings to you on this day! Have a blessed day!

**January 28**—*Always listen twice. First listen to what's being said . . . and then listen to who said it.*—**common expression**

When I read this quote, I was reminded of a story I heard a minister tell many years ago. He told the story about two people who were friends and then had a falling-out. One person made up some very hurtful and damaging accusations against the other and told it to anybody who would listen. After the false stories were told and retold, the only thing more damaged than the friendship was the one person's reputation. Many years went by and the person who had told the false tales, who was in failing health, went to the other person and tried to make amends. "What can I do to correct this?" she asked.

The other person, the one who was damaged by the false accusations, gave an answer that gives us all something to ponder: "I want you to wait for a very, very windy day, a day when it's so windy you can't keep your hat on your head. And I want you to take a sack of feathers and throw them into that gusting wind. Then I want you to wait many years and then go back and retrieve all those feathers."

What a great example and lesson for all of us about the words that we throw out into the wind every day! There are three things that cannot be recalled in life: the moment after it's gone, the time after it's passed, and the most important one, the word after it's spoken. Like today's quote says, listen to what's being said and then listen to who said it. Who said it will be more important than what's being said.

One of the signs of real maturity and growth is when we realize that every situation and comment does not require a reaction or a reply. Many times, silence is the most powerful answer we can give. Chew on your words vigorously before you spit them out, and just like my late mother used to tell me, "Always consider the source."

God's blessings to you on this day! Have a blessed day!

### January 29—*God often uses adversity to direct us, correct us, and protect us.*—Rick Warren

I believe people can enjoy a good life, a happy life, a content life, a rewarding life, and a fulfilling life . . . but nobody has a perfect life. Let me say that again: Nobody has a perfect life. Certainly we all get to see the highlight reel of some folks, but rest assured that everybody deals with the adversity mentioned in this quote.

As I get older I can look at so many places in my life where I thought I had the timing and the circumstances all figured out, only to end up going a totally different direction. Oftentimes when I'm asked to speak, I talk about God directing my path—away from some things and toward others. Regardless of what anybody else thinks, I believe that God has directed my path, and at this moment I'm right where I'm supposed to be. But I have to admit that I didn't always go willingly. You see, I have a tendency to try and do God's work for Him, based on my wants and my timing. I've learned, sometimes the hard way, that's not the way it works. God's direction and timing are always perfect.

I can't count the times in the past few years that I've made the comment: "Boy, God was sure looking out for me (or a member of my family) to keep us away from that situation." And many times the situations I refer to happened decades ago. There's a Bible verse that explains this exactly and straight to the point: "A man's heart plans his way, but the LORD directs his steps" (Proverbs 16:9).

Based on today's quote I'm going to paraphrase that verse to say: "The heart of man plans his way, but the Lord directs, corrects, and protects his steps."

God's blessings to you on this day! Have a blessed day!

## January 30—*Be kind. Be thoughtful. Be genuine. But, most of all be thankful.*—common expression

We've all been asked the question, "Are you a person who sees the glass as half-full or half-empty?" My standard answer through the years, trying to be optimistic, is that I'm a half-full guy. But, a while back—I'm not even sure when it started—I started trying to give thanks to God daily, hourly, sometimes by the minute, for every single thing in my life.

All of a sudden instead of seeing the glass as half-full, I gave thanks that I have a glass that has something in it. I gave thanks that even if the glass is empty, it's always refillable. I gave thanks for work that I didn't want to do, for sore muscles, for strength and endurance, for the desire to learn, to think, to make a difference, to try and reach people by stringing a few words together, and for the sweat on my brow. In all things—let me say that again, in all things—I started giving thanks. And that includes difficult situations, tough days, and contrary people! They all make me stronger!

It was not an overnight transformation, but slowly, a little at a time, I started looking at life differently. I really like the eyes I'm viewing the world through right now. A favorite quote of mine by Maya Angelou says, "A thankful heart is not only the greatest virtue, but the parent of all other virtues." And I give thanks to God for that!

God's blessings to you on this day, and remember that a thankful heart is a happy heart. Have a blessed day!

**January 31**—*Every second brings a fresh beginning, every hour holds a new promise, every night our dreams can bring new hope, and every day is what we choose to make it.*—common expression

I know that January 1 represents a new year and a clean slate, and so people make resolutions to improve and be better at this and that. But, one of the beautiful aspects of life is that we don't have to wait for a new calendar, a new week, a new month, or a new year, because we have the ability to start from any second, any minute, or any hour of any day we choose and start a brand-new beginning.

I particularly love the final nine words of today's offering: "every day is what we choose to make it." Let those nine words sink in. We have that ability every morning to put on a positive attitude, to make the day and shape the day any way we want.

Remember, you can't go back and make a new start, but within you and with God's help, there is the ability to make a brand-spanking-new ending! Today . . . today is called the present, and rightfully so, because it's a present from God. It's a present that contains another chance, a new opportunity and the hope to be a better person. The second your eyes open, every morning that present is waiting on you.

Remember those nine words again—"every day is what we choose to make it." So, the choice is yours and totally yours—what kind of day will you make?

God's blessings to you on this day! Have a blessed day!

**February 1**—*You don't inspire others by being perfect. You inspire them by how you deal with your imperfections.*—common expression

Everybody—and I mean every single person who has lived—has failed at one time or another. Failure is inevitable; it's just part of life. It's what you do when those failures come that matters the most. Do you let it defeat you, or do you use it as a stepping stone and a learning experience and push on?

It's been said that the finest steel has to go through the hottest fire, and so it is with people. Many times, failing or losing reveals much more character about a person than winning. Nobody goes through life without some adversity—some seem to have more than their share—but it's how you handle the adversity that reveals your character. In short, it either defeats you or it defines you. Some people simply hunker down and quit, and others say "watch this," and then pull themselves back up and fight on.

Some people simply refuse to give up. These people use setbacks, failures, obstacles, the doubts and negativity of others, and the word "no" as motivation to reach their goals. Always remember that it's not a failure to get knocked down—failure comes when we refuse to get back up.

God's blessings to you on this day! Have a blessed day!

## February 2—*True courage is to keep traveling on when you can't see the map.*—common expression

I was recently driving down a two-lane highway when I saw a prominently displayed portable flashing sign that read: "Caution: Rough road ahead." My first thought as I drove past the sign was not the road I was traveling on, but of our travels down life's highway. "Wouldn't it be nice," I thought to myself, "if there was a flashing sign to warn us of the troubles and rough roads that are ahead of us in life?" As you know, many times in life we find ourselves in the middle of a rough stretch of road before we know it—a road full of potholes and ruts caused by health issues, the loss of a loved one, relationship problems, family issues, and financial concerns. And those are just a few of the "rough roads" that life can throw our way!

While we might not have a map to guide us through these difficult times, we can always call on the "Map Maker," let go of the steering wheel, and let God take control of the situation.

There are countless instances in God's word where we are instructed "do not fear." We could look at those three little words as our flashing sign and a roadmap from God, that he will provide strength and courage to help us when the road of life turns rough and difficult to travel. While there are no visible flashing signs along life's highway to warn us of rough roads ahead, it should provide immeasurable comfort for all of us to know that we do not need to fear those bumpy, unpaved roads, because Jesus holds the steering wheel and the map of our lives.

God's blessings to you today as you travel down life's highway and remember . . . "do not fear"! Have a blessed day!

## February 3—*Life is an endless echo. What you send out—comes back. What you sow—you reap. What you give—you get.*—Zig Ziglar

While every short sentence in today's quote is meaningful, the very first sentence is the most important: Life truly is an endless echo in every single aspect. Think about the many different situations you will encounter today, this week, this month, or in your lifetime—and then apply those next three sentences. Something as simple as reaching out to an old friend, being kind in a difficult situation, saying a pleasant "good morning" to a stranger, encouraging someone going through a rough time, buying lunch for a stranger, or simply holding a door for somebody you don't know might be the only positive interaction that person has on this day.

I'm going to throw in a second quote by an anonymous writer (at no additional cost) that fits well: "Today will never come again. Be a blessing. Be a friend. Be kind. Encourage someone. Take time to care. Let your words heal and not wound."

So, we get one chance at it on this day, just one chance, that's it. And the plain fact that today will never come again puts even more importance and significance on those three meaningful short sentences—"What you send out—comes back. What you sow—you reap. What you give—you get."

And because life is an endless echo, our actions—good and bad, big and small—will reverberate over and over and over again. What kind of an echo will you send out today? That choice, like it is every single day, is entirely up to you!

God's blessing to you on this day! Have a blessed day!

**February 4—*Be careful how you are talking to yourself, because you are listening.*—Lisa M. Hayes**

I heard a speaker recently talking about two main reasons why people fail—and that those two reasons reside between your ears. They are called "doubt" and "fear." Without question, doubt and fear are the two greatest dream-killers that exist.

While we talk to ourselves, repeating over and over that we can't succeed and can't get ahead, we fail at 100 percent of the things we don't try. We settle for less than we deserve, and the answer is "no" to all the questions we never ask. The saddest summary of a life contains three descriptions: could have, might have, and should have. Make sure your worst enemy doesn't live between your own two ears. Remember, it's not what you are that holds you back; it's what you're telling yourself you're not.

In short, your determination has to be greater than your doubt and your faith has to be greater than your fear. My prayer today is that we evict those dream-killers, doubt and fear, from the room they occupy in our minds. Send them packing today. Give them their walking papers!

God's blessings to you on this day! Have a blessed day!

**February 5—*I am only one, but I am one. I cannot do everything, but I can do something. And I will not let what I cannot do interfere with what I can do.*—Edward Everett Hale**

I love the contrast in each sentence of this quote, but sadly many people (myself included) have, many times in our lives, only used half of each of these sentences. How many times have you thought: "I am only one. . . . I cannot do everything. . . . I cannot do that"? I bet the answer to that question is "many."

As I read through this, the first thought that came to my mind for today's offering was "multiplication." Let me explain. Think about what would happen if every single person applied these three short sentences to every aspect of their lives. Soon, one life would intersect with another and it would be "We are only two, but we are two. . . . We cannot do everything but we can do something." Then those two would overlap with two more and it would be "We are only four, but we are four. . . ." And on and on exponentially! How powerful could that be?

I speak from experience when I say that everything we do in life—and I mean every single thing—has to have a first step involved. A step where we take action and say, "I am only one, but I am one." And of course, that first step is the hardest one. There is never, ever a right time, a perfect time.

My prayer is that whether you're trying to achieve great things or accomplish small things today, this week, or in the future, you will remember these powerful words.

God's blessings to you on this day! Have a blessed day!

**February 6—*The pages of yesterday cannot be revised, but the pages of tomorrow are blank and you hold the pen. Make it an inspiring story.*—anonymous**

Interestingly, the word that caught my attention in this quote is "revised"—a word that is important and used often by writers. In thousands of stories, columns, and even my daily offerings I always "revise"—add or subtract a word, delete a sentence or two that doesn't take away from what I'm trying to say. And on some days when the words don't come easy, I've revised by deleting everything and starting all over again.

Sadly, life is not that way, and it's certainly not as easy as a few strokes on a keyboard. Even though many of us would like to, we can't go back and revise the pages of yesterday. We can't rewrite the pages from the past to make it a more pleasant story to read. We can't edit out words we've said; we cannot edit out difficult people, sadness, mistakes, failures, and unpleasant experiences. As today's quote says, "the pages of yesterday cannot be revised."

But the good news I have to share in this offering is that the pages of tomorrow are a different story. A brand-new ledger is in front of us today—this very moment—and the pages are clean, white, blank, and brand-new. What will my story be today? What will your story be? The most important point I make in today's offering is that we're the authors of our story, and that we hold the pen that will fill the pages of tomorrow.

I recently read a short paragraph by an unknown writer that contained a remarkable sentence—a sentence that caused me to pause and read it over again and again: "Our Redeemer's blood is the ink in the pen that writes the script for our lives." Wow! Let that sentence sink in for a moment. With God's help and direction we can fill the blank pages of tomorrow with the story we want! You're the author. Make it a good one!

God's blessings to you on this day! Have a blessed day!

**February 7—*If your ship doesn't come in . . . swim out to it.*— Jonathan Winters**

It's funny how a short sentence—only ten little words—can trigger a flood of memories and also provide a reminder of a life lesson learned when I was very young. That's the case with today's offering.

When I was a kid my mom and dad took me to church regularly. There was a man who attended—let's call him Joe—who continually talked about God providing him a job. At every opportunity he would stand and say that he wanted church members to continue to pray that God would provide him a job. One Sunday as we were driving home, my mom brought up the subject about Joe and his many requests for the church to pray for him to get a job.

My dad, who was the hardest working man I've ever known and had zero tolerance for anybody lazy, said matter-of-factly: "You know, if Joe would do his part and get off the couch and look for a job, I bet

God would do his part and help him find one." To paraphrase my dad's comment with today's quote: "If Joe's ship wasn't coming in . . . maybe he needed to swim out to it."

I recently read a quote by Mother Teresa that said, "Pray. Not just with your words but with your actions." It's been said that an inch of action will move you closer to your goal than a mile of intentions. I am a big believer in the power of prayer, but I also believe that sometimes it is up to us to provide the action behind those prayers. Sometimes we have to swim out to meet our ship as it's coming in.

God's blessings to you on this day! Have a blessed day!

## February 8—*You are not what you feel . . . you are what you believe.*—common expression

I recently heard a minister speak on this simple sentence. He talked about how most people, on a regular basis, talk about how stressed, hopeless, anxious, and irritable they feel. Facebook has even helped this cause by providing a link where you can add an emotion to a post. The excellent point that he made was that instead of stating what we believe—"God is our refuge and strength, a very present help in trouble" (Psalm 46:1), or "I can do all things through Christ who strengthens me" (Philippians 4:13)—we cling to a feeling, an emotion and, as the old saying goes, "the words we speak become the house we live in." And of course the "house we live in" is referring to what's within you . . . what's inside you . . . what you carry with you every step you take in life.

When I thought about today's offering and what I wanted to write, I was reminded of a quote I used in the past from an unknown author: "There are always two wolves fighting. One is darkness, negativity, and despair. The other is light, optimism, and hope. The question is which wolf wins. The answer is the one you feed."

What a great analogy that defines exactly what every person is faced with daily. Everybody starts each morning with a clean slate and the ability to make that day a good one. Then the wolves start fighting and many people quickly give in to darkness, negativity, and despair —they give in to what they feel and not what they believe.

This quote is a great example why we should wrap ourselves in what we believe and not what we feel. When you feed the wolf of light, optimism, and hope, you will soon begin finding the countless blessings of God in what you might have considered a seemingly ordinary life.

Remember, you are not what you feel; you are what you believe. So, what house will you live in, and which wolf will you feed?

God's blessings to you on this day! Have a blessed day!

## February 9—*Broken crayons still color.*—Trent Shelton

In one way or another we all have some broken crayons in our lives. We've all made mistakes, we've all gotten off course, we all pack some baggage with us from our past, and we all have a few life-related scars.

But the key point in today's offering is that it's what we do with those broken crayons that determine our direction in life. How many times have you seen a person go through a difficult experience and then let that experience defeat them—let it become their stand-by excuse and crutch to put their crayons away and never, ever color again? On the other hand, some people take those same types of difficult experiences and find a way to take tiny pieces of broken crayons and color a beautiful and remarkable picture.

Every one of us has the power within us every single day to pick up our crayons—no matter how many broken pieces there are—and color a new bright, fresh, positive, and happy picture. It doesn't have to be a perfect picture, and it's all right to go outside the lines once in a while. The key thing is this: Always remember that broken crayons still color. So pick up the pieces of your broken crayons, trust in God to guide and direct your efforts, and start coloring a new picture.

God's blessings to you on this day! Have a blessed day!

**February 10—***God gave you 86,400 seconds today. Have you used one of them to say thank you?***—William A. Ward**

I read a story recently that is certainly food for thought about the way we give thanks for our blessings. Consider this: What if you awakened each morning and a bank had deposited $86,400 in your account? The rules of the bank stated that the money you didn't spend that day would be lost, and that the money couldn't be transferred to another account. The next day another $86,400 would be deposited. The second rule is that the bank can close the account at any time with no notice. So, what would you do with the money? Obviously, you couldn't spend all that money on yourself every day, so you'd shower family and friends and probably people you didn't even know with part of your daily windfall.

Now, take away the money aspect and apply it to time—it's the same thing. What time you don't use today on family, friends, doing good, being a better person, helping others, being positive, being kind, and thanking God (and the list goes on and on) is forever lost. A deposit of $86,400 has a monetary value, while those 86,400 seconds each day are priceless—they represent your life!

Today's offering has two short sentences and raises one great big question: Have you used one of those seconds to give thanks to God for those 86,400 seconds you were given today? Well, have you? My prayer is that you take several of those 86,400 seconds you've been given and thank God for another chance, another opportunity, and the gift of another day.

God's blessings to you on this day! Have a blessed day!

**February 11—***A good life is when you assume nothing, do more, need less, smile often, dream big, cherish small joys, laugh a lot, and realize every single day how blessed you are for what you have.***—common expression**

In only one sentence, today's gem provides us with a bonanza of truth and a blueprint for what many people spend a lifetime searching for—the good life.

While I love the list mentioned—assume nothing, do more, need less, smile often, dream big, cherish small joys, laugh a lot—the beauty of this quote is found in the last dozen words: "realize every single day how blessed you are for what you have." And of course, those twelve words come right back to something I've written about often—an attitude of gratitude. Remember, an attitude of gratitude doesn't change the scenery; it merely washes clean the glass you look through so you can clearly see the beautiful colors.

I find it interesting that in defining the good life there is no mention of wealth, status, fame, or fortune. In fact, if you read through this quote slowly, absorb every word, and really let it sink in, you notice that this simple list defining the good life is available to every person every day. Let me say that again . . . every person, every day!

God's blessings to you on this day! Have a blessed day!

## February 12—*Into each life some rain must fall.*—Henry Wadsworth Longfellow

I was driving down the interstate recently, and the dark clouds ahead gave warning that a storm was brewing on the horizon. With one eye on the sky and the other on the road I moved ahead, maybe a little faster than the number on the speed limit sign. In a split second it was like the sky opened up with rainfall. There was no warning, no small prelude of a few sprinkles of rain, just a gully-washer that was so forceful that it felt like it was going to beat the windshield out of my truck. My journey went from 75 mph to a crawl in seconds. Visibility was so poor that I found myself leaning up over the steering wheel just to see the white lines. I also realized that the harder it rained, the tighter I gripped the steering wheel. And then just as quickly as it started, it was over. The pavement was dry, traffic was moving nicely again, I relaxed my death-grip on the steering wheel, and I was again looking forward to my destination.

After I drove through the rainstorm I immediately thought of our travels down life's highway. Many times in life we find ourselves in the middle of a storm caused by health issues, the loss of a loved one, relationship problems, family issues, and financial concerns. The list is endless. One minute the road in front of us is clear and dry, and before we know it visibility is poor, travel is uncertain, and we're just trying to hold on tightly.

Life changes without our permission. Take a look around on any given day and you realize that life can change dramatically from one minute to the next. We can be in the middle of a downpour at any moment. That means it's very important to take nothing and nobody for granted—your family is priceless, your time is gold, and your health is wealth. While there are no visible flashing signs along life's highway to warn us of storms ahead, it should provide immeasurable comfort for all of us to know that we do not fear those storms because Jesus has the steering wheel.

God's blessings to you today as you travel down life's highway—hopefully with no rainfall! Have a blessed day!

### February 13—*Was it a bad day? Or, was it a bad five minutes out of your day that you worried and stressed about all day?*—anonymous

The older I get and the more I observe, I'm convinced that life's struggles do one of two things: They either defeat us, or strengthen us. How many times have we all had that five-minute bad experience that today's quote mentions, and then let it define the rest of the day, or maybe even the rest of the week or month? In some instances, five bad minutes in one day turn into a lifetime of anger and hatred.

Think about today's offering like this: There are 1,440 minutes in each day. Take away the amount of time we sleep and we all have roughly 1,000 minutes each day. If you have a bad five minutes and you let it become the reason to frown and have a sour, bitter attitude, you've given away 995 minutes of your precious time. And that time you gave away is time you could have spent on family, friends, doing good, being a better person, helping others, thanking God for your countless blessings, and the list goes on and on. The saddest aspect is that because of five negative minutes, 995 positive minutes are lost forever.

Keep in mind that happiness and positive thinking is an attitude. By the way we approach that bad five minutes, we do one of two things: We can make ourselves miserable and weak and let it ruin our day, or we can rise above it and remain happy and strong because we know that we have 995 more minutes to focus on the really important blessings in our life. Interestingly, the amount of work is the same.

My prayer is that you take any five-minute obstacle in your daily life and turn it into a 995-minute opportunity to help yourself and count your many blessings.

God's blessings to you on this day! Have a blessed day!

## February 14—*Interrupt anxiety with gratitude.*—common expression

It's often said that the mark of a good writer is the ability to say more with fewer words. In that case, the unknown author of today's quote really packed a punch in this little four-word gem, which gives us a battle plan to deal with the cares of life that sometimes stand out more than the blessings in our life.

I read this quote and I immediately thought about the numbers involved with counting blessings compared to adding up troubles. Everybody encounters a few troubles along the way, that's just part of life. But what if every time we started adding up the troubles we're dealing with, we immediately interrupted the anxiety created by those troubles with gratitude and started counting our blessings? And the beauty of this attack on anxiety is that it really works. Of course, you have to apply this practice to learn that it works.

Let's look at a few "anxiety interrupters" today. You woke up this morning, blessing one; you opened your eyes and could see, blessing two; you placed your feet on the floor and stood up, blessing three . . . and on and on. The list of real blessings to interrupt anxiety in our lives is infinite and unlimited.

The next time you feel anxiety, stress, or any other funk settling in, interrupt it with gratitude and remember that there is always, always something to be thankful about. I recently ran across a quote by Zig Ziglar that ties this thought up nicely: "Today be thankful and think how rich you are—your family is priceless, your time is gold, and your health is wealth."

Make you a list of "anxiety interrupters" today and keep them handy . . . anxiety and stress won't stand a chance!

God's blessings to you on this day! Have a blessed day!

**February 15—*Our reaction to any situation literally has the power to change the situation itself.*—anonymous**

I read this quote through once, and then slowed down and read it slowly through again. After I wrapped my mind around this one-sentence, fourteen-word gem, I thought about the plain, old unvarnished truth in this quote—and I realized that in all the hundreds of quotes I've shared, this might be one of the most powerful.

Think about it like this: On any given day we have no control over other people we deal with, family issues, coworkers, traffic, and what kind of a mood some people happen to be in on that particular day. In short, life can change dramatically from one moment to the next, and it certainly changes without our permission. However, the key to today's offering is found in the first two words: "Our reaction." While we have no control over many things, we have total control over our reaction. And just like the quote says: Our reaction—let me say it again, our reaction—to any situation literally has the power to change the situation itself.

The key point in today's offering is that we don't control the outcomes, but we do control our reactions to them. And certainly sometimes the best reaction is no reaction and the strongest response is no response. I often use the wonderful quote by Dr. Charles Swindoll, who said that life is 10 percent what happens to you and 90 percent how you react to it. And just like today's quote says, we all have within us the power to change that 90 percent simply by the way we react. That's powerful stuff—that's a life-changer!

God's blessings to you on this day! Have a blessed day!

**February 16**—*Every positive change in your life begins with a clear, unequivocal decision that you are going to either do something or stop doing something.*—**Brian Tracy**

The simplicity and clarity of this quote jumped off the page at me. How many times have we all worried, fretted, and stewed over positive changes that we know need to be made in our lives? In today's offering, this one-sentence quote simplifies those needed positive changes down to two words—"either" and "or." Either we're going to do something . . . or we're going to stop doing something. That's it. If we're going to make a positive change, one of those two simple either/or things have to happen. Just like a journey of a thousand miles begins with a first, small step, the journey to make positive changes begins with the first step of either/or.

A lot of times, the choices we are faced with seem confusing and clutter our minds—what-if-this and what-if-that. But, when you look at a choice, using this quote, it really makes it very simple. We either do something or stop doing something, period.

So, it doesn't matter if it's trying to build or renew a relationship with God, trying to get a better job, lose weight, start college, get fit, be more positive, be more thankful, be kinder, or hundreds of other things, that either/or decision has to be the starting point. Let me leave you with this nugget regarding making a positive change in your life: You don't have to be great to start . . . but you have to start to be great.

So, what's it going to be for you today on your positive change? Will it be "either" or will it be "or"?

God's blessings to you on this day! Have a blessed day!

**February 17**—*The only way to get over it . . . is to go through it.*—**common expression**

Most people have been faced with situations in life—death of a loved one, painful break-up, loss of employment, the list is endless—where you would just like to sleep for a year and skip the pain involved. While sticking your head in the sand sounds good, in reality that's not how life works.

Many years ago I had a wise man tell me the exact words in today's quote: "Everybody faces situations where we'd like to go under it, around it, sidestep it, ignore it, or just plain avoid it . . . but the only way to get over it . . . is to go through it." Of course, he was right.

But, I've learned (sometimes the hard way) that there should be a second sentence added to this quote that says: And as you go through it . . . let go and let God.

Today's offering reminds me of another quote that I love, by an unknown author: "The greater your storm, the brighter your rainbow." I recently read a story that pointed out that a rainbow is a promise to everybody who sees it—it's a promise of sunshine after rain, calm after storms, joy after sadness, peace after pain, love after loss, morning after night, and a bright beginning after a painful ending. Be sure to note how many times the word "after" is used in the previous sentence. After . . . you go through it!

Throughout life there are always going to be personal storms. Sometimes those storms are going to rage. For some people, these storms provide a reason to quit or give up. For others who know that God is in control and their rainbow is on the horizon, the storms of life will be used as nothing more than stepping stones to help us keep pushing on and moving forward. We're all going to battle life's storms, but the key thing to remember when we're trying to navigate those choppy waters is that we have to go through the storm and rain in order to get to that bright rainbow—the promise.

God's blessings to you on this day! Have a blessed day!

**February 18—*You'll never get anywhere you're meant to be by traveling yesterday's road. It's a new day; find a new way.* —anonymous**

What a beautiful and truthful message in this quote! And to me, the beauty is found in the three words that are used to describe the past, the future, and the present. In these three short sentences are a blueprint and a roadmap for life.

Forgive the past, whether you have to forgive yourself or somebody else, get past the past, make peace and put it to rest. And whatever you do, don't reside there. The past is a place of reference, not a place of residence. Everybody has a past, but more importantly everybody also has a future. Look to the future with prayer instead of worry. You can worry, fret, and stew about the future, but we are not guaranteed the future, or even tomorrow. And that brings us to the most important sentence in the quote: The wisest thing you can do is to be present in the present . . . gratefully.

Think about that—be present in the present . . . gratefully. It's called the present because it's a gift—a gift from God for us to enjoy with an attitude of gratitude for the millions of tiny miracles that make up our life every single day. Don't forget, "This is the day [the present and your gift] the LORD has made . . . rejoice and be glad in it" (Psalm 118:24).

God's blessings to you on this day! Have a blessed day!

**February 19—*Don't miss the sunshine today worrying about the rain coming tomorrow.*—anonymous**

The beauty of today's offering is that it explains worry in terms we all understand—the weather. Think about that for a second—worrying about things that will never happen is exactly the same thing as walking around with an umbrella on a sunny day . . . waiting for it to rain. It's also been often said that worrying about things that might never happen is like handing over your hard-earned cash for a debt you might not even owe. That gets your attention, doesn't it?

I remember one time when I was very young, telling my mother that I was worried. She gave me advice that I still remember: "You can worry until you make yourself sick and it will not change one thing that is going to happen. Worrying will rob you of your happiness. You need to always remember that 99.9 percent of what you worry about will never happen." When I read this quote. I thought of her wise words from decades past.

One of the most powerful passages about worry can be found in 1 Peter 5:6–7: "Therefore humble yourselves under the mighty hand of God, that He may exalt you in due time, casting all your care upon Him, for He cares for you." Worry is a thief, a liar, and a dream-killer. One thing we all need to keep in mind about worry is that we can fret and stew and even agonize about what might happen and in the end it will not empty tomorrow of its troubles—but it will certainly empty today of its strength.

Let me leave you with this gem today: Enjoy your sunshine today, lay down your umbrella, and quit paying on a debt you may never owe.

God's blessings to you on this day! Have a worry-free and a blessed day!

### February 20—*If you want to improve your self-worth stop giving other people the calculator.*—Tim Fargo

It took some time but I've learned that there are people who roll out of bed every morning with the intention of spreading as much negativity as possible. And then once that negative seed is planted, that voice that lives between our ears takes over and convinces us that we will never reach our goals and accomplish our dreams. That voice keeps people in dead-end jobs, harmful relationships, and a dozen other life-traps.

This is why you can never, ever give the calculator to somebody else. Keep it in your hand, always. Then you have to be strong. Don't listen to the enemy between your ears, and don't let a negative comment from a person who eats razor blades and prunes for breakfast dampen your enthusiasm or crush your spirit.

The key thing is that the detractors and naysayers can't defeat you without your consent. In short, never, ever let yourself be defined by somebody's comment, opinion, or ignorance. Remember, your value doesn't decrease based on somebody's inability to see the good and the worth in you. You hold the calculator that determines your self-worth. It belongs to you and only you!

God's blessings to you on this day! Have a blessed day, and keep a tight grip on your calculator!

**February 21—*The past is a place of reference, not a place of residence; the past is a place of learning, not a place of living.*—Roy T. Bennett**

Sadly, many people have the words "reference" and "residence" reversed. They've set up residence in the past, while the present rolls by them day after day. And certainly, nobody can start a new chapter in their life if they keep rereading the last one.

I've used this illustration before, but it's worth repeating: I heard a minister ask the question one time: Why is the windshield on your car so big while the rearview mirror is so small? The simple answer, he explained, is because while we are driving we should spend almost all of our time looking forward, with only an occasional glance back. He then went on to point out that life is the exact same way: A glance back is all right, but our focus should be on the big windshield of life that is right in front of us.

Remember, you are not defined by your past and you don't reside there. Instead, you are prepared by your past, prepared to keep your eyes on that big windshield in front of you, to plan your future with purpose and to frame your life with faith in God. Remember, we all have a blank 365-page book in front of us, and today is the first chapter. The key thing is that you are the author of that book and you can write the story any way you choose. And remember, don't look back . . . you're not going that direction!

God's blessings to you on this day! Have a blessed day!

**February 22—*A candle loses nothing by lighting another candle.*—James Keller**

When I read this quote, I thought immediately about weddings and church services I've attended where one candle is used to sometimes light dozens of other candles. Certainly, this quote could read: A candle loses nothing by lighting a thousand other candles.

But, can't the same be said about a human life?

Think about the number of people you reach in person or by social media each day, each month . . . each year. And then compare that number to that one candle. Just like lighting candle after candle from one small flame, how many lives could be impacted if we all took just a moment to offer a smile, a handshake, a small act of kindness, a pat on the back, a sympathetic ear, or an encouraging word?

Think about the impact and good will that would generate if every person started each day with the goal of lighting a single candle that particular day. And just like that one solitary candle, we would lose nothing by providing our light to others. As you go about your daily routine today, try to light a few candles along the way.

God's blessings to you on this day! Have a blessed day!

### February 23—*People who worry and stress whether the glass is half-full or half-empty are missing the point. The glass is refillable.* —common expression

If I have learned nothing else, I know that life is a balancing act. On one hand, we need to be kind and considerate, but on the other hand we can't let people run over and use us. We must trust, but not to the point of being deceived. And finally, it's very important to be content and thankful for all we have but we should never, ever stop trying to improve ourselves.

Every person faces challenges, struggles, and problems, and many times at day's end we're beat up from dealing with the balancing act of life. And it's on those difficult days that the question of half-full/half-empty doesn't matter because the glass is empty and there's nothing left in it, period. But, just like today's offering says, the glass is refillable. So, our prayer every single day should be to ask God to refill our glass with all the ingredients required to maneuver the balancing act of life.

The key point in today's offering is simple. If you have a bad day . . . it's just a bad day, it's not a bad life. Through the grace of God, the glass is always, always refillable.

God's blessings to you on this day! Have a blessed day!

**February 24—*Practice the pause. When in doubt, pause. When angry, pause. When tired, pause. When stressed, pause. When you feel like you can't go on, pause. And when you pause, pray.*—anonymous**

Since the key word in that quote is "pause," I'm going to suggest that *you* pause for just a moment today and read it again . . . slowly . . . and let those seven, short sentences sink in and register. What a powerful statement and a true roadmap for dealing with the everyday stress and anxiety of life.

Can you imagine how much different life would be for everybody— how many bad situations would be averted, how many injured feelings would be avoided, how many lives would be altered—if we all just exercised that one moment of pause? And of course, the most important sentence in this quote is the final one—"And when you pause, pray."

Think about it like this: When we doubt, we question. When we're angry, we say things we regret. When we're tired, we make irritable comments. When we're stressed, we make bad decisions. So, instead of letting one emotion create more negative emotion, practice the pause . . . and pray. In fact, those three little words—practice the pause—are going to become a daily goal of mine. When I feel doubt, anger, fatigue, or stress creeping in—things we all experience—I'm going to practice the pause. It might not immediately help the situation, but it will definitely help *me*.

God's blessings to you on you this day! Have a blessed day!

**February 25—*Forgiveness is unlocking the door to set someone free and realizing you were the prisoner.*—Max Lucado**

I recently heard a speaker talking about forgiveness, and he made a comment that stayed with me: "Forgiveness does not change the past, but it does enlarge your future." In other words, forgiveness is a gift you give to yourself. It doesn't make you weak; it sets you free.

Many people have carried anger, bitterness, and hatred around for so long that they're not even sure what they're upset about. They just know they're mad and that they plan to stay mad.

These people are prisoners, and their lives are ruled by resentment and retaliation. When I hear people say that they will never, ever forgive, I think of a quote by Mark Twain: "Anger is an acid that can do more harm to the vessel in which it is stored than to anything on which it is poured."

Perhaps the very best point I can make in today's offering about forgiveness is found in Ephesians 4:32: "[B]e kind to one another, tenderhearted, forgiving one another, even as God in Christ forgave you."

Maybe it's time to enlarge your future, unlock the door, and set a prisoner free—yourself.

God's blessings to you on this day! Have a blessed day!

**February 26—*Courage is being scared to death and saddling up anyway.*—John Wayne**

Nobody is born being afraid, being scared, being fearful. It's a flaw that we all acquire at some point in life. And be assured that regardless of a person's rough, tough exterior, everybody has fears.

Fear crushes ideas and dreams, limits life experiences, and at its worst can cripple a person's mind. But it's how we handle those fears that define us. I am a big believer that many times in life, we have to muster up all the courage we can and face our fears head-on to overcome them.

I do want to quickly add that I also believe that we need God's help when confronting our fears.

Much like beauty, courage is in the eye of the beholder. By this, I mean that we all measure courage in different ways. Many times, professional athletes are singled out for their courage. But I see a lot of courage on a daily basis from average, ordinary folks—people who fight and claw through difficult situations but keep going, keep battling to put one foot in front of the other.

Sometimes true courage is simply taking that (sometimes scary) first step in a totally different direction, knowing that all you are armed with is commitment, desire, a strong work ethic, prayers, and absolutely no guarantee of success. For those who might be considering stepping in a new direction on sheer courage, remember that we fail at 100 percent of the things we don't try, and that the answer is "no" to all the questions we never ask. The saddest summary of a life contains three descriptions: could have, might have, and should have.

If you are facing a fear today and saddling up anyway, my prayer for you is for strength, determination, and courage!

God's blessings to you on this day! Have a blessed day!

## February 27—*Lord, I hate buttermilk.*—anonymous

I speak from experience when I say that we all have times when our faith lags, when we don't understand or like our present circumstances, when we pray for direction but feel like we're floundering. I ran across a short story about those feelings that I want to share with you today. Today's offering is a great example that simple words sometimes pack a powerful message.

Here's the story: One Sunday morning at a small, country church, a young pastor called on one of his oldest members to lead the opening prayer. The old man stood up, bowed his head, and said: "Lord, I hate buttermilk." The pastor opened one eye and wondered to himself where this prayer was going. The old man continued: "Lord, I hate lard." The young pastor was confused and a little perplexed, but the old man continued in a strong, clear voice: "Lord, I ain't too crazy about plain, old flour . . . but after you mix them all together and bake 'em in a hot oven . . . I just love biscuits."

The old man concluded: "Lord, help us realize when life gets hard, when things come up that we don't like, whenever we don't understand what you are doing, that we need to wait and see what you're making. And Lord, after you get through mixing and baking, we know it will be something even better than hot biscuits. Amen."

My prayer today is that when the Lord finishes mixing and baking in our lives it will be better than hot biscuits . . . with sausage and gravy poured over the top.

God's blessings (and hot biscuits) to you on this day! Have a blessed day!

**February 28—*The words you speak become the house you live in.* —common expression**

In only one sentence and ten words this quote is chock-full of truth, wisdom, and honesty. I have read this gem through several times. The house we live in does not mean our structural dwelling located on Any Street, Any Town, USA. Instead, in this instance "the house you live in" refers to what's within you . . . what's inside you . . . what you carry with you every step you take in life.

Today's offering does a wonderful job pointing out that just like virtually everything in life, the house you live in comes down to a single word—attitude. We have the choice every single morning, when our feet hit the floor, to choose our attitude—and our words and actions—for that particular day. We are in control of our attitude from the moment our eyes open; it's our decision alone, and we are the only one who can decide. And certainly, the decisions we make about the attitude we embrace and the words we speak really do become the house we live in.

I want to leave you with a great quote by W. Clement Stone that I believe ties this all together quite well: "There is little difference in people, but that little difference makes a big difference. The little difference is attitude and the big difference is whether it's positive or negative."

Today's quote begs two questions: What words will you speak? What house will you live in?

God's blessings to you on this day! Have a blessed day!

**March 1—*Success is not final. Failure is not fatal. It is the courage to continue that counts.*—Winston Churchill**

Dark rain clouds were rolling across the sky recently, as I was traveling down a residential street heading toward home. As I stopped at an intersection I noticed a woman in one of those little motorized scooters. She was on the sidewalk near the intersection and she was rocking back and forth, sort of flailing from side to side. Her scooter was not moving. I pulled up, jumped out of my truck, and asked her if she was stuck. With an exasperated tone, she said "yes." I asked her if she could stand up, even for a few seconds, so that I could free the scooter. With the same exasperation in her voice she told me she couldn't. I got around behind the scooter and noticed that the back wheels had dropped off in a bad place in the sidewalk. As the first sprinkles of rain fell, I lifted up and pushed forward on the scooter as she hit the forward lever. In a few seconds the wheels gained some traction and she sped off down the sidewalk, yelling "thank you" behind her as she hurried to beat the obvious deluge of rain that was fast approaching.

As I drove off, I thought about the woman's situation—she was stuck in a rut (literally) and just needed a little nudge to get going again. How many people, I wondered, are stuck in a rut (figuratively) and also just need a nudge, a little push, a slight lift to help them gain traction and start rolling in the right direction? Maybe it's an encouraging word that God loves them and cares about where they are in life. Perhaps it's something as simple as a pat on the back, a show of kindness, or a gentle push to steer them in the right direction. We all get stuck in ruts, but as today's offering aptly points out, it is the courage to continue that counts. My prayer is that if you're stuck in a rut, you'll get a little nudge to help you gain the traction you need to get moving again.

God's blessings to you on this day! Have a blessed day!

### March 2—*Your mind is a garden. Your thoughts are the seeds. You can grow flowers, or you can grow weeds.*—Ritu Ghatourey

I'm a visual person, so being able to actually picture in my mind a beautiful flower garden or an ugly patch of weeds really puts this quote in perspective. Think of the contrast between flowers and weeds, and then keep in mind that every single day—in fact, every minute of every day—we have within us the ability to plant the seeds we choose. We can plant positive, helpful, caring seeds or we can plant seeds of negativity, divisiveness, distrust, and bitterness. And the amazing thing is that the choice is ours every day. Every person breathing makes the decision every morning, when they open their eyes, of what type of seeds they will plant that day.

Our prayer should be to ask God to help us, to check us, and to hold us accountable for the work we do daily in our garden. What type garden will you plant today? Tomorrow? In the future? Again . . . because it's certainly worth repeating: "Your mind is a garden. Your thoughts are the seeds. You can grow flowers, or you can grow weeds." As you go about your daily routine today, pause for just a moment and ask yourself what you plan to grow today. You have a clear choice. Will it be flowers, or will it be weeds? The choice is yours, and it belongs to you and only you!

God's blessings to you on this day! Have a blessed day!

**March 3—*It's not what you look at that matters, it's what you see.***
**—Henry David Thoreau**

There is an old adage that says: Beauty is in the eye of the beholder. But when you think about it, everything in life, every single thing, is in the eye of the beholder. Or, as today's offering states: When you change the way you look at things, the things you look at change.

I write and speak a lot about an attitude of gratitude. I am a big believer that developing a mindset that finds gratitude about the small things in our daily life can really change the way we see the world. I know this not because somebody told me, but because I tried it and it really works. It's not easy, but it works!

A few years ago, I began an attitude-of-gratitude process. I started giving thanks daily, sometimes hourly, and often by the minute. Certainly I gave thanks for the many blessings in my life, my children, grandchildren, my job, my income, etc. My thankful list is endless! But I also gave thanks for jobs I didn't want to do, people who are contrary, sore muscles, sweat dripping off the end of my nose, and difficult tasks. In all things I gave thanks!

The transformation was not an immediate one, but after a period of time I literally began viewing life differently. Gratitude doesn't change the scenery; it merely washes clean the glass you look through, so you can clearly see the colors you've been missing.

An attitude of gratitude really works! Let me challenge you to give it a try. Because, as today's gem states: It's not what you look at that matters, it's what you see.

God's blessings to you on this day! Have a blessed day!

**March 4**—*In optimism there is magic, in pessimism there is nothing.*—**common expression**

I heard a story recently about a couple who had identical twin boys. One was a complete optimist about everything, while the other was a total pessimist. The parents sought help with doctors to find out why their sons were so diametrically opposite in their moods. The doctors came up with a plan to try and move the twins away from their optimism and pessimism. The son who was a pessimist was given an expensive, bright, shiny racing bike; and the son who was an optimist was given a neatly wrapped box filled with manure.

The pessimist son took one look at the racing bike and said: "Oh great . . . I'll probably try and ride that and crash and break both my legs." The optimist son opened the box of manure, smiled widely, and headed for the front door. His parents inquired where he was going. He said: "With this much manure . . . there has to be a pony outside somewhere."

Just like today's quote says: Most people are about as happy as they make up their mind to be. There is a ton of truth in that little one-sentence quote. Think about it. You see many people weighted down from the cares of life—they've been handed a box of manure—and they somehow manage to find a smidgen of good in their situation and trudge ahead with a smile and a good attitude.

But, there are others—people who have bright, shining things in their lives—who regardless, make up their minds (in some instances, before they get out of bed) that they're going to be in a foul mood and put everybody else in a foul mood. It's like the old quote that says, "Some people complain when opportunity knocks, because it made too much noise."

We are all the captain of our own ship. We're the author of our own story. There are many things in life we can't control, but there is one thing we can control—and that's our attitude. Make up your mind to have a good day, and you will . . . even if you get handed a box of manure!

God's blessings to you on this day! Have a blessed day!

**March 5**—*Learn from yesterday. Live for today. Hope for tomorrow.*—**Albert Einstein**

In a nutshell, those three short sentences and nine simple words really do sum up how we should approach life. They provide a blueprint, a guide on how to handle those three very important and sometimes tricky areas—the past, present, and future.

First, I think it is so important to emphasize that those three sentences certainly don't and shouldn't carry the same weight. In fact, these three areas are not even close to being equal. You see, I believe we should learn from yesterday but certainly not fix our gaze on yesterday, and that we should hope for tomorrow but not dwell on tomorrow. A glance back and a peek forward are all right, but our main focus and attention should be on today. There is an old adage that I think of and use often, that goes well right here: "Yesterday is history, tomorrow is a mystery, but today is a gift. That's why it's called the present."

And today, well . . . as Psalm 118:24 states: "This is the day the LORD has made. We will rejoice and be glad in it." Let me paraphrase that just a little: This is the day the Lord has made for me . . . and for you, and we are doing a great disservice to our Creator if we do not rejoice and be glad and thankful for this day—this wonderful present—that we have been given. My prayer today is that you enjoy and focus on the present God has given you.

God's blessings to you on this day! Have a blessed day!

**March 6**—*You can never cross the ocean unless you have the courage to lose sight of the shore.*—**Christopher Columbus**

This offering provides a great analogy of life for all of us. In this short, one-sentence quote there is a huge challenge for us to have the courage to leave our comfort zone—the place where we are safe and secure standing on the shore.

The beauty of this quote is that it encompasses all things life-related, from major decisions such as starting or renewing our relationship with God, starting a new career, a new business, or moving a totally new direction in life to many seemingly inconsequential things we can do every day to become a better person and help us lose sight of the shore—things like smile at a stranger, open the door for somebody you don't know, chew on your words before you spit them out, do a random act of kindness for somebody who can't help you, volunteer to help, be kind, make somebody laugh, laugh at yourself, get started back at the gym, or give someone a compliment and mean it . . . and the list could go on and on.

The key word in today's offering is "courage." Having the courage to lose sight of the shore is oftentimes much easier said than done. A definition of courage I use often fits in very well here: "Courage is the commitment and desire to begin . . . with absolutely no guarantee of success. Courage is simply taking that first step."

Regardless of what ocean you're crossing or thinking about crossing, my prayer is that you have the courage to take that first step.

God's blessings to you on this day! Have a blessed day.

**March 7—*The same boiling water that softens the potato hardens the egg. It's not about circumstances but what you're made of that matters most.*—anonymous**

It's been said that circumstances do not make the man . . . they reveal him. As wonderful as life is, it is still filled with problems, trials, twists and turns, and difficulty. It's how we all handle those things that define us. I have learned through the years that sometimes those circumstances are completely out of your control, and that the only way to handle them is to let go and let God—or, to quote the title of the Carrie Underwood song, "Jesus, take the wheel." Maybe that's why 1 Peter 5:7 is one of my favorite verses; Peter advises us to be "casting all your care [or circumstances) upon Him, for He cares for you."

Many people miss this point, but regardless how bad things appear, your present circumstances do not determine where you can go in life.

Instead they only determine where you start! Instead of focusing on the circumstances you cannot change, throw all your positive energy into the circumstances you can change. I am a big believer that any person can change many circumstances in their life simply by changing their attitude. Always remember that life is not about what happens to us nearly as much as it is how we react to it. The last sentence in today's quote is worth repeating: "It's not about circumstances but what you're made of that matters most."

God's blessings to you on this day! Have a blessed day!

## March 8—*Seek to be worth knowing rather than well known.* —Sandra Turley

Today's offering is only one sentence and nine words, but it packs a punch and contains a huge measure of truth. In fact, when you slow down, read it slowly, and put some thought into that little sentence, it's pure gold.

How many times have you heard a person introduced, or read about an individual, and in front or behind their title or name the words "well known" are inserted? Accomplishing something, good or bad, becoming famous or infamous, can make a person well known. Many people are well known because of terrible things they've done.

On the other hand, being kind, considerate, caring, positive, helpful, honest, patient, trustworthy, a true friend, a confidante, encouraging, and motivating can make you worth knowing. In many instances those four little words—"well known" versus "worth knowing"—are literally miles apart. And in the whole scheme of what's really important in life, it is far better to be worth knowing than well known.

God's blessings to you on this day! Have a blessed day!

## March 9—*The blessing of dissatisfaction.*—Kirk Packer

I recently heard a minister deliver a message, and today's quote was the title. I love to string words together, and these four words certainly caught my attention. Clearly, I was interested in what he had to say because the words "blessing" and "dissatisfaction" seem out of place when used together. Certainly, it begged the question: How can being dissatisfied be a blessing?

The sermon was excellent, and talked about how some people are never satisfied and always striving for more, particularly a closer relationship with God. He pointed out that this is OK . . . in fact, it's a blessing to be dissatisfied and to want to be more like Jesus and get more from our Christian experience. The sermon had such an impact on me that I thought about it many times the following week.

But, taking that word "dissatisfaction" one step further, couldn't we apply that to every portion of our lives? In other words, we are to never be too content, never be too satisfied, and never be too comfortable with where we are in life. Always be a work in progress. Along with always striving for a closer relationship with God, we should also always strive to be a better person; always strive to be healthier; always work hard to be a better friend, a better coworker, a more caring person, a more compassionate person, a more understanding person—the list is endless.

I think today's offering is so important to so many people. You see, life is like riding a bicycle—if you stop moving you'll lose your balance. So, whether you're twenty-three or ninety-three, set goals, trust God, dream dreams, trust God some more, keep your balance by moving forward, and always be at least a little bit dissatisfied with where you are in life! Just like riding that bicycle, some dissatisfaction keeps you constantly moving forward.

God's blessings to you on this day! Have a blessed day!

**March 10—***Don't believe everything you tell yourself late at night.*
**—anonymous**

I recently read where the average person has between 50,000 and 70,000 thoughts per day. Let's split the difference and make the number 60,000. Based on that number, even if you're positive 90 percent of the time that still means that you have to sort through 6,000 negative thoughts each day. Wow! No wonder so many folks walk around negative and pessimistic, like the little guy in the cartoon who had a black cloud follow him everywhere he went!

But, that's what makes today's offering so important: Don't believe everything you think.

Think about this: How many times in your life have you uttered the phrase, "I talked myself out of doing that?" Regardless if it involves a job, a relationship, going to church, starting a diet, or going to the gym, the enemies between our ears—commonly known as fear and doubt— win a lot of decisions. And of course that means we lose, because fear and doubt are dream-killers, life-changers, and career-crushers.

Make sure the gatekeeper is in place to filter out those negative thoughts, and replace them with an attitude of gratitude. Then put down the shovel and don't dig up in fear and doubt what you planted in faith. And finally, it's worth repeating again: Don't believe everything you think!

God's blessings to you on this day! Have a blessed day!

**March 11—***Life's problems are like the never-ending waves in the ocean. You can't stop them, but you can learn to surf.* **—anonymous**

In one short sentence, this quote sums up life in general. There are going to be waves in life in the form of trouble, mistakes, missteps, sickness, hardships, and problems. It's how we navigate those "waves" that will make us or break us.

Many people experience a failure (or failures) in life, and then use that as a standby excuse to never try again. It's been said that hardships and failure often prepare ordinary people for an extraordinary destiny. I truly believe that, because it seems that a constant rule for people who have enjoyed success is that they simply refuse to give up. Somehow these people use setbacks, failures, obstacles, the doubts and negativity of others, and the word "no" as motivation to reach their goals. In short, these folks learn that it's not a failure to get knocked down—failure comes when we refuse to get back up. They learn that you cannot stop the waves in life . . . you simply learn to surf through them.

Every day is a new beginning, treat it that way. Don't let the negative words or actions of others affect your smile or your pursuit of a goal or a dream. Trust in God to direct you through rough waters and grab your surfboard and decide that today is going to be a great day!

God's blessings to you on this day! Have a blessed day!

## March 12—*Worrying is like a rocking chair. It gives you something to do but it doesn't get you anywhere.*—Van Wilder

If you pay even a little bit of attention to the daily news, you know there is plenty of upsetting and worrisome stories. In the world we live in, with a never-ceasing 24/7 news cycle, it seems that we move quickly from one crisis and calamity to the next, often so fast that we can't even take a deep breath in between. Sometimes it's hard to digest it all daily and still stay optimistic when you look at the downhill direction it seems we're traveling as a nation.

I am certainly not a theologian, but recently while I was fretting over another dose of bad news a Bible verse came to me that gave me reassurance, one I've heard many times before: "Let not your heart be troubled; you believe in God, believe also in Me" (John 14:1). It calmed me and made me smile to know that the world I think is spinning out of control some days is the same world God created. We can worry about this and that, but the bottom line is this: God is in control, period. Remember (and I'm talking to myself, too) worrying does not empty tomorrow of its troubles; it empties today of its strength. My prayer today is that you remember John 14:1 and tuck it away with you, if even a moment of worry crosses your mind.

God's blessings to you on this day! Have a blessed day!

**March 13—***Every test in our life makes us bitter or better, every problem comes to break us or make us. The choice is up to you and you only, whether you become victim or victor.***—common expression**

I believe people can enjoy a good life, a happy life, a content life, a rewarding life, and a fulfilling life . . . but nobody has a perfect life. Let me say that again: Nobody has a perfect life. Certainly we all get to see the highlight reel of some folks, but rest assured that everybody deals with the tests and problems mentioned in this quote.

Every person—young and old, rich and poor, and every description in between—at some point in their life gets knocked down. It's just a given . . . it's inevitable. But the true character of a person— what separates the victors from the victims—is measured by how we deal with our tests and problems, and how we get back up and move forward.

Issues involving work, finances, relationships, family, and health are only a few of the ways that life can knock us down. One thing that is often overlooked in life is that the strongest people aren't always the ones who win, but the people who don't give up when they lose. And in most instances, these defeats are only a temporary condition. Giving up and becoming a victim is what makes them permanent.

The key word in today's offering is "choice," because we really do have the option every minute of every day to choose what direction life's tests and problems take us. I believe the single most important thing we can do when we're faced with the tests and problems of life is to hand them to God and put our trust in Him. Let go and let God, and in the end we will be the victors and not the victims.

God's blessings to you on this day! Have a blessed day!

**March 14**—*People underestimate their capacity for change. There is never a right time to do a difficult thing.*—John Porter

There's an old familiar adage that says: "A journey of a thousand miles begins with a single step." But really, that phrase can be used with anything we do in life, from small everyday tasks to life-changing decisions. However, just as today's offering points out, that first step is difficult because we all underestimate our capacity for change.

I speak from experience and not something I read when I say that everything we do in life—and I mean, every single thing—has a first step involved. And of course, that first step is the hardest one. There is never, ever a right time, a perfect time.

Even when we're at the end of that thousand-mile journey—or that life-changing decision—the last step will not be as hard or as difficult as that first one. But while that first step is the hardest one, there is also joy, freedom, and excitement in moving in a new direction.

Another quote by an unknown writer that fits in well here states: "To achieve great things or to accomplish small things the formula is the same—start where you are, use what you have, do all you can, and trust in God." I love this quote because it's in the present; there is no procrastination. Start where you are, use what you have, do all you can and—most importantly— trust in God. That means right now!

My prayer is that regardless of whether you're trying to achieve great things or accomplish small things today, this week, or in the future you will have the strength, stamina, and determination to take that difficult first step . . . and then keep on stepping.

God's blessings to you on this day! Have a blessed day!

**March 15**—*This is a wonderful day. I've never seen this one before.*—Maya Angelou

I love this quote because it's a great reminder that, while each new day brings new challenges and maybe a few obstacles, it also brings a fresh slate, a new start, and new opportunities to enjoy life and to be a better person.

One of the greatest aspects about life is that we don't have to wait for a new week, a new month, or new year; we have the ability to wipe the slate clean every single morning. Remember what this quote says: This is a wonderful day that we have never seen before. One of the keys to this quote is that we cannot bring yesterday's problems to today. Remember, worrying does not empty tomorrow of its troubles; it empties today of its strength.

Enjoy this one-of-a-kind day God has given you, because tomorrow will be a different day. That means we get one shot, and one shot only, to do this one right. So smile often, be kind to others, dream big, laugh a lot (and at yourself), hold tight to those you love, and count your blessings, because they are many.

God's blessings to you on this remarkable and unique day that we have never seen before! Have a blessed day!

## March 16—*Laugh when you can, apologize when you should, and learn to let go of what you can't change.*—common expression

Read through this little one-sentence quote again . . . slowly. Three seemingly simple things are mentioned, but these three things are life-changers.

When I read this quote I immediately thought of give-and-take—words used a lot together, but not in the context I see them in this quote. Let's break today's quote down based on give-and- take.

Take . . . the time to laugh! As the old saying goes, it's good medicine and it also refreshes the soul. And this includes learning to laugh at yourself, because you know we all do some pretty silly things sometimes. Secondly, give . . . the apology when you should, and also have the good sense to take or accept the apology when you should. There's a quote that I've used before that says, "Forgiveness is unlocking the door to set someone free, and realizing you were the prisoner."

And the last "give" is the most important—give the things you can't change, your problems, your worries, your cares, your troubles, the difficult people you deal with . . . give it all to God, period. Isn't it amazing that today's quote—eighteen total words—provides a plethora of wisdom and instruction? These are some words to tuck away and remember.

God's blessings to you on this day! Have a blessed day!

**March 17—*Courage doesn't always roar. Sometimes courage is the quiet voice at the end of a long, trying day that says: "Thank you Lord for this day. I will try again tomorrow."*—Mary Ann Radmacher**

Much like beauty, courage is in the eye of the beholder. By this, I mean that we all measure courage in different ways. Many times, professional athletes are singled out for their courage. But I see a lot of courage on a daily basis from average, ordinary folks—people who fight and claw through difficult situations but keep going, keep battling to put one foot in front of the other.

Sometimes true courage is simply taking that (sometimes scary) first step in a totally different direction, knowing that all you are armed with is commitment, desire, a strong work ethic, prayers, and absolutely no guarantee of success. For those who might be considering stepping in a new direction on sheer courage, remember that we fail at all of the things we don't try and that the answer is always "no" to all the questions we never ask.

Perhaps the greatest definition of courage comes from legendary actor John Wayne, who said: "Courage is being scared to death and saddling up anyway."

God's blessings to you on this day as we saddle up for another ride! Have a blessed day!

**March 18 —*Spending time today complaining about yesterday won't make tomorrow any better.*—common expression**

Maybe it's an age thing, but I don't want to be around negative people. And by negative I'm not talking about a person simply having a bad day,

I'm referring to that person (you can name one or two or twenty right now) who walks around every day hating everybody and everything. I'm referring to the type of person who sets out each morning with the sole intent to make every person they come in contact with as miserable as they are.

Now, read the quote again and consider this: Yesterday is gone—and regardless of what took place, what difficulty you experienced, you can't change it. As far as tomorrow, we're not promised tomorrow. But today . . . today is called the present, and rightfully so, because it's a present from God. It's a present that contains another chance, a new opportunity, and the hope to be a better person. The second your eyes open every morning, that present is waiting on you.

My prayer is that you will forget yesterday, don't worry about tomorrow, and truly enjoy the wonderful present you've been given.

God's blessings to you on this day! Have a blessed day!

## March 19—*Difficult roads often lead to beautiful destinations.* —Zig Ziglar

Every person has faced difficult roads as they travel through life. We've all been there, cruising along the straight highway of life, and then out of nowhere comes that rough, bumpy stretch in the road, that sharp curve that is difficult and seemingly impossible to navigate. It could involve family, a relationship, finances, difficult people, loss of employment, health issues, and the list goes on and on.

As I get older, I realize that it's not the times when we're cruising down the wide-open road with great visibility that defines us. Instead, it's those rough patches of road, the sharp curves and hairpin turns when the road is slippery and it's really difficult to see, that shapes our character.

Sometimes you have to slow down to a crawl to navigate these rough patches of life's highway, and sometimes you have to stop completely just to get your bearings. Other times, when you can't stop and you have to keep moving, you have to turn loose of the steering wheel completely—let go and let God!

One of my favorite verses states: "Trust in the LORD with all your heart, and lean not on your own understanding; in all your ways acknowledge Him, and He shall direct your paths" (Proverbs 3:5–6). And that means even if the path is rough, bumpy, and full of potholes.

Let me close today's offering by paraphrasing a portion of that verse: "In all your ways acknowledge him and he shall direct your paths . . . particularly when you're traveling a difficult road. Remember, it's not the end of the road!"

God's blessings to you on this day! Have a blessed day!

## March 20—*Be a fountain, not a drain.*—Rex Hudler

I saw this little one-sentence, six-word quote, and I loved it immediately. The first thing that came to my mind is that those two words—"fountain" and "drain"—are diametrically opposed. They are as far apart as any two words you can find. A fountain springs forth, it gives, it bubbles over—while a drain takes away, it depletes, it vacates.

When I thought about this, I realized that we all have the opportunity every single day to be a fountain or a drain. By the way we approach life and our everyday thinking, we are either a fountain of giving, happy, and positive emotions, or we are a drain, depleting and taking away the energy and optimism from ourselves and those around us. Interestingly, the amount of work that goes into being a fountain or a drain is the same.

There are many, many things in life that we cannot control, but whether we're a fountain or a drain is one of the few things we control daily. From the moment our feet hit the floor every morning we have the option of determining whether we'll be a fountain or a drain. Remember, you can be a drain and complain because rose bushes have thorns . . . or you can be a fountain and rejoice because thorn bushes have roses—the work and effort is the same, and the choice is yours!

My prayer is that today you are surrounded by fountains everywhere you go!

God's blessing to you on this day! Have a blessed day!

**March 21—*You can encounter many defeats in life and still never be defeated.*—Maya Angelou**

The greatest strength of a writer is to be able to say more in fewer words. The writer of this quote has, in one sentence and twelve words, provided a tried-and-true guide for success. You might be wondering how the word "success" factors into a quote that speaks about many defeats in life. One thing that is often overlooked in life is that the strongest people aren't always the ones who win, but the people who don't give up when they lose.

It's been said that the finest steel has to go through the hottest fire, and so it is with people. Many times, failing or losing reveals much more character about a person than winning. Nobody goes through life without some adversity, but it's how you handle the adversity that reveals your character. In short, it either defeats you or it defines you. Some people simply hunker down and quit, while others say "Watch this" and pull themselves back up, square their shoulders, and with God's help hold their head up and fight on.

Remember, no matter how many defeats you've experienced in life, keep your faith, trust in God, push on, and you will never, ever be defeated!

God's blessings to you this day! Have a blessed day!

**March 22—*We don't always control the outcomes, but we do control our reactions to them.*—anonymous**

Let's break today's quote in half and look at it as two separate thoughts. First, take a look around on any given day, and you realize that rarely do we control the outcomes in life. From the moment our feet hit the floor we have no control over other people we deal with, family issues, coworkers, traffic, and what kind of mood some people happen to be in on that particular day. In short, life can change dramatically from one moment to the next, and it certainly changes without our permission.

But it's the second half of the quote that packs the punch for today's offering, because our reaction and our attitude really does determine the ride, especially when life changes in a way that tests us. I used a quote recently that says: "There is little difference in people, but that little difference makes a big difference. The little difference is attitude and the big difference is whether it's positive or negative."

I often use the wonderful quote by Dr. Charles Swindoll: Life is 10 percent what happens to you, and 90 percent how you react to it. The one single, solitary thing we are in control of at all times, every minute of every day, is our attitude. Remember, your attitude, not your aptitude, determines your altitude.

God's blessings to you on this day! Have a blessed day!

## March 23—*No one ever injured their eyesight by looking on the bright side.*—common expression

I read this quote and I immediately thought about the numbers involved with counting blessings, compared to adding up troubles. Everybody encounters a few troubles along the way, that's just part of life. But what if every time we started adding up the troubles we're dealing with, we immediately started counting our blessings and looking on the bright side? And regardless how many troubles you might be experiencing, there is always a bright side.

Let's look on the bright side today, come on. . . . It won't hurt your eyes. You woke up this morning, blessing one; you opened your eyes and could see, blessing two; you placed your feet on the floor and stood up, blessing three . . . and on and on. The list of real blessings in our lives is infinite, and the opportunity to look on the bright side is unlimited.

There's a quote by Maya Angelou I've used before that sums up today's offering nicely: "A thankful heart is not only the greatest virtue, but the parent of all other virtues." Isn't looking on the bright side really just having a thankful heart? I believe that while we're in the middle of the storm, we have to find the silver lining in the dark clouds. It's not easy, I know firsthand. Boy, do I know firsthand. But there is always, always something to be thankful about. If we would all just take a look at the infinite number of tiny miracles in our life, we would realize that the bright side is so bright we should all wear sunglasses.

God's blessings to you on this day! Have a blessed day . . . looking on the bright side!

## March 24—*How will you know if it's the right decision, if you never make it?*—common expression

Many times in my own life I have thought, "I would rather try and fail than to look back with regret in twenty years and wish I had tried."

Certainly, that statement holds true for the major decisions in life. But I think it goes far beyond work, relationships, etc., and even filters down to people carrying resentment, anger, bitterness, hurt, and other negative feelings around with them for years and sometimes for decades. Some people have been mad or upset at each other so long they can't even remember why—they just know they're mad, and they're staying that way.

Many years ago I read a quote by the late comedian/author Erma Bombeck that has stuck with me: "When I stand before God at the end of my life I would hope that I would not have a bit of talent left, and I could say, I used everything you gave me."

That quote should be our measuring stick daily. Use every ounce, every morsel, every scrap, and every smidgen of talent that God gave us. And the key to that is, don't fear failure. The saddest summary of a life contains three descriptions: could have, should have, and might have. Regardless of where you're at in life, don't look back with regret and say "I wish." Don't be a "could have, should have, might have" person. My prayer today is that our faith is bigger than our fear of failure, and that we examine all those "could have, should have, might have" moments in our lives.

God's blessings to you this day! Have a blessed day!

## March 25—*Courage isn't having the strength to go on—it's going on when you don't have any strength.*—Napoleon Bonaparte

Certainly courage can be defined in a lot of different ways, about a lot of different types of battles. But when I read this quote, my initial thought was that this one, small sentence defines perfectly those who fight the daily battles and struggles that life sometimes throw our way. I would like to add one more sentence to this quote: Courage is also defined by those who battled on, pushed forward, and refused to let past mistakes, missteps, and setbacks keep them down.

How many times have you seen a person go through a difficult experience, and then let that particular event define them and every aspect of their life? On the other hand, we also see people who go through the same struggles and use a difficult experience for motivation to become a stronger, better person, to help others, and to achieve their goals. In short, they turn an obstacle into an opportunity.

Many people need to understand that their past has given them the strength, wisdom, and compassion to become the people they are today, so celebrate it. Remember, getting knocked down in life is a given—getting back up is a choice!

God's blessings to you on this day! Have a blessed day!

## March 26—*A good life is when you assume nothing, do more, need less, smile often, dream big, cherish small joys, laugh a lot, and realize and thank God every single day how blessed you are for what you have.* —common expression

If you took a poll of what the definition of a good life consists of, I'm fairly certain there would be a wide variety of opinions. Some folks might add unlimited wealth or social status to their list, but those things don't automatically equate to a good life.

In fact, I would challenge you to add anything to this very complete list. Read through today's offering slowly and think of your own life (I did), and you can see just how spot-on this definition of a good life really is. I love every single word of this quote, but the short string of words that ties everything together is this: Realize and thank God every single day for how blessed you are for what you have. All the other examples of a good life are wonderful and accurate, but the attitude of gratitude to recognize and to give thanks to God for those daily blessings provides the exclamation point.

The older I get, the more I am convinced that an attitude of gratitude—giving thanks for all things in your life—is the most important and by far the most life-changing we can acquire. I should point out that an attitude of gratitude does not change the scenery; it merely cleans the glass you look through daily so you can see the bright colors you've been missing.

God's blessings to you on this day! Have a blessed day!

**March 27—*Strength doesn't come from what you can do. It comes from overcoming the things you once thought you couldn't do.*— Rikki Rogers**

Certainly, today's quote could be defined in a lot of ways, but when I read this I didn't equate the word "strength" with physical ability. Instead, I believe the author was pointing out the mental strength, the strength of our character, that it takes to face the many challenges that life tosses our way.

One of the greatest quotes about strength illustrates my point: "A river cuts through rock not because of power but because of persistence."

If you asked a group of people to define the word "strength," more than likely you would hear words like "power" and "force," but I doubt you would hear the word "persistence." You see, I'm convinced that any strength developed in life, both physical and mental, comes from persistence. I've learned through the years, while traveling down a few bumpy roads, that persistence is a wonderful and much-needed quality.

Persistence, in a nutshell, means you never, ever give in and that you never, ever give up regardless what you're facing. Persistence means that if you get knocked down seven times, you get up eight. I believe, with God's help, that persistence is one of the greatest virtues any person can have or develop. I'm convinced that persistence is a key component of strength, which allows us to overcome the things we once thought we couldn't. My prayer today is that we can all roll along like that river, cutting through obstacles in our path—not by power, but by being persistent.

God's blessings to you on this day! Have a blessed day!

**March 28—*Two things define you: your patience when you have nothing, and your attitude when you have everything.*—common expression**

It's often said that a person's true character is most accurately measured by how you treat those who can do nothing for you. I thought of that gem when I first read today's offering.

I recently read a story about a very successful advertising executive, who handled multi-million-dollar deals on a daily basis. She was asked what has led to her success. She said it came down to two very simple words: "Be nice."

That's it: Be nice.

She explained that without exception, she applies that simple two-word philosophy to every single person she meets in the course of every day—and many of those people, she said, she just meets in passing. Her point is that by doing this it has developed an attitude in her that draws people to her and makes her business thrive. What a concept, huh? Just . . . be nice.

Think about it for a second: What if everybody had that attitude every minute of every day about every person you come in contact with, particularly those who can do nothing for you? What if every person practiced the "be nice" approach to every single person they met every day? What a remarkable difference that would make in the world! My prayer for you today is a simple one: Be nice!

God's blessing to you on this day! Have a blessed day!

## March 29—*Gratitude is a quality similar to electricity—it must be produced and discharged and used in order to exist at all.*—William Faulkner

When I read this quote, I thought of the comments I heard a speaker make recently. He noted that electric companies produce electricity and deliver it up to the outside of our homes, where it stops. From there, it is up to us to flip on a switch inside the home to produce light. In short, even though electricity has been produced, if we don't flip on the switch, we will be standing in the dark.

And just like today's offering states, "gratitude is a quality similar to electricity—it must be produced and discharged to exist at all." And just like the electricity in your home, you're the one that has to flip the gratitude switch. Remember, a thankful, grateful heart is not only the greatest virtue—it's the parent of all other virtues.

In my daily offerings I share a lot of quotes and write about the importance of attitude. I don't think I can emphasize the importance of attitude enough. I have often pointed out that our attitude is the one thing we are in control of every single day. I'm convinced that an attitude of gratitude is the most important and by far the most life-changing we can acquire—sort of like flipping on a light switch in a dark room!

God's blessings to you on this day! Have a blessed day!

## March 30—*The worst prison to be locked in is the what-other-people-think prison.*—anonymous

There is an old adage that states: No good deed goes unpunished. This little gem simply means that no matter how honest, sincere, and noble your actions are and no matter how much good you try to do, somebody will find fault. The key, of course, is to learn to ignore the naysayers, detractors, and pessimists, and stay focused on the goal in front of you. Of course, this is easier said than done, and in order to accomplish this and avoid "prison" time you have to make sure to avoid the what-other-people-think prison.

You see, there are people who roll out of bed every morning with the intention of spreading as much negativity as possible. Once that negative seed is planted, the dream-killers—doubt and fear—take over and begin telling you over and over again that you're not good enough, smart enough, or talented enough to accomplish your goals. And then, with those thoughts in your mind, you get locked up in the what-other-people-think prison, worrying and fretting about what others might think of your every action. Being locked in this prison keeps people from fulfilling dreams, shackled in dead-end jobs, bound by harmful relationships, and handcuffed in dozens of other life-traps.

The key way to avoid getting locked up in this prison is to always remember that people cannot dim your light and they cannot dull your sparkle without your consent. In short, never, ever let yourself be defined by somebody's comment, opinion, or—let me go ahead and say it—by their ignorance. Remember, your value doesn't decrease based on somebody's inability to see the good and the worth in you.

God's blessings to you on this day! Have a blessed day!

### March 31—*Our days are happier when we give people a bit of our heart rather than a piece of our mind.*—Rita Ghatourey

Today's quote reminds me of a conversation I had with a friend recently. He was talking to a school administrator about a problem involving his child. He felt like the administrator was short, condescending, and borderline rude. He said he bit his tongue to keep from giving the school official a piece of his mind, but instead stayed calm and kind. He concluded the story by telling me that he spoke with the administrator a week later; she apologized about the way she had handled the first meeting, saying that she was dealing with some serious illness in her family and was going through a very difficult time. In the end, everything worked out well.

What if a war of words had developed during the first encounter? Certainly irreparable damage could have been done. Instead, just like today's quote says, our days are happier when we give people a bit of our heart rather than a piece of our mind.

Hearing that story reminded me of another quote I've used in the past, by Marvin J. Ashton: "If we could look into each other's hearts and understand the unique challenges each of us faces, I think we would treat each other much more gently, with more love, patience, kindness, and care."

Today's offering is a reminder that everybody, and I mean everybody, faces challenges and deals with problems and obstacles. Some of these are small, some large, and some monumental. Keep in mind as you go about your daily travels that the people you deal with who might seem irritable, short-tempered, or distracted could be facing one of those life-altering or life-threatening situations.

Since we can't look into each other's hearts, maybe the best solution is to always strive to give people a bit of our heart rather than a piece of our mind.

God's blessings to you on this day! Have a blessed day!

## April 1—*Service is the very purpose of life. It's the rent we pay for living on the planet and not something you do in your spare time.* —Marian Wright Edelman

I believe some people have the idea that the word "service" mentioned in this quote means that we have to do grand things, involving a large number of people. If you can pull that off, that's great; however, a quote I read recently attributed to Mother Teresa sums up, I believe, what service is all about: "If you can't feed hundreds of people, then feed one."

As an example, a while back I was asked to speak at a graduation ceremony at a state-operated youth camp in a neighboring community, a detention center that is part of the Department of Corrections. There were eight graduates, who had all made some serious mistakes before they reached the age of twenty-one. All eight had earned their high school diploma while incarcerated and were preparing to head back to real life. In my comments to them I planted some seeds and hopefully said something those young men will remember, tuck away, and keep. Going back to Mother Teresa's words about feeding one, I would have liked to have spoken to eight hundred or eight thousand, but on that particular day my service was to speak to eight. To paraphrase Mother Teresa: If you can't speak to eight hundred, then speak to eight.

I believe even something as small and seemingly inconsequential as a kind word, a kind gesture, a smile, a pat on the back, reaching out to someone going through a rough time, or just taking the time to talk to somebody is a service that we can all practice every single day. By doing these things consistently, day after day, we can keep our rent paid up for the wonderful privilege of living on this planet.

God's blessings to you on this day! Have a blessed day!

**April 2—*If you want to know how rich you are, add up how many things you have that money cannot buy.*—common expression**

Perhaps the best thing I can add to today's quote is to tell you to read it again and again, and then every single day add up all the blessings in your life that do not have a price tag attached.

First and most importantly, remember that your faith guarantees you eternal life and was purchased for you on an old rugged cross. Then add in your family and friends—they're priceless. Your time is gold, and your health is wealth. Interestingly, all the things on that list—which, by the way, are the most important elements of life—cannot be purchased.

I'm going to ask for some audience participation today. It's easy sometimes to look around and feel as though you've come up short—that you're not exactly where you should be or want to be. I want you to take a moment, stop what you are doing, clear your mind, and take inventory of your life and the wonderful, marvelous, beautiful things that God has given you—things that cannot be bought. If you're like me, when you start adding up those things that money can't buy it won't take long to determine that you are a rich person!

God's blessings to you on this day! Have a blessed day!

## April 3—*The greater your storm, the brighter your rainbow.* —anonymous

As wonderful as life is, it's still filled with problems, trials, twists, turns, and difficulty. In short, life is filled with storms, some big and some small. I've learned through the years that sometimes the storms of life are completely out of our control, and that the only way to handle them is to let go and let God

I recently read a story that pointed out that a rainbow is a promise to everybody who sees it—it's a promise of sunshine after rain, calm after storms, joy after sadness, peace after pain, love after loss, morning after night, and a bright beginning after a painful ending.

Throughout life there are always going to be personal storms, and sometimes those storms are going to rage. For some people, these storms provide a reason to quit or give up. For others who know that God is in control and their rainbow is on the horizon, the storms of life will be used as nothing more than stepping stones to help us keep pushing on and moving forward. I love the quote by President Franklin Roosevelt that says: "A smooth sea never made a skilled sailor." We're all going to battle life's storms, but the key thing to remember when we're trying to navigate those choppy waters is that we have to ride out the storm and rain in order to get to that bright rainbow—the promise.

God's blessings to you on this day! Have a blessed day!

**April 4**—*The secret to happiness is to count your blessings while others are busy adding up and telling everybody about all their troubles.* **—William Penn**

In another life I worked as a coal miner. I started working 650 feet underground when I was eighteen years old; it was quite an education. I worked with one elderly gentleman who gave me some great advice one day about people who feel compelled to tell everybody about all their problems.

His advice was simple: "If somebody asks you how you're doing, always say 'I'm doing great,' and then move on." Obviously, my question back was, "Why?" His answer is a classic—funny but true: "If somebody asks how you're doing and you start whining and complaining and telling them every trouble and problem you have, well . . . keep in mind that 70 percent of the people you're talking to don't care and the other 30 percent are glad you're having trouble."

Without question, that sage advice has served me well for more than forty years. By the way, I'm doing very well today, thanks for asking. My prayer is that we will all spend much, much more time today and every day counting our blessings, and far less time adding up our troubles.

God's blessings to you on this day and Have a blessed day!

**April 5**—*Every failure is a lesson. If you are not willing to fail, you're not ready to succeed.*—**anonymous**

Many times, failing or losing reveals much more about a person's character than winning. Nobody goes through life without some adversity—some seem to have more than their share—but to me, it's how you handle the adversity that reveals your character. In short, it either defeats you or it defines you.

Here's where today's quote comes into play. When faced with adversity, some people say, "Watch this," and fight on. Others simply hunker down and quit. Again, you have not failed until you quit trying.

One of my favorite quotes regarding failure states: "Don't fear failure. The saddest summary of a life contains three descriptions: could have, should have, and might have."

Regardless of where you're at in life, don't quit trying, don't fear failure, and don't look back with regret and say "I wish." Don't be a "could have, should have, might have" person. My prayer today is that our faith is always bigger than our fear of failure, and that we all examine our lives in those "could have, should have, might have" areas.

God's blessings to you on you this day! Have a blessed day!

## April 6—*I firmly believe that the only disability in life is a bad attitude.*—Scott Hamilton

I have often written and spoken about the importance of a good attitude. I don't believe there is anything more important than attitude, period. Stop just a moment and think about it: Our attitude has an impact on every single thing that we do every day. While a lot of folks worry about the clothes they put on each morning, many would be better off to concentrate more on the attitude they dress themselves in each day. A home, a business, a church, a work environment, and our relationship with every single person—attitude is the make-or-break difference.

I recently read a quote by W. Clement Stone that stated: "There is little difference in people, but that little difference makes a big difference. You see, that little difference is attitude and the big difference is whether it's positive or negative."

The interesting thing about developing a positive or a negative attitude is that the amount of work is the same. That last sentence might not be completely correct, because based on some of the negative people I've dealt with in my own life, it might take more work to be mad all the time. There are many, many things in life that we cannot control, but our attitude is one of the few things that we control daily. You have a choice every day, even before your feet hit the floor, to determine what attitude you will embrace that day.

So, this morning and every morning when you get spiffed up to face the day, make the big difference the little difference and add a positive attitude to your daily wardrobe.

God's blessings to you on this day! Have a blessed day!

## April 7—*Action always, always beats intention. Go the extra mile! That road is never very crowded.*—common expression

As a kid I used to hear my mother say, "The road to hell is paved with good intentions." At that time I didn't understand what she was talking about. Like many other things she told me, I sure understand it now.

Think about how much better our lives would be if we put action in place of everything we intended to do. Applying action to small, simple things—smiling at a stranger, taking a second to hold a door open for somebody we don't know, making a phone call to an old friend, offering a word of encouragement to somebody going through a rough time, or simply being pleasant to everybody we encounter daily—would make the world a far better place, and us far better people.

And of course, that sage advice of applying action over intention also holds true for big decisions such as renewing or strengthening a relationship with God, living healthier, furthering your education, coming to terms with a troubled relationship, or moving away from a dead-end job. It's a given that if we all choose action over intention, we're going to see a lot more people traveling on "extra-mile road."

My prayer is that when it comes down to action or intention, we make the harder choice and the better choice, and always choose action over intention.

God's blessings to you on this day! Have a blessed day!

**April 8**—*Sometimes the smallest step in the right direction ends up being the biggest step of your life. Tip-toe if you must, but take the step.*—**Naeem Callaway**

There's an old and often-used phrase that says, "A journey of a thousand miles begins with a single step." But really, that phrase can be used with anything we attempt, from small everyday tasks to life-changing decisions, to a journey of a thousand miles.

Everything we do in life, and I mean every single thing, has to have a first step involved. If it's starting or leaving a job, reaching out and beginning or renewing a relationship with God, heading to the gym, or any of thousands of things that we do daily to try and move in the right direction . . . they all begin with a first step. And as the quote says, tip-toe if you must, but take the step.

And of course, that first step is always the hardest and most challenging one to take. Even when we're at the end of that thousand-mile journey, the last step will not be as hard or as difficult as that first one. But while that first step is the hardest one, there is also joy, freedom, and excitement in moving a new and right direction. And if you encounter obstacles along the way, throw them on the ground and use them as stepping stones!

My prayer is that regardless if you're trying to achieve great things or accomplish small things today, this week or in the future you will have the strength, stamina, and determination to take that difficult first step . . . and then keep on stepping.

God's blessings to you on this day! Have a blessed day!

**April 9**—**The fears we don't face become our limits.**—**Robin Sharma**

Have you ever considered a life-changing decision about a new direction in life, or a new career, and before you could register the first thought fear took over and your new ideas were quickly scrapped? If you're like many people, the answer to that question is a resounding "yes."

Simply stated, fear is a dream-killer and a career-crusher; it deeply limits our ability to achieve our goals. At its worst, fear can cripple a mind and literally ruin a person's life.

Fear, joined often by his twin brother Doubt, keeps people in dead-end jobs, harmful relationships, and countless other life-traps. These two culprits often take up residence between a person's ears and begin a nonstop loop of the "you're not _____ enough" chants. The words that normally fill in that blank include "smart," "good," "young," "talented," "gifted," etc.

The interesting thing about fear is that when confronted, it simply flees and moves on to another victim. In fact, fear is a lot like the playground bully: all blow and no go.

The single, simple point in today's offering is to encourage you to never, ever let fear limit your life opportunities. Stand up to fear, evict it from between your ears, put out "no trespassing" signs and then happily release the limits in your life.

God's blessings to you on this day! Have a blessed day!

### April 10—*A pessimist is someone who complains about the noise when opportunity knocks.*—Oscar Wilde

I recently read a book by Kent Keith entitled *Do It Anyway*. It's a book with ten paradoxical commandments. The first one is: "People are illogical, unreasonable, and self-centered. Love them anyway." The others involve kindness, honesty, doing good each day, etc. It's good stuff.

After a recent short conversation with an individual, I added an eleventh paradoxical commandment. During a casual encounter, on a beautiful spring day, here's the conversation:

Me: "What a beautiful day it is, I'm sure happy to see that sunshine today."

Other person: "Yeah . . . but it's supposed to rain and maybe storm later in the week."

Me (with a sigh): "Well . . . I'm just going to enjoy the sunshine today and not worry about later this week. (Quickly walks away.) Have a great day."

Here's another commandment that would fit well in the book: "Some people are going to be negative, pessimistic, and oftentimes critical. Be positive and optimistic anyway." My prayer today is that instead of thinking about rainy days when the sun shines, you'll instead remember those glorious, sun-drenched days when it's pouring down rain.

God's blessings to you this day! Have a blessed day!

## April 11—*It's never too late to become who you might have been.* —George Elliott

Sometimes inspiration appears in unique places. That was my thought recently when I had a brief but inspirational exchange with a young lady who was working as a cashier at a business.

Another employee said something about age, and the young cashier mentioned that she had an upcoming birthday. Then she said something that really caught my attention.

"I'm not where I want to be in my life," she said with some apparent disappointment in her voice. "I really thought I would be farther along at this point. I haven't finished college yet . . . and I thought I would be graduated and have a good job by now."

I asked her how old she was going to be, and she told us she would be twenty-three years old. I chuckled out loud and told her she was "a child," but saw a great opportunity to practice a little of what I preach daily. "Even though you didn't ask for it, I'm going to give you some advice," I told her. "I'm sixty-three, and I'm not where I want to be in my life. Every person, regardless of age, needs goals and dreams and ambition to do things or you quit growing and learning. As long as you're moving forward, I'd say you're right where you're supposed to be . . . and happy early birthday to you."

I think this offering is so important to so many people. You see, life is like riding a bicycle: If you stop moving, you'll lose your balance. So whether you're twenty-three or ninety-three, set goals, trust God, dream dreams, trust God, strive to be better than you were yesterday, and keep your balance by moving forward! And most importantly, keep on trusting God!

My prayer, to go along with today's offering, is that regardless of whether you're trying to achieve great things or accomplish small things, we will all have the energy, strength, stamina, and determination to set new goals and dream new dreams!

God's blessings to you on this day! Have a blessed day!

**April 12—*There are three things you cannot recover in life: the word after it's said, the moment after it's missed, and the time after it's gone.*—common expression**

Those three things—words, moments, and time—are priceless items that every one of us has within our control each day. However, as the quote says, they are also the three things in life that you cannot take back, call back, or bring back.

So choose your words wisely. They can heal or hurt, encourage or discourage, and brighten or ruin somebody's day. Those little seemingly inconsequential words are powerful. They can heal or hurt, unite or divide, and bring people to a common goal or a bitter divisiveness.

Take advantage of every moment you have in life because someday the moments we embrace will be memories and the moments we miss will be regrets. And finally, don't waste time (and energy) worrying and fretting over things that in the entire scheme of life do not matter. God deposits 86,400 seconds into your life account each day—use them wisely; each one is precious.

Words, moments, and time—wonderful items at our disposal daily—cherish each of them.

God's blessings to you on this day! Have a blessed day!

## April 13—*If God brings you to it . . . he will bring you through it.*
### —common expression

There are days when we all have to fight through a funk, through the blahs, to go about our daily routine. A while back I was having one of those days. I tried every trick I knew, but couldn't seem to shake the overall worried, stressed, and anxiety-filled mood that surrounded me.

I was working at home, and in the middle of the afternoon I glanced over on my desk and noticed a prized (but often neglected) possession—my mom's old Bible. I reached over and picked it up, and thought maybe I would open it to a page and a verse would just jump off the page to help me. I've heard of people doing that before, but nothing really caught my attention. For some reason I thumbed through her Bible all the way to the back, where there was a couple of blank pages. On one of those pages, in my late mother's handwriting was this: "When you're feeling down always read Psalm 46:1. Read it, and then believe it." She signed her name—Geraldine Muir—under what she had written. My mother passed away eighteen years ago, and that was the first time I had seen her handwritten message. I quickly located the verse and it read: "God is our refuge and strength, a very present help in trouble."

There will be those who will say that the message I found that day was just a coincidence, a chance occurrence. But I see it differently. I believe that God loves me so much that the message written many years ago was designed specifically for me to read on that day at that moment. My mom prayed a zillion prayers for me during her life, despite the fact that I often fought against her as hard as I could. The message I found is just another example of her trying to point me in the right direction.

So, today let me leave you with a message from Geraldine Muir: "When you're feeling down read Psalm 46:1. Read it, and then believe it."

This is another great reminder that God knows and cares what is happening in our lives. That's such a powerful verse, let me repeat it— "God is our refuge and strength, a very present help in trouble." What a wonderful promise!

God's blessings of refuge and strength to you this day! Have a blessed day!

**April 14**—*It's Friday . . . but Sunday's coming.*—**Rev. B. D. Scroggins**

More than thirty years ago I heard B. D. Scroggins—a minister I love and respect—deliver a sermon by this title, and all these years later I still recall that powerful and beautiful message. He talked about how those who loved and followed Jesus must have felt as the man they believed was the Son of God was beaten, mocked, cursed, and nailed to a cross while wearing a crown of thorns. He detailed what must have gone through Mary and the disciples' minds —the questions, doubt, worry, anguish, and hurt. Of course, as he pointed out, they didn't know it but Sunday was coming! And then on that glorious Sunday, Jesus' resurrection demonstrated that Satan had not defeated him, but instead Jesus had won the victory over sin, death, and the grave. Certainly, it's the greatest love story ever told!

And isn't it the same for us more than two thousand years later? All of us still go through periods and moments where it's "Friday" and those same feelings—the same questions, doubt, worry, anguish, and hurt— sometimes get the best of us.

But, just like the joy on resurrection morning when the stone was rolled away, I can share that same good news with you today, because regardless of what's happening in your life or what Friday-moment you're facing, Jesus is still King and for certain—Sunday's coming. My prayer is that you push through those Friday moments with your eyes firmly fixed on that old rugged cross, and your mind fully aware that Sunday's coming.

God's blessings to you this day! Have a blessed day!


**April 15**—*When thinking about life, always remember this: No amount of guilt can change the past and no amount of anxiety can change the future.*—**common expression**

Read this quote again and consider this: Rehashing, rereading, or reliving yesterday will not change or alter one thing that happened. At the same time, worrying, fretting, and being anxious does not empty tomorrow of its troubles; instead, it empties today of its strength.

That leaves today—and that's why today is called the present, and rightfully so, because it's a present from God. It's a present that contains another chance, a new opportunity, and the hope to be a better person. The second your eyes open every morning, that present is waiting on you as your gift to enjoy.

And it is a gift, a gift made especially for you. And the beauty of receiving this gift is that we all hold the power to make this day anything we want it to be. We can't change the past, we can't predict the future, and we cannot change the fact that people will act in a certain way. But we have in front of us a blank sheet every morning, and we hold the pen and can write any story we want that day. My prayer is that we all take time to enjoy and be thankful for our gift—today.

God's blessing to you this day! Have a blessed day!

**April 16—*I may not be where I want to be, but thank God I'm not where I used to be.*—Joyce Meyer**

I recently was reading a short story and there was a verse included that really grabbed my attention: "for in Him we live and move and have our being" (Acts 17:28). But as I read on, this verse was paraphrased by an unknown writer in a way that literally jumped off the page at me. He wrote: "Our Redeemer's blood is the ink in the pen that writes the script for our lives." Read that single sentence again, very slowly, and let every word sink in.

Maybe it's because I'm a writer and I love to try and string words together to reach out to people, but I found this one short sentence remarkable. As I read it through a few times, I thought of Jesus taking a crumpled, dirty piece of paper (our life)—and because of the blood He shed on the cross, turning it into a bright, shining manuscript. I also thought of another quote I've used that says that every new day is a blank piece of paper. Because of the old rugged cross, the good news today is that Jesus holds the pen—he's the author!

Thank you, Jesus . . . thank you for the ink in the pen that writes the script for our lives.

God's blessings to you on this day! Have a blessed day!

**April 17**—*Scars show us where we've been, they do not dictate where we are going.*—**David Rossi**

I don't know of any person who has gone through life and not picked up a few scars. These scars—the invisible ones we carry from life's struggles—are evidence that we lived, made mistakes, healed, and hopefully learned. We have the option every day to choose what direction those scars will take us.

I'm convinced that life's scars do one of two things: They either defeat us or strengthen us. How many times have you seen a person go through a bad experience—and again, we all have a few scars—and then let that particular event defeat them and become their reason to frown and have a bitter, sour attitude about every aspect of life? On the other hand, we also see people who go through the same struggles and use their scars for motivation to become stronger, better people who help others and to achieve their goals. In short, dealing with the scars of life really comes down to a choice. Do they become an obstacle or an opportunity? My answer to that question is clearly: opportunity.

To paraphrase today's quote, "Scars only show us where we've been, the roads we've traveled, and the people we've dealt with, but they absolutely do not make us who we are today or defeat our future." While people like to remind us often of our mistakes, I am thankful beyond words that it's God, through his son Jesus Christ, who is in control of forgiving those mistakes, erasing our scars, and wiping the slate clean.

God's blessings to you on this day! Have a blessed day!

**April 18**—*There are always two wolves fighting. One is darkness, negativity, and despair. The other is light, optimism and hope. The question is: which wolf wins? The answer: the one you feed.*—**common expression**

What a great analogy that defines exactly what every person is faced with every single day. Everybody starts each morning exactly the same way—with a clean slate and the ability to make that day a good one. Then the wolves start fighting and many people quickly give in to darkness, negativity, and despair.

This quote is a great example why we should wrap ourselves in an attitude of gratitude each and every day. When you feed the wolf of light, optimism, and hope, you will soon begin finding the countless blessings of God in what you might have considered a seemingly mundane and ordinary life.

Remember, embracing and practicing an attitude of gratitude doesn't change the scenery; it just washes clean the glass you look through so you can clearly see the bright colors and beauty in your life.

So, I leave you with a single, simple question today: Which wolf will you feed?

God's blessings to you on this day! Have a blessed day!

**April 19**—*Every day is a new beginning. Problems and mistakes from yesterday are just memories of lessons learned.*—**anonymous**

Sometimes inspiration appears in the strangest places. Recently one morning, I was at the local convenience store getting my daily shot of caffeine—my kickstarter. A lady was checking out in front of me and was talking to the cashier, a young man in his early twenties. She must have known him because she called him by name. She was kidding him, asking if he "was pushing all the right buttons" on the cash register where he deals with gas/lottery, etc. He laughed and said "no," and said he had to "clear the register and start all over a couple of times."

As I listened to them talk, I immediately thought of how life is just like that conversation. There is not a day goes by that we all hit the right buttons. Sometimes we say the wrong thing, we're quick to anger, we're negative, and we lean toward bitterness and resentment. Sometimes, as my mother used to tell me, "we talk when we should be listening." But the beauty is that, just like the young man who had to clear the register, we also have the ability, through Jesus Christ, to clear our own personal register and start all over again at any time of any day.

Remember, nobody can make a brand-new start, but everybody has the option to make a brand-new ending. And you can start this day, this hour, this minute, this very second, and hit the clear button.

God's blessings to you on this day! Have a blessed day!

### April 20—*The struggle you're in today is developing and building the strength you will need for tomorrow.*—common expression

A few years ago I was asked to speak at the funeral of a young man who died in his mid-twenties. In one of the saddest, most difficult conversations I can recall, his grief-stricken mother, who was not affiliated with any church, told me she remembered one particular verse from attending Sunday School as a child. That verse was Matthew 11:28, which states, "Come unto Me, all you who labor and are heavy laden, and I will give you rest." She asked me to incorporate that verse into what I said.

I worried and anguished over what to say on that sad day, and finally I decided to break the verse down into three parts. I believe this simple verse (with God's help) brought a small measure of comfort to a struggling family.

If you break this simple sentence down, it contains a plea for everybody, "come unto me"—that's everybody, every person without restriction. It also contains a wonderful promise—"I will give you rest." And for those who have gone through difficult times, that rest is so welcome for both the body and the mind.

But I believe the key words in this verse are "all who labor and are heavy laden." You see, regardless of what you're facing—from a rough work week to a parent trying to come to terms with the death of a child, and every situation in between—these seventeen words offer an unconditional invitation to everybody. The plea and the promise are important, but the invitation to "all"—"all who labor and are heavy-laden"—is the game-changer.

So, regardless what kind of week you've had or what kind of week is in front of you, remember the plea, the promise, and most of all, remember the invitation.

God's blessings to you on this day! Have a blessed day!

## April 21—*If you don't like the road you're walking, start paving another one.*—Dolly Parton

Almost every person has been there—cruising along the straight highway of life with everything going great, and then suddenly we find ourselves on a bumpy road, full of potholes and deep ruts. It could involve family, a relationship, finances, loss of employment, or health issues. The list of problems we often face on the bumpy road of life is a long one.

I understand more each day that it's not the good times, the days we're on cruise control and rolling down a nice smooth highway that defines us. Instead, it's those days when there's sharp curves and hairpin turns, when the road is slippery and it's really difficult to see, that shape our character.

When these difficult times happen, we sometimes have to ease on the brakes and slow down, and other times we have to jam on the brakes hard and come to a complete stop just to get our bearings. And then there are times when you have to turn loose of the steering wheel completely—let go and let God!

One of my favorite verses states: "Trust in the LORD with all your heart, and lean not on your own understanding; in all your ways acknowledge Him, and he shall direct your paths" (Proverbs 3:5–6). Let me paraphrase that last sentence: "In all your ways acknowledge him and he shall direct your paths . . . particularly when you're trying to pave a new road in your life.

God's blessings to you on this day! Have a blessed day!

**April 22**—*Among the things you can give and still keep are your faith, your word, a smile, and a grateful heart.*—Zig Ziglar

There is an old adage that says, "You make a living by what you get, and you make a life by what you give." A lot of folks will automatically say, "I don't have anything to give anybody." My answer to that would be, sure you do! Just look at today's quote again. All four of those give-away items—your faith, your word, a smile, and a grateful heart—are priceless, and mean so much more than giving away material possessions.

You can give a few minutes to call a friend going through a difficult time, maybe just to listen and be a sounding board and to let them know God cares about them and every single situation in their life. You can give a smile (it won't cost you anything) or even a pat on the back, a hug, or just a kind word. Sometimes even the smallest gesture can change a person's entire outlook that day. And the amazing thing is that while you're helping somebody else, you are also helping yourself more than you will ever know.

We all get so caught up trying to making a living, but my prayer today is that we all try to find a few minutes each day to make a life, give back, and pay it forward. And keep in mind, the things I've mentioned today are things you can give away and still keep. No act of kindness, no matter how small, is ever wasted.

God's blessings to you on this day! Have a blessed day!

**April 23**—*You didn't come this far . . . to only come this far.*
—common expression

Looking back on the past year, I've been blessed to speak more than any time in my life. What a joy and a blessing that has been!

Regardless of the venue or the age of those in attendance, I always talk about purpose. I believe every person has a purpose in life. And just like our attitude, I also believe that our purpose is something we control, it's in our hands daily and I believe it's something that can make or break us. You might be saying: I'm not sure what my purpose in life is. For those who want to use that excuse, consider this. Think about what a great world it would be if we all started each day with the simple, single-minded purpose of being kind to each other, smiling more, complaining less (or not at all), being helpful, being positive, and just trying to be a better person than we were yesterday. If you're looking for some purpose . . . there's a great place to start.

Once again, let me remind you. Place your hand over your heart. Feel that? That's called purpose. You're alive for a reason, or, as today's quote says: "you didn't come this far . . . to only come this far."

God has deposited 24 hours, 1,440 minutes, 86,400 seconds into your account for this day. How will you spend it? Will you use it wisely? Will it be wasted? What is your purpose?

God's blessings to you on this day! Have a blessed day!

**April 24—*You may not control all the events that happen to you, but you can decide not to be reduced by them.*—Maya Angelou**

Perhaps the greatest mystery of life is when bad things happen to good people. Several years ago I talked with a lady who had lost a son in a tragic accident. She told me that in the years following his death she became a bitter person, to the point of screaming and questioning God why her good son died when bad people continue to thrive. She said it became difficult to even drive down the main street of the town where she lived, because she would see people battling life's demons and agonize about why they were alive and her son was dead. Just as the quote says today, she let an event that she did not control reduce her to a person she didn't like or know. The bright side to this story is that she sought help for herself, and with God's grace, she was able to regain her focus and even help people who were dealing with the same loss she experienced.

While that example is an extreme, today's one-sentence quote holds true for anything—big or small—out of your control that happens to you. It's your choice whether or not you are reduced by those things. I used a quote in the past by Zig Ziglar that says: "Every test in our life makes us bitter or better and every problem comes to break us or makes us. The choice is up to you and you only, whether you become victim or victor."

Just like the lady who lost her son, it comes down to choice—does a test or a problem become an obstacle or an opportunity? In life you have three choices—you give in, give up, or give it all you got. Don't be a victim—be a victor! Don't give in and don't be reduced by things out of your control.

God's blessings to you on this day! Have a blessed day!

**April 25—***In this world we do not see things as they are. Instead, we see things as we are, because what we see depends mainly on what we are looking for.***—John Lubbock**

When I read this quote, I thought about (of all things) the weather. Let me give you an example: Coming off the blistering heat of summer, everybody looks forward to fifty-degree weather, so we can get out our hoodies and look forward to football weather and roaring bonfires. But, in contrast, after surviving another bitter winter, we all look forward to fifty-degree weather so we can get out the shorts and flip-flops and bask in the warm weather. It's the same fifty degrees, so what's the difference? The answer can be found in today's quote, "we do not see things as they are . . . we see things as we are."

How many times in your life have you uttered the phrase, "I talked myself out of doing that?" Regardless if it involves a job, a relationship, a career change, going to church, starting a diet, or going to the gym, those two pesky little enemies that camp out in our head—commonly known doubt and fear—win a lot of decisions based on the way we see things, and not the way things are. I know people who have all the intangibles— intelligence, work ethic, personality, skill, etc.—but can't overcome the fear factor. And of course that means they lose, because fear is a dream-killer, a life-changer, and a career-crusher. Keep in mind that courage is not the absence of fear—everybody has fears. But instead, courage is the triumph over fear—seeing things as they are and not as we are. My prayer is that we all try to see things as they are and not as we are!

God's blessings to you on this day! Have a blessed day!

## April 26—*Take care of the rocks first.*—anonymous

A philosophy professor stood before his class with some items on the table in front of him. When the class began, he picked up a very large, empty mayonnaise jar and proceeded to fill it with rocks that were about one inch in diameter.

He then asked the students if the jar was full. They agreed that it was. So the professor then picked up a box of pebbles and poured them into the jar. He shook the jar lightly. The pebbles, of course, rolled into the open areas between the rocks. He then asked the students again if the jar was full. They agreed it was.

The professor then picked up a box of sand and poured it into the jar. Of course, the sand filled up the remaining open areas of the jar. He then asked once more if the jar was full. The students responded with a unanimous "Yes."

"Now," said the professor, "I want you to recognize that this jar represents your life. The rocks are the important things—your family, your health, your faith—things that if everything else was lost and only they remained, your life would still be full. The pebbles are the other things that matter—like your job, your house, your car. The sand is everything else, the small stuff.

"If you put the sand into the jar first," he continued, "there is no room for the pebbles or the rocks. The same goes for your life. If you spend all your time and energy on the small stuff, you'll never have room for the things that are important to you. Pay attention to the things that are critical to your happiness. There will always be time to go to work, clean the house, give a dinner party, or fix the disposal."

The moral here today is simple: take care of the rocks first, the rest is just sand.

God's blessings to you today! Have a blessed day!

**April 27—*Be grateful each day for small things, big things, and everything in between. Count your blessings, not your problems.*** **—anonymous**

Today's offering packs a powerful punch in only two short sentences. I loved it the second I read it, primarily because I've lived it.

How about some audience participation today? Let's break this very meaningful one-sentence quote down together. First, you have to focus on those small things, right along with the big things and the "everything in between" things. And that requires us to develop a different mindset. Let's start with the basics: You woke up this morning, your eyes opened, your feet hit the floor, and you can read this. And on that initial list, be sure not to forget the caffeine that provides you a jumpstart every morning. You had countless blessings in a matter of seconds today. Then move to the three most important things you can have in life—faith (free to those who ask), family (priceless), friends (worth more than gold)—and the list just goes on from there. Again, you have to focus on how good the good is, and that means focusing on the really important things in life.

When you get focused and develop a different mindset about what is and what isn't important and how good the good is, an attitude of gratitude will emerge and your problems will seem trivial compared to your blessings.

God's blessings to you on this day! Have a blessed day!

**April 28—*A bird sitting in a tree is never afraid of the branch breaking, because its trust is not on the branch but on its own wings.*—anonymous**

I think this simple one-sentence quote provides a great analogy about life in general. Many of us are sometimes sitting on one of life's many shaky branches—health issues, the death of a loved one, work-related problems, difficult relationships, children issues, addictions, etc. It's at these times that we have to trust God to be our wings, to lift us up from that branch we find ourselves sitting on. And that's not always easy; in fact sometimes it is very difficult, because many times it seems that shaky branch is ready to break.

I recently read a short verse that stated: "Nowhere, not one single place in the Bible does it say, 'go figure it out on your own,' but over and over again it says, 'Trust in God.'"

So, the simple point behind today's offering is really pretty simple: Don't try to fix it yourself, don't try to figure it out . . . trust God. My prayer is that regardless of what wobbly perch we're on today, tomorrow, or in the future, we'll learn to put our trust and faith in God and let him be our wings.

God's blessings to you on this day! Have a blessed day!

### April 29—*Faith isn't a feeling. It's a choice to trust God even when the road ahead seems uncertain.*—Dave Willis

As a frequent visitor to Facebook and social media sites I am sometimes overwhelmed with the difficult times that many, many people face. In recent months several families I know have faced health concerns, sickness, strife, and uncertainty. Add in the stress involved with just normal day-to-day living and there are a lot of people with a lot on their plate and struggling mightily. While reading yet another post about a family facing difficult medical odds, a beautiful verse came to mind: "casting all your care upon Him, for He cares for you" (1 Peter 5:7).

Let's examine the wonderful words that make up that verse. The key word and the beauty in this verse is *all*. It doesn't say cast "some" of your cares, or only your big cares, or to prioritize your cares and take the top three—it says to cast "all" your care upon God. What a truly wonderful promise, and what a beautiful gift that the Creator of the universe cares that much about us!

And while the word "all" is the key to the sentence, the last five words—"for He cares for you"—provide the exclamation point. What a comforting and glorious promise to carry with us every minute of every day, regardless of what life throws our way! My prayer is that you will remember today, this week, and always, that regardless of where you are or what you are facing, God cares about you. And just like today's quote says, faith isn't a feeling, it's a choice to trust and believe God even when the road ahead seems uncertain and unsure.

God's blessings to you on this day! Have a blessed day!

### April 30—*A moment of patience in a moment of anger can save you hundreds of moments of regret.* —common expression

While it seems so simple, I didn't learn until just a few years ago that I do not have to respond to everything that is said to me. Wow, what a concept! In fact, one of the greatest lessons I've learned in life is that no answer is sometimes the strongest, loudest, and most powerful answer you can give. Or, as my late mother used to say: "Sometimes it's better to chew on your words before you spit them out."

And of course, here in the twenty-first century that also holds true for social media, where some people clearly need a speed bump between their keyboard and their brain. Lately I have started asking myself the question, "In the whole scheme of life, is replying to somebody's ignorant/antagonistic/wrong comment going to change anything?" The answer is, of course, always a resounding "no." So reel in that moment of anger, practice that moment of patience, and in the process save yourself many, many moments of regret. As Mark Twain said, "Speak when angry and you'll make the best speech you'll ever regret."

My prayer today is that we all learn the reward of practicing a moment of patience in a moment of anger and that we also install a keyboard speed bump.

God's blessings to you on this day! Have a blessed day!

**May 1—*Yesterday is history, tomorrow is a mystery, and today is a gift. That's why it's called the present.*—Bill Keane**

This short two-sentence quote, only eighteen words total, provides us a template, a guide, on how to approach the past, present, and future.

Rehashing, rereading, or reliving yesterday will not change or alter one thing that happened. The past is a place of reference and a place to glance back at occasionally, it's not a place of residence and a place where we want to fix our eyes. At the same time, worrying, fretting, and being anxious does not empty tomorrow of its troubles; instead, it empties today of its strength.

So, that just leaves today, the present, as your gift to enjoy. And it is a gift, a gift made especially for you, but it's a gift that cannot be enjoyed if you are daily reliving the past or fretting about the future. And the beauty of receiving this gift is that we all hold the power to make this day anything we want it to be. We can't change the past, we can't predict the future, and we cannot change the fact that people will act in a certain way. But we have in front of us a blank sheet every morning, and we can write any story we want that day. My prayer is that we all take time to enjoy and be thankful for our gift—today.

God's blessings on you this day! Have a blessed day!

**May 2—*Too busy is a myth. People make time for the things that are really important to them. Be stronger than your excuses.*—Mandy Hale**

I read a short story recently that said in every aspect—every single, small detail—life boils down to either finding a way to do something or an excuse not to do it. Think about that phrase for just a moment—you either find a way or you find an excuse—and then plug in the details of every single, small thing you do in your daily life.

Regardless if it's attending church, going to the gym, doing a little extra at work, spending more time with your family, building a closer relationship with God, etc.—it really does come down to finding a way to get things done or finding an excuse not to do it at all. When I saw the quote I shared today, particularly the last five-word sentence, "Be stronger than your excuses," I immediately thought of that story. "Find a way . . . or find an excuse."

In the fast-paced world we live in, it's not easy for anybody, but being stronger than our excuses and finding a way instead of an excuse is a very good first step to a better, more productive, and, more importantly, a more satisfying life. It's also a great way to do away forever with the "too busy" myth!

God's blessing to you on this day! Have a blessed day!

**May 3**—*Gratitude turns what we have into enough, and more. It turns denial into acceptance, chaos into order, confusion into clarity—it makes sense of our past, brings peace for today, and creates a vision for tomorrow.*—**Melody Beattie**

Today's quote is a little longer than what I usually share, and if you're like me you probably read fast and sometimes just skim over the words. To get the full meaning please read it slowly, pause at each comma, and then pause a little longer at every period. I think this quote is powerful, and certainly a guide for developing an attitude of gratitude.

In these daily offerings I share a lot of quotes and write about the importance of attitude. I have often pointed out that our attitude is the one thing we are in control of every single day. Certainly, an attitude of gratitude is the most important and by far the most life-changing virtue we can acquire. As this quote points out, an attitude of gratitude "turns what we have into enough, and more. It turns denial into acceptance, chaos into order, confusion into clarity—it makes sense of our past, brings peace for today, and creates a vision for tomorrow."

There's a familiar quote that asks the question: "What if you woke up today with only the things that you thanked God for yesterday?" Perhaps the best way to know the answer to that question is to give thanks to God each day for all things. A great way to measure your blessings is to start when you open your eyes every morning, and just go from there. You'll soon find out that your day is made up of countless tiny miracles and blessings, one right after the other!

God's blessings to you on this day! Have a blessed day!

## May 4—*Sometimes you win and sometimes you learn.*—John Maxwell

Everybody has tasted defeat and experienced setbacks—that's just a part of life. It's what we do with those difficult times, and what we learn from those setbacks, that either defines us or defeats us.

It seems that a constant rule for people who have enjoyed success is that they simply refuse to give up. Somehow these people use setbacks, failures, obstacles, the doubts of others, and the word "no" as a learning experience and motivation to reach their goals. It's not a failure to get knocked down—failure comes when we refuse to get back up.

Have you ever had a ring of keys and you were unsure which one was the right one to unlock a door? Isn't it uncanny how many times it's the very last key that finally works? It's often the same way with trying to reach a goal. Many times, we have to try a lot of different keys to unlock the door to our future. Remember, if Plan A doesn't work, learn from it and remember that there are twenty-five more letters in the alphabet. And if you use up those twenty-six letters, after Plan Z . . . you can start back with Plan 1A! Sometimes you win and sometimes you learn!

God's blessings to you on this day! Have a blessed day.

## May 5—*Some people live in a bitter, angry, hate-filled world. Some people live in a friendly, caring, love-filled world. Interestingly . . . it's the same world.*—Jose N. Harris

There are people, and we can all name them, who have to work hard to be as miserable and negative as they are each day. These are the kind of people who will let you know quickly that it is supposed to rain tomorrow when you comment how beautiful the weather is today.

There are many, many things in life that we cannot control, but our attitude is one of the few things we control every minute of every day. I love the quote that says: "Life is 10 percent what happens to us and 90 percent how we react to it." Remember, you can complain because rose bushes have thorns, or you can rejoice because thorn bushes have roses—the work and effort is the same, and the choice is yours!

Let me paraphrase today's quote this way: "Happiness and positive thinking is an attitude. By the way we approach life and our everyday thinking we either make ourselves miserable and weak or happy and strong. Interestingly, the amount of work is the same."

God's blessings to you on this day! Have a blessed day!

**May 6—*Don't fear failure. The saddest summary of a life contains three descriptions: could have, should have, and might have.*—Louis E. Boone**

It's often been said that it is far better to try and fail than to look back years and years later with deep regret and say, "I wish I would have done that."

I think that quote goes far beyond the major events in life—work, relationships, etc.—and even filters down to people carrying resentment, anger, bitterness, hurt, and other negative feelings around with them for years and sometimes for decades. Some people have been mad or upset at each other so long they can't even remember why—they just know they're mad and they're staying that way.

Regardless of where you're at in life, don't fear failure and don't look back with regret and say, "I wish." Don't be a "could have, should have, might have" person. My prayer is that our faith is bigger than our fear of failure and also that we all examine our life in those "could have, should have, might have" areas.

God's blessings to you this day! Have a blessed day!

**May 7—*When writing the story of your life, don't let somebody else hold the pen.*—anonymous**

When I read this quote, I immediately thought of a quote that I've used in the past: "Tomorrow is the first blank page of a 365-page book. Write a good one." In a different variety of words, that's exactly what today's offering is saying—you hold the pen in your hand; you are the author, and what is or isn't written on all those blank pages is determined by you and you alone. Always remember that at any given moment you have the power to say, "This is not how my story is going to end."

And I want to emphasize the part about "what is or isn't written" because what will fill those blank pages for all of us really boils down to two things: we either accept conditions as they exist in our life or we accept the responsibility to change them. One or the other is what we will write, period. Will the pages of your story be filled with optimism, kindness, purpose, motivation, positive thoughts, and understanding? Or will those pages be filled with pessimism, doubt, fear, resentment, excuses, and blame?

Again, you are the writer, you hold the pen, and regardless what happens in your life, the words that fill those pages will be determined by you. For all those embarking on any type of new journey, new goal, or new endeavor, let me remind you one more time that at any given moment you have the power to say, "This is not how my story is going to end."

God's blessing to you on this day! Have a blessed day!

**May 8—*Leave a little sparkle wherever you go.*—common expression**

I used a quote a while back that stated, "Don't let anyone dull your sparkle." And certainly, there are people who roll out of bed every morning with the intention of trying to dull somebody's sparkle that day. The key point I wrote earlier is that these people can't dull your sparkle without your consent, and you can never let yourself be defined by somebody's comment or opinion.

So, now that nobody is going to dull our sparkle, let's look at today's little seven-word quote that packs such a strong meaning. I guess it could be looked at as Part 2 in the "Sparkle Series."

First, think what a different world it would be if everybody would leave a little—just a little —sparkle wherever they go. You might be saying, "I don't have any sparkle, and I'm not even sure what that means." Well, everybody has "sparkle"—and I mean everybody. Every person has within them the ability to be kind, considerate, thoughtful, compassionate, and understanding. Everyone can offer a smile, a handshake, a hug, a pat on the back, a word of encouragement, or a random act of kindness. And that list doesn't scratch the surface of "sparkle" that we can leave wherever we go.

So, get out there today and leave a trail of sparkle behind you!

God's blessings to you on this day! Have a sparkly and a blessed day!


### May 9—*Comparison is the thief of joy.*—Theodore Roosevelt

Many people grow up with the belief that they will marry their high school sweetheart, get a college degree and a great job, get married and have perfect children, and then live happily ever after in the house on the corner. And of course, there's a white picket fence around the yard.

Sadly, when problems, trials, and difficulties happen—when life happens—any variance away from that dream causes many people to feel they failed. The situation is compounded when they start comparing their lives to others, and just like this quote states, "Comparison is the thief of joy." If you get caught up in the comparison trap it's a certainty that you will bog down, start feeling sorry for yourself, and lose focus on your own life. You are you—your life is your life. Your road to happiness is not going to be like anybody else's, so don't try to live somebody else's life or live your life comparing it to others. God didn't give us an easy life or a hard life; he gave us all a life—and what we do with it is up to us.

Instead of comparison, we really do have the option to choose what direction life's tests and problems take us. We've all seen people face what looked like an impossible situation and then become the victim or the victor. Again, it came down to choice—does a test or a problem become an obstacle or an opportunity? The third time is the charm, so let me remind you one more time: Don't fall into the comparison trap; it will steal your joy.

God's blessings to you on this day! Have a blessed day!

## May 10—*Don't dig up in doubt what you planted in faith.* —Elizabeth Elliot

Every person—I don't care who they are or how much self-confidence they seem to show—has doubts and fears failure.

Think about it: How many times have you taken a leap of faith, felt good about your decision, and then let those twin enemies that sometimes resides between your ears (doubt and fear) convince you that your decision is destined to fail? In other words, what you planted in faith you dug up in doubt?

When I read this particular one-sentence gem I thought of another quote that I've used in the past. I first saw this quote a while back and I can't count the times since that I've thought of it when making a decision: "What if I fail . . . but what if I fly?" Regardless if it's a big decision or small decision, it's a great question to ask.

Put down the shovel today and quit digging up in doubt what you planted in faith. Instead, tend to the faith you planted with prayer, trust in God, hard work, prayer, high energy, prayer, and positive thoughts! And add some more prayer . . . just for good measure!

God's blessings to you on this day! Have a blessed day!

**May 11—***You never know how strong you are until being strong is the only choice you have.***—common expression**

I read this quote and I thought about a comment made by a minister years ago. He said most people he counsels who are going through a tough time want to continually look back and dwell in the past— rehashing all the bad things that happened.

He said he always encourages them to remember how they feel today but to look ahead exactly one year and then strive to be better, healthier, stronger, etc., 365 days later. I know from experience that when you're going through a tough time, looking ahead one full year can be mind-boggling. If that's the case, then shorten the book—make it a thirty-day book, a seven-day book, or even a twenty-four-hour book . . . and then write a good one.

Regardless of the length of your "book," today is a blank page and the very first chapter. The key thing to remember and focus on is that you are the author, and that with God's help you have within you the strength, intelligence, talent, and ability to write the story any way you choose. And remember, don't look back . . . you're not going that direction.

God's blessings to you on this day! Have a blessed day!

**May 12—***Every weakness you have is an opportunity for God to show his strength in your life.* **—common expression**

Despite what you might think, there is not a single person on the planet, not one, who doesn't have a weakness in their life. Certainly, there are those who come off not showing a chink in their armor, but you can be assured there's one there.

While I will admit to many weaknesses, today's offering highlights one that I face daily. I have a great platform to speak and write about my belief and trust in God through his son Jesus Christ. But oftentimes I hold back and temper what I want to say, mainly because I've made a multitude of mistakes in my own life and those mistakes make me feel inadequate and not worthy to speak about something as perfect as God's love and plan of salvation for all of us.

I recently ran across a Bible verse that has helped me, one of those that you find that makes you know it is tailor-made for your situation. It reads: "My grace is sufficient for you, for My strength is made perfect in weakness" (2 Corinthians 12:9). Think of that: God's strength made perfect in our weakness. What a wonderful promise!

God's blessings to you on this day! Have a blessed day!

## May 13—*Happy moments–Praise God. Difficult Moments–Seek God. Quiet Moments–Worship God. Painful Moments–Trust God. Every Moment–Thank God.*—**Rick Warren**

The mark of a good writer is to say more in fewer words. Here, the author used only twenty words to lay out a blueprint for life and a guide for virtually any situation we will encounter in dealing with life. Contained in these few words is a plan for us to go by, regardless of what is happening in our life. The key point, and the constant in these twenty powerful words, is that God is always with us—always! Any emotion; any situation good, bad, or in between; every triumph; every heartbreak; every victory; every defeat every day, every minute, every second—God is there.

The final line in this gem reminds me of the question we often hear: What if we awakened today with only what we thanked God for yesterday? Read through these wonderful words again, and then ponder that question. My prayer today is that we all tuck these twenty life-changing and powerful words away and keep them with us for daily guidance.

God's blessing to you on this day. Have a blessed day!

**May 14—***The good life is a process, not a state of being. It's a direction, not a destination.***—Carl Rogers**

I think this quote does a great job of simplifying the difference between the wants and needs of life. Looking through materialistic eyes we could all say, "I want this, and I want that." However, in the real scheme of life those things pale in comparison to the actual needs involved in the making of a good life. I love the line that says the good life is a direction, not a destination. That means we're never going to fully reach our destination, but that we should keep pushing on toward that direction.

Certainly smiling often, dreaming big, and laughing a lot are important, but being able to recognize the blessings in life and to be thankful for what you have is the most important on any list we could compile about "the good life." Being able to give thanks for what we have in our life is really pretty easy when you slow down and simply look around because our "thankful list" is really never-ending. Remember, a thankful heart is a happy heart. In all things give thanks.

Isn't it interesting that a detailed list of the good life contains nothing about wealth, fame, or fortune? Certainly, this writer has his priorities in place!

God's blessings to you on this day! Have a blessed day!

**May 15—***I'm on the hunt for who I've not yet become.***—common expression**

One of the rewards of getting older is to look back and sort out your younger life. Many, many times I thought I had things all figured out, only to see my life (and my steps) head a totally different direction. Back then, I found it confusing and troubling when things didn't work out, because I thought I had everything planned out so perfectly. I recently read a verse that sorts this out perfectly: "A man's heart plans his way, but the LORD directs his steps" (Proverbs 16:9).

Looking back, I see how blessed and fortunate I was that some of my plans didn't work out. I didn't know it at the time, or was too headstrong to see it, but I believe Proverbs 16:9 was a huge part of my life, steering me in certain directions and away from others.

While there are those who believe that life is a long line of coincidences and chance occurrences, I'm confident that God has directed my life and my paths to this very moment. And yes, I believe He loves me that much! Perhaps the only thing left to say in today's offering is: "Thank you Lord for directing my steps in the past, and I'm excited about the path in front of me!"

God's blessings to you today as you travel on your path! Have a blessed day!

**May 16—*Ability is what you're capable of doing. Motivation determines what you do. Attitude determines how well you do it.* —Lou Holtz**

Regardless of how small or large the task, those three simple sentences will always come into play . . . always. And to me, attitude is by far the most important—because, with a good attitude, your motivation will be strong and your ability will exceed what you think you're capable of doing.

And if we're all in agreement that attitude determines how well we do things, consider this paragraph written by author Charles Swindoll about attitude. It's the best definition ever about the importance of attitude:

> The longer I live, the more I realize the importance of choosing the right attitude in life. Attitude is more important than facts. It is more important than your past; more important than your education or your financial situation; more important than your circumstances, your successes, or your failures; more important than what other people think or say or do.

It is more important than your appearance, your giftedness, or your skills. It will make or break a company . . . a church . . . a . . . home.

You have a choice each day regarding the attitude you will embrace. . . . You cannot change the years that have passed, nor can you change the daily tick of the clock. . . . You cannot change the decisions or reactions of other people. And you certainly cannot change the inevitable. . . . What you *can* do is play on the one string that remains—your attitude.

I am convinced that life is 10 percent what happens to me and 90 percent how I react to it. The same is true for you.[1]

As Swindoll said, you are in charge of your attitude, so use it well and use it wisely.

God's blessings to you on this day! Have a blessed day!

### May 17—*A blessing is a circle of light drawn around a person to protect, heal, and strengthen.*—John O'Donohue

Every quote I've used is different, and intended to be inspirational and motivational. But, I usually end every one of these devotionals the same way: God's blessings to you on this day! Have a blessed day!

I'm a visual learner, so today's quote jumped off the page at me with such a special meaning and it also gave me a portrait of what our blessings look like.

When we factor this quote into those two simple sentences, or to the phrase "God bless you" or to a comment I use often when I say "I'm a blessed man" it gives us a literal view of a blessing from God. Think of that, a blessing is a radiant, beaming circle of light that surrounds and encircles us and provides a hedge, a shield, and a wall of protection,

[1] Charles R. Swindoll, "Attitudes," *Insight for Living*, http://store.insight.org/p-1390-attitudes-gift-set.aspx.

health, and strength around each of us. In only one sentence and sixteen words this quote paints a beautiful, remarkable picture that we should all embrace daily—a picture of God's love and care for us.

Imagine that circle of light—that blessing—drawn around you, your children, grandchildren, and friends! It is with you everywhere you go! What a beautiful picture and what a comfort!

God's "circle of light" around you today! Have a blessed day of protection, health, and strength!

## May 18—*The future belongs to those who believe in the beauty of their dreams.*—Eleanor Roosevelt

Each year I enjoy the pictures and comments on social media about high school and college graduations. How exciting that a new class of graduates are ready to tackle the world. Today's offering is for everybody, but really geared toward graduates. A couple years ago I was asked to give a commencement speech at an area high school. This is the condensed version.

Two of the most important words in your vocabulary should be "purpose" and "choice." The best advice I can give about purpose is to find your passion—your purpose will be found there. And when you combine your purpose and your passion, it will more than likely lead directly to your profession. The choices you make today, next week, next year, and beyond the safe walls of a high school or college will come back and bless you and bless others, or they could come back and bite you. Simply stated, the choices you make in life will make your life, so choose wisely.

Finally, let me offer a laundry list of advice to graduates (and everybody else). In no particular order: Get a job; work hard; give back; don't whine; ask questions; be kind to others and be kind to yourself; don't be afraid to take the path less traveled; have a purpose; say what you mean and mean what you say; assume nothing; learn to laugh at yourself; choose wisely; dream big; smile at people you don't know; laugh often; be on time; do more with less; look people in the eye when you talk to them; remember there are always two sides to every story; never forget that you are capable of much more than you think. And last: Thank God every single day how fortunate you are to have the world at your feet.

God bless you on your journey—you *are* the future and we're counting on you! There is a big world with unlimited opportunities and challenges out there waiting on you . . . go get 'em. Congratulations again to all graduates!

God's blessings to you on this day! Have a blessed day!

**May 19—*There are really only two primary choices in life: to accept conditions as they exist, or to accept the responsibility for changing them.*—common expression**

A lot of times choices we are faced with seem confusing and they clutter our mind—"what-if" this and "what-if" that. We can literally make ourselves sick worrying and fretting about decisions we're facing. But when you look at a choice, using this quote, it really makes it very simple. We either accept conditions as they are, settle, and make a choice that is easy and safe; or we recognize that the only people who can change a situation, or at least try to change it, are us.

Many times, accepting the responsibility to try and change a condition takes us out of our comfort zone, which is always a very good thing. And of course, as the old adage goes, you are free to make either of these two choices you wish; however, you are not free from the consequences of that choice.

My prayer is that this simple quote might help someone today, this week, or in the future who is facing a difficult choice.

God's blessings to you on this day! Have a blessed day!

**May 20**—*Appreciate where you are in your journey, even if it's not where you want to be. Every season serves a purpose.*—*common expression*

Never underestimate the power of a church sign!

I started working as an underground coal miner right out of high school, a job that I held for more than twenty years. At the age of thirty-nine the mining industry fizzled and I was out of a job. Being a divorced father with a high school diploma, and three children under ten years old, does not provide for a great resume.

I enrolled in college for the first time in my life and was a much better college student than I was a high school student. I found that I had some raw talent for writing and speaking and decided, with the encouragement of a very special instructor, that I would try and combine those two things into a new career. To support myself and my family I was working three (or was it four?) part-time jobs. One of them was delivering pizza on weekends. The days were long, my plate was full, and often my faith and enthusiasm wavered.

On one particular Saturday night I was ready to throw in the towel on my goal of trying to carve out a career as a writer/speaker. On this particular night everything that could go wrong did, and I was in the middle of one gigantic pity party. On my last delivery of the night I passed a church and just happened to see the sign in front. The letters on the sign looked like they were three feet tall when I passed. I circled the block and then made a complete stop in the road and read again what the sign said: "Poverty of purpose is worse than poverty of purse."

On that night I didn't have two nickels to rub together, but I had a purpose, so I prayed and plowed ahead. A year later I embarked on a twenty-five-year career as a writer for two area newspapers and a broadcaster for a regional radio station.

Today's quote is worth mentioning again: Appreciate where you are in your journey, even if it's not where you want to be. Every season serves a purpose (I was a darn good pizza dude). And speaking of purpose, always remember that poverty of purpose is worse than poverty of purse.

God's blessings to you this day! Have a blessed day!

## May 21—*Failure is ceasing to try.*—anonymous

Life is full of failures, some big and some small, and some private and some very public. But, it's what we do with those failures that define us. In reality there are only two choices regarding failure—you can either curl up in a ball and quit, or you can square your shoulders, pick yourself back up, and try again. That's it—those are your choices when you fail. With a healthy dose of determination and stubbornness and a bigger dose of God's help I have always chosen the latter, and I hope you do too!

Perhaps Winston Churchill summed up failure best: "Success is moving from failure to failure without loss of enthusiasm." You have to love a quote about failure that begins by defining success! My prayer is that we do not let failure, big or small, public or private, be a stopping point in our life. Instead, make it a new enthusiastic beginning, a starting point!

God's blessings to you on this day! Have a blessed day!

## May 22—*If you hang out with chickens you're going to cluck, and if you hang out with eagles you're going to fly.*—Steve Mariboli

We've all heard today's quote many times before, and it always brings a smile or a chuckle. But sometime, just think about your day and the people you come in contact with and you will see that this little one-sentence gem is spot-on accurate.

We all deal with and encounter daily those people who walk around with black clouds over their heads. You know the ones I'm talking about: Everything is bad, nothing is good, the sky is falling, and the world is out to get them. It might be a beautiful day today . . . but they will remind you that it is going to rain in a few days.

I can be around people like this and in a matter of minutes I can physically feel it start wearing on me and I'm ready to cluck. On the other hand, being around people who are optimistic, forward-thinking, and ready to face and overcome any obstacle can make you believe you can soar with the eagles.

While this is a cute quote, clearly there is immeasurable truth in it. In short, don't let negative people who made up their mind to be mad before they got out of bed—the "cluckers" of the world—rob your happiness. Limit your time with the "chickens" and try instead to surround yourself with "eagles." Then . . . fly high!

God's blessings on you this day! Have a "cluck-less" and a blessed day!

## May 23—*A ship is safe in harbor, but that's not what ships are for.* —John Shedd

This quote provides a great analogy of life for all of us. As human beings certainly, we can all stay safe in our own little "harbor," but just like a ship, that's not what we're made for either. In this short, one-sentence quote I see a huge challenge for us to leave our comfort zone, a place where we are all safe in our own harbor.

And the amazing thing is that there are so many little, seemingly inconsequential things we can do every day to help us venture out of our safe harbor—things like smile at a stranger, open the door for somebody you don't know, chew on your words before you spit them out, do a random act of kindness for somebody who can't help you, volunteer to help, be kind, make somebody laugh, laugh at yourself, get started back at the gym, renew or strengthen your relationship with God, give someone a compliment and mean it . . . and the list could go on and on.

Sometimes leaving our safe harbor and navigating through the choppy waters of life to help somebody else or give back makes our own daily sailing adventure a lot smoother. My prayer today is that we all venture out of our safe harbor. Remember, a smooth sea never made a skilled sailor!

God's blessings to you on this day! Have a blessed day!

**May 24—*You make a living by what you get; you make a life by what you give.*—Winston Churchill**

Please read over today's quote again, and be sure to pause for a second or two when you reach the semi-colon that separates these two thoughts. I ask you to do that so you can distinguish the contrast between making a living and making a life. You see, what we gather in life is important, but it pales in comparison to what we scatter . . . what we give back.

You might be thinking, "I don't have anything to give anybody." Sure you do! You see, I believe the word "give" in this quote means much, much more than material possessions. There are so many things we can give daily—the list is never-ending. You can give your time to call a friend going through a difficult time, to listen to that friend. You can give a smile, a pat on the back, a hug, or even just a kind word. Sometimes even the smallest gesture can change a person's entire outlook that day. And the amazing thing, while you are helping somebody else, you are also helping yourself . . . you're making "a life."

We all get so caught up trying to making a living, but my prayer today is that we all try to find a few minutes each day to make a life and give back. You know . . . leave a little "sparkle" behind you everywhere you travel!

God's blessings to you this day! Have a blessed day.

**May 25—*Comparison creates doubt. Doubt is fuel for fear. And fear stands in the way of everything you want.*—anonymous**

How many times have you had a positive thought about embarking on a new journey in life, a new direction, and immediately doubt and fear took over and your ideas and dreams were tossed to the side? If you're like most people, me included, this has happened often. Because it's "that voice" in your head that says you're not good enough, smart enough, gifted enough, talented enough—you fill in the word in front of "enough"—that keeps all of us from being the best people we can be. That voice keeps people from reaching out to God, and it keeps people in dead-end jobs, harmful relationships, and dozens of other life-traps. Doubt and fear are the two culprits behind many dreams that were never realized!

Be strong and don't let doubt and fear set up residence between your ears. Always remember that it's not what you are that is holding you back, it's what you think you're not.

God's blessings to you on this day! Have a blessed day!

## May 26—*Sometimes it's better to react with no reaction.*—common expression

No matter how hard we try, there are situations in our lives that we simply cannot control. We can't change the fact that some people will act a certain way, that we will cross paths with negative people, and that there are days when everything seems to go wrong and you'd like to just go back to bed and pull the covers over your head.

However, the one thing we can control every single day is our attitude and the way we react. I don't believe there is anything more important than attitude. I preach it daily, and I try my best to practice what I preach! While a lot of folks worry about the clothes they put on each morning, many would be better off to concentrate more on the attitude they dress themselves in each day. A home, a business, a church, a work environment, and our relationship with every single person—attitude is the make-or-break difference in all those.

We have the ability within us every single day to decide what our attitude will be that day. Almost every day I think of the quote that says: Life is 10 percent what happens to us and 90 percent how we react to it. We are all in charge of our attitude . . . put on a good one today! The key to today's offering is that we're not going to control all that happens to us on any given day, but we have the power within us to control how we react! That's good stuff!

God's blessings to you on this day! Have a blessed day!

**May 27**—*I believe I am here for a reason and my purpose is far greater than my challenge.*—**common expression**

There is an old saying that states, "You've put your cart before the horse." Of course, this is just an old-fashioned way of saying that we sometimes get our priorities out of line.

I am a big believer that the words "purpose" and "challenge" often fall into that category with many people. Oftentimes we begin a new project with great enthusiasm and vigor—knowing that what we are working toward is a big challenge, but that our purpose to succeed carries us, motivates us, and inspires us to keep pushing forward. In those days, our purpose is far out in front of the challenges involved.

But, as the days, weeks, and months—sometimes even years—drag on, we grow tired, weary, and sometimes even pessimistic about the challenge in front of us. When this happens, the challenge becomes larger than the purpose—the cart is now before the horse—and we falter, letting the size of the challenge in front of us diminish our purpose until we give in or give up.

The key point in today's offering is to strive to always keep your purpose in front of your challenge. Keep in mind that if you are on a journey of one hundred miles and got to the fifty-mile mark before deciding to quit, you would have to travel fifty miles back to fail—when you could travel fifty miles forward and succeed. The time and distance is the same. Don't be consumed with how far you have to go; instead, stay focused on how far you have come.

God's blessings to you on this day! Have a blessed day!

**May 28**—*To be ready to fail is to be prepared for success.*—**anonymous**

More than a few times in my life I have embarked on work-related journeys where I knew, going in, that the potential for failure not only existed but was probable. Certainly, it might be a character flaw in me but I found each of these endeavors both exhilarating and frightening. I used both emotions to push myself harder to work for a positive outcome.

The two times that really stand out in my mind—once when I launched a monthly forty-eight-page regional magazine, and the other I ran for countywide political office—I used the "regret factor" to convince myself that it was the right thing to do. Both of these endeavors— both successful, by the way—were things that I wanted to do in my life and feared that if I didn't try I would one day look back and say, "I wish I would have done that." To me, failure was a preferred option over that!

So, as today's quote states, I was ready to fail but I was prepared for success.

The key point in today's offering is to never, ever let fear of failure dictate your life and defeat you from reaching for your lifelong dreams! Boot doubt and fear from that spot they sometimes occupy between your ears, roll up your sleeves, and get to work preparing for success!

God's blessings to you on this day! Have a blessed day!

## May 29—*Most people are about as happy as they make up their mind to be.*—**Abraham Lincoln**

When you first read this quote it makes you smile or chuckle, but when you think about it for just a second it is spot-on accurate.

I worked in the coal industry many years ago with an elderly gentleman who was cantankerous on a good day. When we worked midnight shift and it was near the end of the shift, he used to say, "I'm going home this morning, and if my wife has made breakfast I'm not eating a bite. And if she hasn't made breakfast I'm going to throw a fit."

While a part of what he said was in jest (I hope), there are a lot of people who are this way about everything. In short, they're going to be mad and negative no matter what. Or, just like Ol' Abe said, they are going to be "as happy [or mad and miserable] as they make up their mind to be." In short, don't let negative people, who have made up their mind to be mad and negative regardless, rob your happiness. My prayer is that you often remember this one-sentence gem and make up your mind to be happy.

God's blessing to you on this day Have a blessed day!

### May 30—*A thankful heart is a happy heart. In everything give thanks.*—common expression

I've mentioned often that my parents seemed to have an old-fashioned saying for every situation that came along in life. When talking about blessings I've heard my dad say countless times, "If you can sit up and take nourishment . . . you are blessed and have a lot to be thankful for." So, that's a good place to start today.

Certainly we will always be met by challenges, and we will always encounter worries and difficulties. That's just life; nobody escapes those challenges, worries, and difficulties. It's how we handle them, how we react to them, that makes the difference. Do we let those things rob our joy, or do we look beyond that and add up and give thanks for our countless blessings?

In everything—your feet hitting the floor this morning, the ability to read this offering, your health, family, friends, and a loving, forgiving, caring God—we all have countless reasons to give thanks. How about giving thanks for the electricity that comes into your home that provides power for that cup of coffee that you savor each morning? The second sentence to today's offering is the kicker: In. Everything. Give. Thanks.

The first time you feel yourself getting out of sorts today or this week, instead of having a "high-speed-come-apart," pause and give thanks for the blessings in your life—and there are many. Sometimes you just have to wipe the glass clean to see them! It will change your outlook; it really works!

God's blessings to you on this day! Have a blessed day!

**May 31**—*Take care of your thoughts when you're alone and take care of your words when you're with people.*—**Eleanor Roosevelt**

Taking care of your thoughts when you're alone is easier said than done. In our minds, we worry and stress about things that never happen, we beat ourselves up over mistakes we've made, and then we convince ourselves that we can't before we even try. In the end, we allow the doubts in our minds to defeat our goals, dampen our plans, and kill our dreams.

I recently read where the average human mind registers an average of 70,000 thoughts per day. Think about this: If only 10 percent of those are negative—and that's probably far too low of a percentage—then we have to sort through 7,000 negative thoughts each day. That's a lot of "sorting."

The second portion of the quote, taking care of our words, is actually easier than controlling our thoughts—even if it means biting your tongue until it bleeds. One of the greatest lessons I've learned in life (I wish I would have learned it decades ago) is that I don't have to respond just because somebody says something to me.

Silence is, in fact, the most powerful answer a person can give. This is a quote that all of us could use and practice every single day (and I'm at the top of the list). Taking care of our thoughts and words will help us go a long way in developing an attitude of gratitude and living a better life!

God's blessings to you on this day! Have a blessed day!

**June 1**—*Failure does not happen when you fall down, failure happens when you refuse to get back up.*—**Chinese proverb**

Some of the greatest success stories in American history—including Henry Ford, Walt Disney, and Abraham Lincoln—happened after multiple crushing failures. What if these three men—icons in American history and folklore—had refused to get back up after being knocked down by failure? And certainly there are many, many other success stories where folks had achieved great success because they simply refused to give up or give in after repeated failures.

The fear of failure, and particularly the fear of failing more than once, is a dream-stealer that keeps people in the same old rut day after day. Another quote that fits well here: "Success is not final. Failure is not fatal. It is the courage to continue that counts."

There is another old adage that says, "fall down seven times … get up eight." Regardless of how many times we fall down in life—and there are countless ways to fall down—we have to find a way to get back up. It doesn't matter how many times you fall down, failure does not happen until you refuse to get back up!

So, what are you waiting for? Get back up, dust yourself off, grab your bootstraps, and get back in the saddle! There are many successes waiting for you!

God's blessings on you this day! Have a blessed day!

### June 2—*The only time you should ever look back is to see how far you've come.*—Kevin Hart

The past—some people get stuck there, and others can't seem to turn it loose. And while some don't like to admit it, we all have a past. And of course there are those who never miss an opportunity to remind us on a regular basis about our past miscues and missteps. In short, putting the past behind us and keeping it behind us is a monumental task for many, many folks. That's why today's one-sentence gem is so important. It explains that we won't be focused on the past if our vision is in the right direction.

The best analogy I've ever heard about the past involved a windshield and a rearview mirror. I heard a speaker ask why a windshield is so big, while a rearview mirror is so small. The answer, he said, is because while driving we should spend almost all our time looking forward, with only an occasional glance back. He then noted that life is the same way, we should spend almost all our time focused on what's in front of us with only a look back once in a while. After all, what's behind you should never be your focus because that's not the direction you should be going. My prayer today is that we all keep our eyes fixed on what's in front of us—that big picture!

God's blessings to you on this day! Have a blessed day!

**June 3**—*Some people will always throw stones in your path, but it depends on you what you make of them. So, what will you build . . . a wall or a bridge?*—**anonymous**

It's a fact that life is full of stone-throwers—those folks who seem to find joy in planting a doubt in your mind, raining on your parade, remembering a past mistake, or pointing out that there is a greater chance of failure than success in what you are trying to accomplish. The older I get, the more I'm convinced that in order to stay positive, focused, and moving forward we have to distance ourselves from, and ignore, negative people.

There's an old adage that speaks volumes about this topic: A negative thinker sees a difficulty in every opportunity, but a positive thinker sees an opportunity in every difficulty.

So, what will you build . . . a wall or a bridge? Negative people are a daily part of life, but don't let the stones they throw become a wall to hinder or stop your plans, your dreams, and your goals. Instead, when they lob a negative stone your way use it, with God's help, to build a positive bridge to a better life.

God's blessings to you on this day! Have a blessed day!

**June 4**—*Strength doesn't come from what you can do. Strength comes from overcoming the things you thought you couldn't do.* —**anonymous**

There are many definitions of "strength," but I think today's quote is one of the best and provides a great measuring stick to determine how strong we are in handling life's many challenges. In addition, there is great joy in overcoming the things you thought you couldn't do.

It seems that a constant rule for people who have enjoyed success is that they simply refuse to give up. Somehow these people use setbacks, failures, obstacles, the doubts of others, and the word "no" as motivation to reach their goals. In short, it's not a failure to get knocked down; failure comes when we refuse to get back up.

Have you ever had a ring of keys and you were unsure which one was the right one to unlock a door? Isn't it uncanny how many times it's the very last key that opens the door? It's the same way with trying to reach a goal: Many, many times we have to try a lot of different "keys" to unlock the door to our future.

Remember, if Plan A doesn't work . . . there are twenty-five more letters in the alphabet.

God's blessings to you on this day! Have a blessed day!

## June 5—*The secret to happiness is counting your blessings while others are adding up their troubles.*—William Penn

Let me pose a question to you in today's offering: What are you thankful for today?

Wait! Before you give me the standard answers, think about that question and really give it more than a passing thought. First, start from the moment you opened your eyes this morning, to the ability to think about what your plans are today (probably still in bed), to your feet hitting the floor to take a first step, to a cup of coffee, to the quietness and beauty of early morning. What are you thankful for today? You might want to grab a pen and notebook, because if you answer honestly about all the people, all the freedoms, the beauty, wonders, excitement, the physical and mental ability you have . . . and on and on . . . that make up your life, it will take you a while.

Every person will encounter a few troubles along the way; that's just life. But I challenge you to list your blessings on one side of a page and your troubles on the other. I can guarantee that your blessings far exceed your troubles. The list of real blessings in our lives is infinite. Life is a succession of tiny miracles stacked on top of each other! So using two key words in today's offering, start counting and quit adding.

There is a quote I've used in this space before that sums up today's thought nicely: "A thankful heart is not only the greatest virtue, but the parent of all other virtues."

God's blessings to you on this day (and they are many)! Have a blessed and thankful day!

### June 6—*Knowledge is knowing what to say. Wisdom is knowing when to say it.*—common expression

Two short sentences, one right behind the other, make up today's offering. But my, oh my, how far those two sentences are apart. And that vast difference is created by one word in each sentence—what and when.

Looking at that quote, it seems our prayer should be for a measure of both knowledge and wisdom—the knowledge to know what to say, combined with the wisdom to know exactly when to say it. Certainly, gaining the knowledge to know what to say is not nearly as difficult as mastering the art of knowing when to say it. For some people, me included, learning to bite your tongue is a great way to attain the wisdom to know when to talk and when to shut up.

As many people my age can attest, we are often reminded as we grow older of sage advice our parents dispensed on a regular basis. Reading today's offering reminds me of a gem my mother tossed my direction on a regular basis. I can still remember her saying often, "The good Lord gave you one mouth and two ears for a reason!" And then she would quickly point out that my mouth will close, but my ears won't! As always, words of wisdom! My prayer is that we all gain knowledge and wisdom with our daily words, to know what to say and when to say them!

God's blessings to you on this day! Have a blessed day!

## June 7—*Today is the tomorrow you worried about yesterday.* —Dale Carnegie

Today's offering is a little bit of a tongue-twister, but it really carries a powerful punch. I challenge you to read it again slowly. Today (take a pause) is the tomorrow (take another pause) you worried about yesterday.

Now that you've read it slowly and have a handle on the significance, let's go back and look at yesterday and all the worries we had about "tomorrow." Of course, that tomorrow is now today, and 99.9 percent of the things we stewed and fretted about never came to fruition. I heard a speaker say recently that worrying about everything (including tomorrow) is like carrying an umbrella around with you on a sunny day on the chance that it might rain.

We can worry ourselves sick about this, lose sleep about that, and stress out about everything imaginable, but the bottom line is this: God is in control, and worrying does not empty tomorrow of its troubles; it empties today of its strength.

Isaiah 41:10 gives us a wonderful promise to hang on to on the days when we worry about tomorrow: "Fear not, for I am with you; be not dismayed, for I am your God. I will strengthen you, yes, I will help you, I will uphold you with my righteous right hand." That's a great promise to anchor ourselves in yesterday, today, and tomorrow!

God's blessings to you on this day! Have a blessed day!

## June 8—*The difference between a stumbling block and a stepping stone is decided by how high you raise your foot!*—Benny Lewis

When I first read this quote, I immediately thought of the question we've often heard: "Is the glass half-full or half-empty?" The way a person answers that question explains a lot about how they approach life.

In this instance, where some people might see a stumbling block in their path, others know that by stepping a little higher they can turn an obstacle into an opportunity, a bitter experience into a better life, and a test into a testimony. This quote reminded me of another gem I've used before: Don't carry your mistakes around with you. Instead, place them under your feet and use them as stepping stones.

As you travel along life's pathway today, tomorrow, and in the future, my prayer is that if you run into a stumbling block you can do some "high-steppin'" and turn it into nothing more than a stepping stone. And oh, by the way, the answer to the question about whether the glass is half-full or half-empty? It doesn't matter—the glass is always refillable!

God's blessings to you on this day! Have a blessed day!

**June 9**—*Happiness and positive thinking is an attitude. By the way we approach life and our everyday thinking we either make ourselves miserable and weak or happy and strong. Interestingly, the amount of work is the same.*—common expression

I recently read a story that our brains are wired for survival; therefore, picking out the negatives in our life is what we instinctively do each day. You probably just had the same thought as me that some folks work overtime each day picking out the negatives in life. These are the people that we all deal with, who seem to have a problem for every solution. The story went on to say that we can actually rewire our brains by focusing on positives for sixty seconds, three times a day, for forty-five consecutive days. The story didn't use one of my favorite phrases, but this is exactly how we can develop an "attitude of gratitude"—washing life's window clean to see what we have been missing.

There are people—we can all name them—who have to work hard to be as miserable and negative as they are each day. These are the kind of people who, when you comment how beautiful the weather is, quickly let you know that it's supposed to rain next week. The last sentence is the "kicker" to this quote—the amount of work in developing a negative or a positive attitude is the same. In reality, it might actually take more effort to be negative and pessimistic on a daily basis.

Remember, you can complain because rose bushes have thorns . . . or you focus on the positive and rejoice because thorn bushes have roses. The work and effort is the same, and the choice is yours! My prayer is that the work you put in on you results in becoming happy and strong.

God's blessings to you on this day! Have a blessed day!

### June 10—*Your present circumstances don't determine where you can go, they merely determine where you start.*—Nido Qubein

This quote holds so much truth and instruction in only one sentence. Many of us, myself included, have been in difficult situations where you feel as though your present circumstances—the problems swirling around you—are the determining factor in what your future holds.

You can get beat down to the point that you convince yourself that this is the way your life is always going to be. Instead, as this wonderful quote points out, those trying circumstances should be looked at as the starting point, the beginning, and a genesis to a new page in your life's story.

Every day—in fact, every minute—starts a new page in your life story. You hold the pen in your hand and you are the author of your story. Don't let circumstances hold you back. Instead, let them be the starting point to success, achievement, and happiness.

God's blessings to you on this day! Have a blessed day!

### June 11—*A flower does not compete with the flowers next to it. It just blooms!*—Zen Shin phrase

This quote illustrates one of the great misconceptions of life—measuring success. Many people feel like they have failed at life because they continually measure their success against friends, coworkers, family members, and highlight-reel pictures that some people post on social media.

In my estimation, success is not measured by what you do compared to what others do. Instead, success is measured by what you do with the ability that God gave you. And I truly believe every person is gifted; however, some people never open the present.

The only person we should be in competition with, and the only person we should try to be better than, is the person we were yesterday! So, get out there and open the present God gave you, and just like a beautiful flower . . . bloom!

God's blessings to you on this day! Have a blessed day!

### June 12—*Ambition is the path to success. Persistence is the vehicle you arrive in.*—Bill Bradley

As a young writer many years ago, I was often told by editors to "write tight"—in other words, to put as much punch as possible in as few words as possible. I thought of that when I read these two powerful sentences. In only thirteen words, the writer delivered a perfect and accurate description about what it is going to take to travel the path to success, and the mode of transportation it will take to get there. Any young person embarking on an education or work-related journey need to get acquainted with these two words—without question, ambition and persistence will carry you a long, long way in life..

Let me remind you of one of my favorite verses that goes perfectly with today's offering: "I can do all things through Christ who strengthens me" (Philippians 4:13). Remember, that verse doesn't say, "I can do some things," or "a few things." It says, "I can do *all* things." A healthy dose of ambition and unwavering persistence, coupled with Philippians 4:13, is a guaranteed recipe for success!

My prayer today is that any time you're working toward success and encounter a difficult moment, you'll recall these two perfectly worded sentences, and the verse that reminds us that *all* things are possible through Christ.

God's blessings to you on this day! Have a blessed day!

**June 13—*Anger is a feeling that makes your mouth work faster than your brain.*—anonymous**

Everybody gets mad and feels anger; it's impossible to live day to day and deal with the struggles and difficult people that come our way on a regular basis and not feel anger from time to time. The key is how we channel that anger, what we do with it, and how it impacts our life.

I love the quote by Mitch Albom in *The Five People You Meet in Heaven* concerning anger: "Holding anger is a poison. It eats you from inside. We think that hating is a weapon that attacks the person who harmed us. But hatred is a curved blade. And the harm we do, we do to ourselves."[2]

It's been said that harboring anger and hatred is like drinking poison and expecting the other person to die. How many times in life have we seen people get angry with each other and then devote the rest of their life trying to demean, discredit, and destroy the other person? We've all seen people that couldn't tell you what they're mad about, but they're mad and they're going to stay that way! Their lives turn into a constant "get-even" mentality.

In all the words I write in my life, none will be more powerful and honest than the next sentence: Our lives will be much, much better if we spend our time trying to get even with those who helped us, while we happily ignore those that hurt us. It's not easy, but with God's help, a strong will, and a heaping helping of determination, overcoming anger can be accomplished!

God's blessings to you on this day! Have a blessed day!

---

[2] Mitch Albom, *The Five People You Meet in Heaven* (New York: Hyperion, 2003), 141.

**June 14**—*You ought to be thankful a whole heaping lot . . . for the people and places you're lucky you're not.*—**Dr. Seuss**

This quote, with a little rhyme attached, is clever and rolls off the tongue easily, but it's also spot-on accurate. As I get older, I can look at so many places in my life where I thought I had the timing and the circumstances all figured out, only to end up going a totally different direction. Oftentimes when I'm asked to speak I talk about God directing my path—away from some things and toward others. Regardless of what anybody else thinks, I believe that God has directed my path, and at this moment I'm right where I'm supposed to be. But I have to admit, I didn't always go willingly. You see, I have a tendency to try and do God's work for him based on my wants and my timing. I've learned, sometimes the hard way, that's not the way it works. God's direction and timing are always perfect.

I can't count the times in the past few years that I've made the comment: "Boy, God was sure looking out for me (or a member of my family) to keep us away from that situation." And many times, the situations I refer to happened decades ago. There's a Bible verse that explains this exactly and straight to the point: "A man's heart plans his way, but the LORD directs his steps" (Proverbs 16:9).

It's been said that a thankful heart is not only the greatest virtue, but the parent of all other virtues. And while I am truly thankful for all of the many blessings in my life, I'm also thankful for some things *not* in my life. Or, to paraphrase today's quote: "Today I'm thankful a whole heaping lot . . . for the people and places I'm lucky I'm not."

God's blessings to you on this day! Have a blessed day!

**June 15**—*Life is not a race, but a journey to be savored each step of the way.*—*common expression*

The key word in today's quote is "savored"—a word that I don't associate much with the fast pace of life in the twenty-first century. To put it bluntly, it sure doesn't seem like many folks are even enjoying, let alone savoring, life these days.

A lot of folks spend their days dwelling on the past, while others are continually planning for the future. Certainly, a glance (a quick glance) back is all right, and it never hurts to plan ahead, but don't do either while letting today slip right through your fingers. I have mentioned often in my daily offerings that today is called "the present" clearly for a specific reason—it's a gift from God to use any way you choose!

When you awaken each morning, "the present" is waiting for you, your slate is clean, and you can and should savor each step of your journey. Remember, it's not a race. You have the ability every single morning to mold, shape, and make each day into what you want it to be. You can dress yourself in an attitude of gratitude, get your sparkle on, and leave a wide trail of it everywhere you go. Then you can add a wide smile to your wardrobe to savor every moment of your day—a day made especially for you and a present from God!

God's blessings to you on this day! Have a blessed day!

**June 16**—*It's a great day to have a great day!*—**common expression**

I recently woke up one morning, and immediately when my eyes opened I started thinking about the long list on my plate for that day. It was a Wednesday—my longest, busiest, most tiring day—and on this particular "hump day" I had a couple other tasks that just added to my worry and concern. Keep in mind that within a few minutes—while still in bed—I had worked myself into a tizzy before my feet even hit the floor.

Almost in the same instance that I was trying to prioritize my crisis list for the day, a simple verse came to my mind: "[T]hose who wait on the LORD shall renew their strength; they shall mount up with wings like eagles, they shall run and not be weary, they shall walk and not faint" (Isaiah 40:31).

As I pondered that wonderful verse, I asked myself a very important question: "How can I 'mount up with wings like eagles' if I'm stressed out and worried about whether I get my work list done or not?" As I felt a calmness settle in (rare for me), I decided that I was going to rejoice in this (beautiful) day, work hard, and do all I could do—what didn't get done would just have to stay undone for right now. There will always be another day, and if there's not, well then . . . it won't matter anyway, will it?

God's blessings to you on this day that the Lord has made just for you! Have a blessed day!

## June 17—*Maturing is realizing how many things don't require your comment.*—anonymous

In all my years, one of the greatest things I've learned is that I don't have to respond to every negative or hurtful comment that is said to me or aimed in my direction. It took me many years and more than a few verbal battles, but I've found that most of the time the very best response is no response at all and the loudest answer is silence. I suppose it can be blamed on human nature, but we all have the tendency and a desire to want to get the last word—but many of us know that there is never a last word. I say something, you respond and try and top me, and the war of words is on.

Think about it and then try to imagine how much different life would be for everybody, how many bad situations would have been averted, how many hearts would not have been broken, how many dreams wouldn't have been shattered if we all just exercised that one moment of patience? My prayer today is that we all learn to exercise that moment of patience, chew on our words, and bite our tongue until it bleeds to keep from responding in anger.

God's blessings to you on this day! Have a blessed day!

**June 18**—*The miracle of gratitude is that it shifts your perception to such an extent that it changes the world you see.*—**anonymous**

There is a 180-degree difference between hearing about something and actually experiencing it. We could all read countless geography books, but until we actually visited an area and experienced it we wouldn't have a real-life, firsthand experience.

I used that illustration in today's offering because developing an attitude of gratitude is exactly the same. I am convinced that an attitude of gratitude is the most important and by far the most life-changing we can acquire. I believe it because I've lived it . . . period!

A few years ago, after reading about the importance of taking care of my attitude daily, and giving thanks for all things—and I mean all things—in my life I decided to give it a try. It wasn't easy at first, because who wants to give thanks for difficult jobs and the sweat dripping off the end of my nose? But I stayed with it, and soon I began to see a change in the way I viewed the world and my daily surroundings. I even gave thanks for contrary people and sore muscles—they both make me stronger!

I want to point out again that an attitude of gratitude does not change the scenery; it merely cleans the glass you look through daily so you can see the bright colors you've been missing. Or, as a familiar quote states: "Gratitude helps us see what is there instead of what isn't."

God's blessings to you on this day! Have a blessed day!

**June 19**—*Purpose is the reason for your journey. Passion is the fire that lights the way.*—**common expression**

Looking back on the past couple years, I've been blessed to speak more than any time in my life. What a joy and a blessing that has been!

Regardless of the venue or the age of those in attendance, I always talk about purpose. I believe every person has a purpose in life. And just like our attitude, I also believe that our purpose is something we control; it's in our hands daily and I believe it's something that can make or break us.

You might be saying: "I'm not sure what my purpose in life is." For those who want to use that excuse, consider this: Think about what a great world it would be if we all started each day with the simple purpose of being kind to each other, smiling more, complaining less (or not at all), being helpful, being positive, and just trying to be a better person than we were yesterday. If you're looking for some purpose, there's a great place to start.

Once again, let me remind you: Place your hand over your heart. Feel that? That's called purpose. You're alive for a reason. God has deposited twenty-four hours, 1,440 minutes, 86,400 seconds into your account for this day. How will you spend it? What is your purpose?

God's blessings to you on this day! Have a blessed and purposeful day!

## June 20—*Worrying is literally betting against yourself.*—common expression

It would be amazing to know the number of people who go through life afraid, worried, and stressed to the max on a daily basis. We all have fears, we all battle worries and anxiety, but it's what we do with those fears and worries that can make a difference in our lives.

When fear creeps into my mind, I am always reminded of a verse that begins with two wonderful words from God: Fear. Not. As I have pointed out in the past, those two little words located in Isaiah 41:10 are only one time out of many, many times that the Bible reminds us to "fear not." The remainder of the verse is powerful: "Fear not, for I am with you; be not dismayed, for I am your God. I will strengthen you, yes, I will help you, I will uphold you with my righteous right hand" (Isaiah 41:10).

If you're like me, you might have read through that verse quickly. I would encourage you to slow down and savor those meaningful words and messages of hope: "Fear not . . . I am with you . . . be not dismayed . . . I am your God. . . . I will strengthen you . . . I will help you . . . I will uphold you with My righteous right hand."

Maybe, along with all these wonderful promises and messages of hope, the real lesson in today's offering is for me (and maybe you too) is to slow down, don't be afraid, and understand that God is in control. My prayer is that no matter what you're going through or what mountain you're facing, you will slow down and remember the message and promise of Isaiah 41:10.

God's blessings your way on this day! Have a blessed day!

### June 21—*Today give a stranger a kind word or one of your smiles. It might be the only sunshine they see all day.* —anonymous

Many times in life it's the little, seemingly insignificant things that matter the most—things like a kind word, a smile, or even a random act of kindness. How many times have you gotten up in the morning and your mood changed (good or bad) because of a negative or positive comment? If you're honest, it happens often.

I am a big believer that there is very little difference in people; however, that little difference is attitude and the big difference is whether it's positive or negative. So, as you go through you day, smile at people, hold a door open for someone, strike up a conversation, ask somebody how they're doing—in short, throw a little sunshine out there today, and I guarantee it comes right back to you.

Do you remember the wonderful quote by Mother Teresa regarding the importance of kind words? She said, "Kind words can be short and easy to speak, but their echoes are truly endless."

In just one simple sentence this quote speaks volumes. Think about it: It takes virtually no effort to say a kind word—maybe even something as simple as "good morning" to a stranger—or to take the time to ask someone how they're doing. Those few seconds you spend could be the only positive words that person hears on that particular day, or maybe for many days, so certainly the echoes are truly endless. My prayer is that we will all take the time to add a few kind words to our daily vocabulary. It's a small investment that could have a huge dividend.

God's blessings to you on this day! Have a blessed day!

**June 22—*Everyone you know is fighting a battle you know nothing about. Be kind. Always.*—common expression**

I recently ran into a long-time acquaintance and greeted the person in the same way I had for many years. I immediately noticed a difference in their demeanor and greeting back to me. After we parted company, I wondered if I had done something to offend the person and even considered calling to find out. I decided against that idea and put the matter out of my mind on that day. A few days later, I heard that my friend was going through some serious health issues. Certainly that explained our unusual encounter.

When I read through today's quote, I was reminded of that meeting. Every person we encounter is fighting a daily battle of some kind. Some of the battles are monumental; others are small. The list of problems is countless and those affected are young, middle-aged, and elderly. In short, everybody faces obstacles in their lives daily and that's what makes it imperative for us to be keenly aware of how we treat others.

The three little words that finish today's quote are so important: Be kind. Always.

In a world where you can be anything, be kind—because no act of kindness, regardless how small, is ever wasted!

God's blessings to you on this day! Have a blessed day!

**June 23**—*It doesn't matter how many times you fall. What matters most is how many times you stand up, shake it off, and keep moving forward.*—**common expression**

As a youngster I heard my dad use a phrase that goes along with this one: "If you get knocked down seven times, you get back up eight." Back then I wasn't certain what that meant, but as I grew older and faced a few life battles, the meaning became very clear.

Every test in life—and we all face many of them—will either make us better or bitter. Every problem in life will either make us or break us. Every time we get knocked down, we have the choice to stand up and be the victor, or stay down and be the victim.

Sometimes one quote will cause me to think of another quote. I recently found one that parallels this one: The same boiling water that softens the potato hardens the egg. It's not about circumstances, but what we're made of.

With God's grace and strength and a healthy dose of our own determination and common sense, we have the ability to face any test and be better and not let any problem break us. In the end, we will be a victor and not a victim.

Seven times? Eight times? It doesn't matter, because with God's help we can stand up, shake it off, keep moving forward, and plan on being the victor!

God's blessings to you on this day! Have a blessed day!

**June 24**—*Everyone has inside of him or her a piece of good news. The good news is that you don't know how great you can be, how much you can love, what you can accomplish and what your potential is.*
—**Anne Frank**

I heard a speaker recently talking about this very thing. He agreed with the points of this quote but added that there are two main reasons why people don't experience the "piece of good news" that is talked about in this quote. Those two reasons reside between your ears, and they are called doubt and fear.

Without question, doubt and fear are the two greatest dream-killers that exist. In short, your determination has to be greater than your doubt, and your faith has to be greater than your fear.

We fail at 100 percent of the things we don't try. The answer is "no" to all the questions we never ask. Today's offering reminds you once again to make sure your worst enemy doesn't live between your own two ears. Remember, it's not what you are that holds you back—it's what you think you're not. My prayer today is that we all evict those dream-killers, doubt and fear, from the room they occupy in our minds and strive to find that piece of good news.

God's blessings to you on this day! Have a blessed day!

**June 25—*The definition of insanity is to keep doing the same thing over and over again and expecting a different result.*—common expression**

In every aspect of a person's life—spiritual, physical, emotional, work, relationships, etc.—if you do what you've always done, you shouldn't be surprised that the end result is always the same.

Yet people are surprised, sometimes shocked and stunned, that nothing changes. To me, that mentality represents one of the true wonders of life. Reread the one-sentence gem that makes up today's quote. There are people who have spent an entire lifetime proving this definition 100 percent correct.

I think that spot-on definition goes far beyond the major events in life—work, relationships, etc.—and filters down to people carrying resentment, anger, bitterness, hurt, and other negative feelings around with them for years and sometimes for decades. Some people have been mad or upset at each other so long they can't even remember why—they just know they're mad and they're staying that way.

It's often been said that it is far better to try and fail than to look back years and years later with deep regret and say, "I wish I would have done that." The key point in today's offering is that in order to change what you always get, you're going to have to do something different from what you've always done! My prayer is that we all have the courage to stop the insanity and make necessary changes in our lives.

God's blessing to you on this day and Have a blessed day!

## June 26—*If you find a path with no obstacles, it probably doesn't lead anywhere.*—**Frank A. Clark**

Perhaps it's because I know that as soon as my feet hit the floor a very busy and long day will start, I always lay in bed a few minutes and think of the day in front of me—what's on my plate, what needs to be done first. However, on a recent morning my thoughts focused instead on the fact that a lot of people have a difficult week in front of them: funerals of dear family members, funerals of lifelong and loyal friends, stress at work, medical issues, difficult relationships, roller-coaster rides with health problems, financial problems . . . and the anxiety-filled list just goes on and on.

While I thought of all that and how a lot of folks will be starting the day with a sense of dread, a verse, one of my favorites, came to mind: "I can do all things through Christ who strengthens me" (Philippians 4:13). It's only one short sentence, but it's ten power-packed words of unlimited hope, promise, fulfillment, and expectation regardless what we are facing. My prayer is that if you are facing a tough week—and aren't we all—you will take these ten words with you and use them frequently. I can do all things—not a few things, not most things, not a limited list of things, but *all* things—through Christ who strengthens me.

Couple this wonderful verse with today's quote and we have the assurance of knowing that regardless of the obstacles placed in our paths, we can turn to Jesus Christ for our strength!

God's blessings to you this day! Have a blessed day!

**June 27—*If it's important to you, you will find a way. If not, you will find an excuse.*—Ryan Blair**

I'm going to challenge you this morning with the two short sentences that make up today's offering. Take these two sentences and apply them to every aspect of your life, every decision you make about what you do and what you choose not to do. If you're honest with yourself, you have to admit that it is 100 percent accurate—we either find a way or we find an excuse.

I know I quote my parents and their old-fashioned phrases a lot, but when I thought about the truth behind this quote, I remembered hearing my mom say countless times, "Where there's a will there's a way," which in essence is the same thing as above. If you have the will (and it's important), you will find a way to get it done. I suppose I could add a sentence to that: Where there's no will, there's an excuse. For some folks, and I understand this completely, sometimes putting the will and the way together is very difficult.

In every single aspect of our life—our relationship with God, family, friends, work, exercise, etc.—today's quote should be our measuring stick. Do we find a way, or do we make an excuse?

God's blessings to you on this day! My prayer is that whatever you're facing today, tomorrow, or in the future you find a way to put the will and the way together. Have a blessed day!

**June 28—*The secret to getting ahead is getting started.*—common expression**

One of the wisest comments I've ever heard came from a minister talking about people who are going through difficult times. He said most people want to flip a switch and make their lives OK again, and that simply is not going to happen. He said he always tells these people to set very short-term goals that will lead to a long-term accomplishment.

For instance, if it's Monday and you're going through a rough spot in life, look ahead to next Monday and try to stay on course and make improvements in your life from one week to the next. Then look ahead to the next Monday and the next, and the next, with the big-picture goal to look ahead six months or a year and see how far you've progressed. A quote I've used often speaks volumes about this topic: You are not defined by your past; you're prepared by your past.

Remember, opportunity often comes disguised in the form of misfortune or temporary defeat. My prayer today is for strength and determination to you if you're trying to forge a brand-new ending!

God's blessings to you on this day! Have a blessed day!

### June 29—*Be kind. Be thoughtful. Be genuine. But, most of all be thankful.*—common expression

We've all been asked the question: Are you a person who sees the glass as half-full or half-empty? My standard answer through the years, trying to be optimistic, is that I'm a half-full guy. But, a while back—I'm not even sure when it started—I started trying to give thanks to God daily, hourly, sometimes by the minute, for every single thing in my life.

All of a sudden, instead of seeing the glass as half-full, I gave thanks that I have a glass that has something in it. I gave thanks that even if the glass is empty, it's always refillable. I gave thanks for work that I didn't want to do, for sore muscles, for strength and endurance, for the desire to learn, to think, to make a difference, to try and reach people by stringing a few words together, and for the sweat on my brow. In all things—let me say that again, in all things—I started giving thanks. And that includes difficult situations, tough days, and contrary people! They all make me stronger!

It was not an overnight transformation, but slowly, a little at a time, I started looking at life differently. I really like the eyes I'm viewing the world through right now. A favorite quote of mine says: "A thankful heart is not only the greatest virtue, but the parent of all other virtues." And I give thanks to God for that!

God's blessings to you on this day, and remember that a thankful heart is a happy heart. Have a blessed day!

**June 30—*Life is a series of thousands of tiny miracles. All you have to do is notice them.*—common expression**

A few years back, I had some vision issues where I was seeing double. This happened particularly often when I was reading. After several tests it was determined that the nerves and muscles that allow our eyes to view up and down had weakened on one side and my left eye was drooping just a tiny little bit and that was causing me to see one line with one eye where it was supposed to be and the other line a little lower with the eye that was drooping. It was drooping so little that it was barely recognizable to the eye doctor. They were able to make an adjustment to my glasses to correct this problem. The doctor explained about the dozens of nerves just in our face that have to work properly for our eyes and mouth to work properly.

Every time I see this quote about life being a series of thousands of tiny miracles, I am reminded of my vision issues. Can you imagine how many things have to work properly on our body just to be able to get out of bed every morning? When you take time to ponder just that part of your day, every day, it becomes very easy to agree that, yes, life is a series of thousands of tiny miracles. And keep in mind that all takes place before we ever head out to meet the day!

Certainly, the second sentence holds the key: "All you have to do is notice them." That's the kicker in today's offering. If we would all just take the time to look around us on a daily basis—and I mean really take a good, hard, long look—at the beauty and the wonder, all those tiny daily miracles will become very real and very apparent in all our lives.

God's blessings to you on this day! Have a blessed day!

**July 1** —*Faith sees the opportunity; doubt sees the obstacles. What you see is what you get.*—anonymous

When I read this quote, I thought of the old adage: When life hands you lemons, the best thing to do is to make lemonade. The key point in today's offering centers on the way you handle every life situation. It is up to you—the decision is yours to either suck on the lemons or make lemonade.

Keep in mind those two "O-words"—opportunity and obstacle—because they certainly come into play here. I'm convinced that life's struggles do one of two things: They either defeat us or define us. How many times have you seen a person go through a bad experience ,and then let that particular event defeat them and become their reason to frown and have a bitter, sour attitude about every aspect of life?

On the other hand, we also see people who go through the same struggles and use a difficult experience for motivation to become a stronger, better person, to help others, and to achieve their goals. In short, they turn obstacles into opportunities.

My prayer is that regardless of the situation in your life, you will seize the opportunity and push the obstacle out of your path.

God's blessings to you on this day! Have a blessed day!


**July 2**—*Tomorrow–Another chance! A new beginning!*—common expression

Sometimes, if you're paying attention, life's little lessons appear in unique places. Let me explain.

Last summer I helped coach the seven-year-old girls' softball team my granddaughter is on. While at times it resembled herding cats, it was a very rewarding experience and a joy. During a game one of our key players, our leadoff hitter, started off the game by striking out. She had been one of our mainstays all summer, so it was a little unusual. She came up to bat the second time and struck out again. She came up to bat the third and fourth times and struck out again. By the fourth at-bat I could tell she was hesitant to even swing the bat. Clearly, it was a difficult day for her.

The way our schedule was set up, we played at the exact same time the very next night, so twenty-four hours later she was stepping into the batter's box again. I watched her as she dug in, got set, and she was determined and confident. She promptly got a hit and came around and scored a run. The second time up she got a hit, and the third and the fourth. While I compared the two performances on consecutive days I thought to myself: "In a twenty-four-hour span, this little seven-year-old girl has experienced a microcosm of life."

All of us, every single person, have days when we swing and miss and strike out . . . sometimes multiple times in one day. But just like my leadoff hitter, the very next day you have another chance to step up to the plate (of life), dig back in, and swing for the fence.

Every single morning, when our feet hit the floor we have the option of how the day will go—and this option is based solely on our attitude. Isn't that remarkable that we can wipe the slate clean every day, no matter how many times we struck out yesterday, and try again? Certainly we will face struggles and problems almost every day, but again we have the option, with God's help, of how we handle them. Remember, disappointments, struggles, and problems are inevitable—but letting them defeat you is optional.

God's blessings to you on this day! Have a blessed day!

## July 3—*Action always, always beats intention. Go the extra mile! That road is never very crowded.*—common expression

As a kid I used to hear my mother say, "The road to hell is paved with good intentions." At that time I didn't understand what she was talking about, but I sure do now. Think about how much better our lives would be if we put action in place of everything we "intended" to do.

I know from my own life that week after week after week we can have wonderful intentions about going to church, renewing a relationship with God, losing that extra twenty pounds, going to the gym, or exploring other job opportunities. But until we apply action, our goals, dreams, and plans will just remain "good intentions." And as my late mother often pointed out, I know what road those good intentions end up paving!

Even applying action to simple things—smiling at a stranger, making a phone call to an old friend, offering a word of encouragement to somebody going through a rough time, or simply being pleasant to everybody we encounter daily—would make the world a far better place and us far better people. My prayer is that when it comes down to action or intention we will all choose action—and hopefully we can get more people traveling on the extra mile.

God's blessings to you on this day! Have a blessed day!

## July 4—*Failure is not the opposite of success. It is a* **part** *of success.* **—anonymous**

If you spend any time reading and studying people who are successful, you'll find that the common denominator for many on their road to success is failure. Every person who trudges through life experiences failure. It's what you do with those failures—yes, that's "failures," which means more than one—that makes the difference.

Failure is something we can avoid only by saying nothing, doing nothing, and being nothing. Failure is not an undertaker, defeat, or a dead end. Instead, failure should be looked on as our teacher, a small delay and slight detour on our way to success.

I recently read a quote by an unknown writer that talked about failure that hits the nail on the proverbial head: "It's impossible to live without failing at something unless you lived so cautiously that you might as well not lived at all. In which case, you failed by default."

Failure is a temporary condition—giving up is what makes it permanent. Don't be afraid to fail . . . be afraid not to try!

God's blessings to you on this day! Have a blessed day!

**July 5—*Some people cause happiness wherever they go . . . others whenever they go.*—Oscar Wilde**

If we're being honest, we all know those people who make us cringe a little when we see them approaching. These are the black-cloud, dooms-day, chicken-little folks who bombard every person they come across with a string of negativity. These folks—they surely must gargle with razor blades every morning—will complain long and loud to anyone who will listen.

In only one sentence and eleven words, today's offering is a great example of the type of person we should all strive to be versus the type of person we really, really don't want to be. Many times in my daily ram-blings, I remember words of wisdom from my late mother. She seemed to have a saying for every occasion and many of them still cross my mind daily. I can still recall her saying, "If you can't say anything good about somebody, don't say anything at all . . . or say that you heard they were a good whistler." Many folks we cross paths with daily would be better off to practice that sage advice.

Our goal every morning should be to strive to be a "wherever" per-son, and we should work hard to never become a "whenever" person.

God's blessings to you on this day! Have a blessed day!

**July 6—*Stay away from negative people. They have a problem for every solution.*—Albert Einstein**

Run from negative people, and try to avoid contact with them at all costs.

That might sound like a harsh statement, but keep in mind that a constant dose of negativity can contaminate your mind, steal your joy, and hang a dark cloud over an otherwise sunny day. I work hard these days to limit my contact with the naysayers who, as today's quote points out, have a problem for every solution!

Don't you know people just like that? If you mention that it's a beautiful day, they will quickly give you a weather update that includes lots of clouds and rain. If you tell them all the things going right in your life, they'll quickly tell you all that could go wrong. If you walk on water, the haters will say it's because you can't swim.

So, let me add a little more to today's offering: If you can't be positive, kind, nice, pleasant, cheerful, or cordial, then at least be quiet. My prayer is that we all strive to see the many blessings and the positive things in our life—because there are many!

God's blessings to you on this day! Have a blessed day!

### July 7—*Every second brings a fresh beginning, every minute is a blessing from God, every hour holds a new promise, and every day is what you choose to make it.*—common expression

I love that this quote breaks down the unlimited blessings of every second of every minute of every hour of every day. Each day really is a new beginning and a gift from God—that's why it's called the present, a brand-spanking-new present given to us each day. But we need to treat it that way by staying away from what might have been, ignoring the naysayers and pessimists of the world, and staying focused on the positive and the present. And remember that it's impossible to have a good day today if you haul all your baggage from yesterday, last week, and last year along with you.

Here's a list for you today as you enjoy your "present": Thank God often for your blessings; smile often; dream big; laugh out loud; laugh at yourself; give someone a compliment and mean it; hand out a random act of kindness; hold the door for somebody you don't know; smile at every person you see; and realize every second, all day, how blessed you are.

Do not let the negative words or actions of others take away your purpose or your smile. It's a great day . . . to have a great day!

God's blessings to you on this day! Have a blessed day!

**July 8—*Speak when you're angry, and you'll make the best speech you'll ever regret.*— Mark Twain**

There are two things in life that can't be taken back, can't be recalled—time and words. While time is extremely important, I believe it pales in comparison to words. The career path that God has provided for me has allowed me to use both spoken words and written words to reach out to people, so I see every day the power that words have, both good and bad and positive and negative.

Say a kind word to somebody and you can make their day; make a hateful comment and you can ruin their day. Words are powerful and everlasting. Words can heal and unite, or damage and divide. Be careful with your words; once they are said they can only be forgiven, not forgotten.

Again, today's quote is one that I wish I had learned (and practiced) years ago, but better late than never, I suppose. Choose your words wisely, chew on your words if necessary, roll them around in your mind, or bite your tongue . . . but don't speak in anger. We've all heard the phrase that you can't un-ring the bell; the same holds true with what you say, because you also can't un-say words. Once those angry, hurtful words are said, just like time you can't recall them; you can't bring them back.

Today's offering is worth repeating: Speak when you're angry, and you'll make the best speech you'll ever regret. My prayer today is that we all strive to live a life where we never have to regret the words we say!

God's blessings to you on this day! Have a blessed day!

**July 9—*God has a purpose for your pain, a reason for your struggles, and a reward for your faithfulness. Don't give up!*—common expression**

I'm convinced that one of the greatest attributes a person can have is a healthy dose of stubbornness. Let me clarify that I'm not talking about being stubborn just to be contrary or cantankerous, but being stubborn in developing a mindset that says: I. Will. Not. Give. Up. Ever. Regardless.

Sometimes you have to shut out the voices of others that say "you can't" and tell you to give up, and other times you have to battle against those two dream-killers—doubt and fear—that take up residence in your head from time to time. It's that voice in your head that keeps you from moving forward and from reaching your goals. It's what keeps people from advancing in their career and stuck in dead-end jobs, not to mention harmful relationships and dozens of other life-traps.

Remember, the difference between an opportunity and an obstacle is your attitude. Your faith has to be greater than your fear of failing. My prayer is that we all develop a good streak of stubbornness when pushing toward our goals.

God's blessings to you on this day! Have a blessed day!

## July 10—*Life is like riding a bicycle: To keep your balance, you must keep moving forward.*—common expression

I love this quote and the comparison of life to riding a bicycle. While it's clever and catchy, it's also spot-on accurate because finding a balance in life and moving forward are both game-changers.

Finding a balance in life can be tricky. On one hand we want to be compassionate and caring of others, but we have to remain diligent that we are not pushovers. We need to be trusting but not to the point of being taken advantage of by others. We need to strive to help those in need . . . but be smart enough to determine that sometimes those in need . . . need to help themselves a little bit. Yes, just like riding a bicycle, life is a balancing act!

Regardless where you are trying to improve or make progress in your life—even if it seems like the pace is slow, you're not making great strides, and you're only inching forward—keep moving, maintain your balance, and keep on keeping on! Remember, two steps forward and one step back is still progress!

God's blessings to you on this day! Have a blessed day!

## July 11—*Clear your mind of "can't."*—Samuel Johnson

The second I read this quote I thought of a children's book from many decades ago called *The Little Engine That Could*. It was a wonderful book that taught youngsters for many decades about the importance of hard work, motivation, and a never-give-up attitude. Like me, many people grew up with images of that little engine chugging up the hill saying, "I think I can. . . . I think I can."

Life is full of obstacles, challenges, and problems, and in order to overcome them we have to develop a mentality just like that children's book taught. We have to keep pushing and keep chugging along, telling ourselves over and over, "I think I can. . . . I think I can." And in order to think we can we must, just like today's offering says, clear our mind of "can't."

The next time that word "can't" creeps into your mind, think of that little engine and tell yourself over and over, "I think I can. . . . I think I can." And while I've only mentioned the little engine chugging up the hill, remember those great images from the book of the little engine coasting down the hill saying, "I knew I could. . . . I knew I could."

God's blessings to you on this day! Have a blessed day!

## July 12—*The reason people give up so fast is because they tend to look at how far they still have to go, instead of how far they've already gone.*—common expression

I am a big advocate of looking forward and keeping our focus on what's ahead. However, a glance back (not a locked-in stare, but a small peek) to see how far you've come, how much you've grown, and how much you've improved can be refreshing, rewarding, and motivating. Particularly if there's a goal that you are trying to reach, and you glance back and see what you've accomplished, it makes the finish line look so much closer.

Always keep in mind why the windshield is so much bigger than the rearview mirror on your vehicle: The windshield is bigger because we should keep our focus on the big picture in front of us. It's all right to glance in the rearview mirror as long as you're moving forward, but almost all our focus should be on what's in front of us.

So, go ahead, take a little peek back, it's OK . . . then eyes straight ahead!

God's blessings to you on this day! Have a blessed day!

### July 13—*In Christ we find: Purpose for the pain. Strength for the struggle. Faith for the fight.*—anonymous

Let's face it, not everybody is on top of their game every single day. We all have those mornings when nothing seems to go right and we'd really rather not deal with anything or anybody. We've all had those mornings—the ones where the alarm doesn't go off, you stub your toe, and then spill your coffee. On these mornings, going back to bed and pulling the covers over your head seems like the best option.

But, it's on those days when you feel overworked and underappreciated that you have to remember that this day is a gift to you from God, and that what you do with it is entirely up to you. Wrap your mind around that for just a second—the Creator of the universe has given you this day! And the beauty of today's offering is that in Christ we find the necessary ingredients—purpose for the pain, strength for the struggle, faith for the fight—to help and guide us through those days when "life happens." Most importantly, always keep in mind that this is a day the Lord has made. Just. For. You.

So, enjoy this one-of-a-kind day! Smile often, be kind to others, dream big, laugh a lot (and at yourself), remember that every person faces unique challenges every day, and count your blessings because they are many.

God's blessings to you on this day! Have a blessed day!

## July 14 —*Old ways won't open new doors.*—common expression

One of the great mysteries of life is when people—intelligent people—practice the same harmful habits over and over again while expecting a different result. The truly amazing aspect of this phenomenon is that these same intelligent people are astounded, totally mystified that even though they do the same thing over and over, nothing ever changes and the results are the exact same. These folks haven't learned that "Old ways won't open new doors."

As is often the case, one quote triggers a memory of another one that fits well, and such is the case with today's offering. There's a wonderful quote that spells out exactly what must happen in order to reverse the insanity of people doing the same thing over and over and expecting things to change: "If you want something you've never had, you have to do something you've never done." One of my favorite verses states: "Trust in the LORD with all your heart, and lean not on your own understanding; in all your ways acknowledge Him, and He shall direct your paths" (Proverbs 3:5–6). Let me paraphrase that last sentence: "In all your ways acknowledge him and he shall direct your paths . . . particularly when you're trying to get rid of old ways and open new doors."

My prayer for all of us is that regardless of whether we are trying to achieve great things or accomplish small things, with God's help and grace, we will have the strength, stamina, and determination to open new doors and do something we've never done.

God's blessings to you on this day! Have a blessed day!

## July 15—*Living life is the art of drawing without an eraser.*—John W. Gardner

I read that simple ten-word sentence and loved and understood it immediately. For some people, me included, the picture of life that we sometimes draw is not pretty. And many people—again, I will include myself—have sometimes gotten way outside the lines in our attempt to "draw" our life. Sometimes those lines can get skewed and way out of whack before you know it happened. You look up one day and say, "Wow, how did I get this far off course?" Many people will clearly understand this—and if you don't understand, there's no point in me trying to explain.

Today I am thankful beyond words that God, through his son Jesus Christ, doesn't use an eraser where you might still see traces of those lines. Instead, all it takes is one simple prayer, and he will wipe the page clean. Bright. White. Shining. Clean. Now keep in mind that some people will always remember those ugly marks you made outside the lines and remind you of them often, but with God the slate is clean. Again. Bright. White. Shining. Clean.

My prayer is that if you are outside the lines and sometimes making a mess of "drawing" your life, you would call on Jesus—the one who can give you that clean slate.

God's blessings to you on this day! Have a blessed day!

## July 16—*You are your only limit.*—common expression

Only one short sentence and five words, but this quote packs a powerful punch.

How many times in your life have you uttered the phrase, "I talked myself out of doing that"? Regardless if it involves a job, a relationship, a career change, going to church, starting a diet, or going to the gym, the enemy between our ears—commonly known as fear—wins a lot of decisions based on the way we see things and not the way things are. Again, you are your only limit! I know people who have all the intangibles—intelligence, work ethic, personality, etc.—but can't overcome the fear factor. And of course that means they lose because fear is a dream-killer, a life-changer, a career-crusher—and as today's offering points out, your only limit.

Keep in mind that courage is not the absence of fear. Everybody has fears. Instead, courage is the triumph over fear, seeing things as they are and not as we are.

My prayer for you today is that you exit your safety zone, challenge your limits, and overcome the fear that keeps you from accomplishing your goals.

God's blessings to you on this day! Have a blessed day!

## July 17—*If you find yourself in a hole, the first thing to do is stop digging.*—Will Rogers

Today's little fifteen-word gem has been used through the ages as a great illustration about the "holes" we sometimes dig for ourselves in various areas of our life. And let's be honest, nearly everybody who reads this has found themselves in a hole at one time or another, many times trying to figure out how they got there.

Every time I see today's quote I think of an amusing story about two men who were digging a hole in the middle of the road. When they started filling the hole back in they didn't have enough dirt even though they shoveled back in what had been shoveled out. As they stood there scratching their heads and looking at the hole, another guy walked up. They told him about their problem, and he replied, "You should have dug the hole deeper."

Digging a proverbial hole for ourselves is something many of us have done in the past—or maybe we're still digging. There are only two simple rules that apply when this happens.

Rule 1: Be smart enough to recognize you've dug a hole.

Rule 2: Quit digging.

If you find yourself in a hole—whether you did the digging or not—my prayer today is that with God's help you lay your shovel and this burden down.

God's blessings to you on this day! Have a blessed day!

**July 18—*You don't have to be great to start . . . but you have to start to be great.*—Zig Ziglar**

Recently I was standing in line at an area business. A young girl, obviously new on the job, was having some minor difficulties with a cash register and was clearly flustered. Another employee came to her assistance as the line grew longer. When it came my turn, I held the line up a little longer when I asked her if it was her first day on the job. She said "yes."

"I'm going to tell you something that maybe nobody else has told you," I said, loud enough for everybody in line to hear. "Everybody has had a first day on the job, I don't care if they've worked thirty years at the same place there was a first day. You'll be fine—good luck to you!"

As I exited the store, it dawned on me that what I just told the young girl doesn't just apply to a new job. I don't care if you're trying to build a relationship with God, trying to get a better job, lose weight, leave an addiction behind, get fit, be more positive, be more thankful, be kinder, be a better person, or hundreds of other things—there has to be a first day, a start day. And again, just like today's offering states, "You don't have to be great to start . . . but you have to start to be great."

God's blessings to all those trying to start a new chapter on this day! Have a blessed day!

**July 19—*People often say that motivation doesn't last. Well, neither does bathing. That's why it's recommended daily.*—Zig Ziglar**

Every morning on the fifteen-minute drive to work I say a prayer for my family, for the people I work with, the people I will encounter that day, and the situations I will face. I pray for God's blessings "to me and through me." Every single morning that's my routine, and just like the morning shower I took a few minutes earlier, it's something I need to do daily. It's my way of motivating myself for the day. It's amazing how much strength and confidence that little daily chat with God brings me.

I love this quote because it's clever and absolutely spot-on. Just like soap, water, and shampoo we need motivation daily, sometimes hourly. So get up, get a shower, thank God for this day, count your blessings, be thankful, be kind to each other, smile at people you don't know, laugh out loud, hold the door open for somebody, measure your words, focus on positive things, count your blessings (I know I wrote that earlier, but do it often during the day), dream big, stay in charge of your attitude, push negative thoughts and negative people away, pass on a random act of kindness, and strive for one thing: to be a better person than you were yesterday. And just for good measure, count your blessings again.

God's blessings to you on this day! Have a blessed day!

### July 20—*Two things prevent us from happiness: living in the past and observing others.*—anonymous

This one-sentence nugget points out and identifies the two ways that we can guarantee that we lose our happiness—looking in the rearview mirror and measuring our life against others.

Living in the past—or rehashing, rereading, or reliving yesterday—will not change or alter one thing that happened. At the same time, worrying, fretting, and being anxious does not empty tomorrow of its troubles; instead it empties today of its strength.

The second half of this wonderful quote talks about how "observing others" or living a life of comparison is another way to steal our happiness. Simply stated, living a life where we continually measure our life against the highlight reel of others is a sure-fire way to feel inadequate and like a failure. Keep in mind that today is called the present, and rightfully so, because it's a present from God. It's a present that contains another chance, a new opportunity, and the hope to be a better person—a better person in our own eyes and not in comparison to others. The second your eyes open every morning, your present is waiting on you as your gift to enjoy.

And it is a gift, a gift made especially for you. And the beauty of receiving this gift is that we all hold the power to make this day anything we want it to be. We can't change the past, we can't predict the future, and we cannot measure our life against others. But, we have in front of us a blank sheet every morning and we hold the pen; we can write any story we want that day. My prayer today is that we stay "present" in the present, and realize that comparing our life to others will steal our joy.

God's blessing to you this day! Have a blessed day!

## July 21—*Bitterness and resentment only hurt one person, and it's not the person we're resenting, it's us.*—anonymous

Today, I'd like to add an illustration for you to ponder. First, pick up a sixteen-ounce bottle of water and then hold your arm straight out, so that the water is parallel to your shoulder. What would happen if you held it there for five minutes? You're right, probably nothing. But what if you held it there an hour? Four hours? What about eight hours?

It goes without saying that the longer we held the one-pound bottle of water, the more our arm would ache, probably to the point of feeling like it was paralyzed. The interesting part of this illustration is that the weight of the water never changes—the length of time we hold it is where problems begin to arise and the pain starts.

This is exactly the same thing that happens with anger and bitterness. It will start as something small and maybe even insignificant, but the longer we hold on to it the more hurt and damage it will cause. A great quote that ties in well here states: "Holding on to anger is like drinking poison and expecting the other person to die."

Turn loose bitterness and anger and set a prisoner free—yourself. Choose to be better rather than bitter.

God's blessings on you today! Have a blessed day!

## July 22—*Be stronger than your excuses!*—common expression

I read a short piece recently that said, in every single aspect, life boils down to either finding a way to do something or an excuse not to do it. Think about that previous sentence for just a minute, and then plug in anything you do in life—church, gym, a little extra effort at work, a closer relationship with God, etc.—and it really does come down to finding a way to get things done or finding an excuse not to do it at all.

When I slowly read over the little five-word gem I shared today—"Be stronger than your excuses!"—I immediately thought of that phrase, "Find a way . . . or find an excuse." Applying that simple sentence to every part of our daily routine would be life-changing. It's not easy for anybody, including me, but being stronger than our excuses and finding a way instead of an excuse is a good first step to a better, more productive life.

My simple prayer today is that we all find a way to be stronger than our excuses.

God's blessings your way on this day and Have a blessed day!

## July 23—*In order to succeed in life you need three bones, a wishbone, a backbone, and a funny bone.*—Reba McEntire

There is no doubt that the three bones in this quote will carry you a long way in life. The wishbone (I'm going to call it a purpose-bone) keeps us moving forward, striving to do better and be better than we were yesterday, and the funny bone helps us to laugh at life and particularly at ourselves.

Without question, the backbone is the toughest, most difficult one of the three, because it often requires us to reset boundaries and stand up to difficult situations. At one time or another we've all used the phrase: "[Insert name] needs to grow a backbone." Of course, for some people that is easier said than done.

Regarding all three of these important bones, it's imperative to always remember that God will give you strength for every battle, wisdom for every decision, and peace that surpasses understanding.

My prayer is that we all start a daily workout program to develop our wishbone, backbone, and funny bone. It will be some of the best exercise we can get.

God's blessings to you on this day! Have a blessed day!

**July 24—*Sometimes you will never know the true value of a moment or a person until that moment or that person becomes a memory.*
—Dr. Seuss**

This quote is spot-on accurate and also carries a wonderful message for us all. That message, however, is wrapped in sadness.

In the hustle and bustle of daily life we all take people and moments—very special people and moments—for granted.

We're all guilty of this. It's not intentional or that we don't care; it's just that we're all going a hundred miles an hour in different directions, trying to take care of the daily challenges and obstacles of life. And sadly, life doesn't come equipped with flashing lights or ringing bells to remind us to cherish a moment or a loved one as long as we possibly can.

Perhaps a second line should be added to today's offering that says: "So slow down . . . and then stop and smell the roses." Take the time today, tomorrow, and every day to smell a few roses!

God's blessings to you on this day! Have a blessed, rose-smelling day!

**July 25—*The next chapter doesn't begin until you turn the page.*—
common expression**

Borrowing a line from rock legend Bob Seger, it's important in life to
learn to turn the page. We've all had those days—some of us many consecutive days—when we felt we gave our best, and at the end of the day
still feel beat up, beat down, and worn out by life's difficulties.

One thing I've learned is that we have to put each day to rest and
start fresh each morning with a renewed energy. As today's quote states,
it's impossible to reach the next chapter—and every day is a new chapter—unless you turn the page. Otherwise, it's easy to start dragging
one bad day to the next and then the next and the next, and soon we're
dragging a trunkful of bad days with us everywhere we go. And that's a
lot to pack around day after day after day.

Remember, every day is a new beginning, another chance. Every
morning starts a new, bright, clean page in your life story. The beauty
of this is that you are the author and you hold the pen in your hand.
Let me say that again: You hold the pen in your hand. With God's
help you have the ability and strength to write any story you want.
Leave the baggage of a bad yesterday behind, and write a great story
today!

God's blessings to you on this day! Have a blessed day!

**July 26—*A bird sitting in a tree is never afraid of the branch breaking,
because its trust is not on the branch but on its own wings.*—Maya
Angelou**

I think this simple one-sentence quote provides a great analogy about
life in general. Many of us are sometimes sitting on one of life's many
shaky branches—health issues, work-related problems, difficult relationships, financial problems, and the list goes on and on.

It's at these times that we have to trust God to be our wings to lift us
up from that branch we find ourselves sitting on. And that's not always
easy; in fact, sometimes it's very difficult because many times it seems

the branch is ready to break. Remember, faith is not knowing what the future holds but knowing who holds the future—the "branch" we're sitting on!

I recently read a short quote that stated: "Nowhere, not one single place in the Bible does it say, go figure it out on your own, but over and over again it says, trust in God."

So, the point in today's offering is this: If you're sitting on a shaky branch or a wobbly perch, don't try to fix it yourself, don't try to figure it out . . . trust God to be your wings.

God's blessings to you on this day! Have a blessed day!

**July 27—*If you want something you've never had, you have to do something you've never done.*—common expression**

This single-sentence quote plays out every single day for people who want desperately to make changes in their lives. Regardless if it's starting to attend church again, trying to renew a relationship with God, looking for a new job, ending a harmful relationship, or any of a countless list of needed changes, the giant obstacle for most folks can be found in the fact that it requires us to do something we've never done. Sadly, many people will never attempt to change and will instead keep doing the same harmful thing over and over again while expecting a different result.

That, of course, is the definition of insanity!

How many times have you had a positive thought about embarking on a new journey in life, a new direction, and immediately doubt and fear took over and your ideas and dreams were tossed to the side? If you're like most people, me included, this has happened often.

And it's the voice in your head that says you're not good enough, smart enough, gifted enough, talented enough—you fill in the word in front of "enough"—that keeps all of us from being the best people we can be.

Let me rearrange the words in today's quote as a final thought on this offering: If you are ever going to have something you've never had, you must make a life change and do something you've never done!

God's blessings to you on this day! Have a blessed day!

**July 28—*The only person you should try to be better than is the person you were yesterday.*—common expression**

This wonderful quote provides a huge life lesson in only one sixteen-word sentence. Think about it like this: What if every person started every single day with the goal to be a better person than they were the previous day? What a great world it would be if we all started each day with the simple purpose of being kind to each other, smiling more, complaining less (or not at all), being helpful, being positive, and just trying, as today's quote states, to be a better person than we were yesterday!

I believe every person has a purpose in life. And just like our attitude, I also believe that our purpose is something we control; it's in our hands daily and I believe it's something that can make or break us. More importantly it's something that can make us a better person today than we were yesterday!

Let me remind you again to place your hand over your heart. Feel that? That's called purpose. You're alive for a reason and you didn't come this far . . . to only come this far. Remember that small incremental steps made daily result in big progress over the long haul! Every day focus on progress, not perfection!

God's blessings to you on this day! Have a blessed day!

**July 29—*My past has not defined me, destroyed me, or defeated me . . . it has only strengthened me.*—Steve Maraboli**

We all have a past, but more importantly we all also have a future. However, putting the past behind us—where it belongs—is the trick. How many times have you seen a person go through a bad experience, and then let that particular event from their past define them and become their reason to frown and have a bitter, sour attitude about every aspect of life? These folks can't enjoy the present or look to the future because they are focused on the rearview mirror! For these folks the past is not a place of reference, it's their place of residence—they live there!

On the other hand, we also see people who go through the same struggles and use a difficult experience for motivation to become stronger, better people, to help others and to achieve their goals. These folks turn the past into a plus and an opportunity to help others. Many times, failing or losing reveals much more character about a person than winning. Nobody goes through life without picking up a few scars—some seem to have more than their share. But to me it's how you handle the adversity that reveals your character. Some people hone in on the past and stay there and others use those life-related scars to gain strength and then pull themselves back up, square their shoulders, hold their head up, and help others.

My prayer today is that you take any obstacle in your past and turn it into an opportunity to help yourself and others, and that you also use the struggles in your life to become a stronger person.

God's blessings to you on this day! Have a blessed day!

**July 30—*Your life is not yours if you constantly care what other people think.*—common expression**

One of the worst prisons a person can be locked up in is the "what-other-people-think" prison. There are many, many people who spend their entire day, every day, trying to gain the approval of people who get out of bed each morning with the sole purpose of spreading as much negativity and criticism as possible.

The key point in today's offering can be found in the first five words of today's quote: "Your life is not yours." And truly your life is not yours if you constantly hand other people the calculator to determine your self-worth!

The key point that you must remember is that the detractors and naysayers can't defeat you without your consent; it's impossible—you have to grant them permission. In short, never, ever let yourself be defined by somebody's comment, opinion or—let me go ahead and say it—their ignorance. Remember, your value doesn't decrease based on somebody's inability to see the good and the worth in you. You hold your self-worth calculator in your hand. It belongs to you and only you!

Take your life back, and don't give a second thought to what others think. Remember that your worth is found in God, not the opinions of others!

God's blessings to you on this day! Have a blessed day!

## July 31—*Sometimes the easiest way to solve problems is to stop participating in the problem.*—common expression

Have you ever come in contact with a person who focuses on a problem and can't turn it loose? We've all met these folks; they become so consumed with talking about their problems that it becomes the focal point of their lives. You can try to steer the conversation in another direction, but they will hang on like a bulldog chewing on a bone and simply refuse to turn loose.

Today's offering is one of those quotes that should make us all pause and examine the words and topics we use daily—what we focus on the most in our conversation. Certainly, it is easy to zero in and talk about a problem while completely ignoring the countless joys all around us. For many people it's an addiction to talk about problems, and many times the problems belong to somebody else.

There is an immeasurable amount of truth in today's gem. For many people the simplest way to solve many problems in their own lives would be to simply quit participating in those problems. Instead of becoming consumed with a problem, they should instead wrap themselves in an attitude of gratitude and become consumed with the many, many blessings that make up their lives. A quote I used in the past fits well right here: "Talking about our problems is our greatest addiction. Break the habit. Talk about your joys!"

God's blessings to you on this day! Have a blessed day!

### August 1—*What you tell yourself everyday will either lift you up or tear you down.*—anonymous

It's been a running joke for decades that people are not crazy when they talk to themselves . . . it's when they start answering themselves that it becomes a concern. Regardless what category you fall into, it's a given that we all talk to ourselves in one way or another.

But what is it that we tell ourselves?

When we talk to ourselves—many times repeating over and over that we can't succeed and can't get ahead, that we're not very smart and certainly unlovable—we fail at 100 percent of the things we don't try. We settle for less than we deserve, and the answer is "no" to all the questions we never ask. Remember, it's not what you are that holds you back; it's what you're telling yourself you're not.

When I thought about today's offering and what I wanted to write, I was reminded of an anonymous quote I used in the past: "There are always two wolves fighting. One is darkness, negativity, and despair. The other is light, optimism, goodness, and hope. The question is: which wolf wins? The answer: the one you feed."

What a great analogy that defines exactly what every person is faced with daily. Everybody starts each morning with a clean slate and the ability to make that day a good one. Then the wolves start fighting and many people quickly give in to darkness, negativity, and despair—they give in to what they feel and not what they believe.

So, be careful what you tell yourself every day . . . because you are listening!

God's blessings to you on this day! Have a blessed day!

## August 2—*Don't carry your mistakes around with you. Instead, place them under your feet and use them as stepping stones.*—common expression

Mistakes—now there's a topic I'm qualified to write about. I love this quote because it's a great illustration that we should strive with all our might to turn the negative of a mistake into a positive path to become a better person. However, I think this quote stops just a little short.

I would add one more step—the most important one when talking about past transgressions. Before you place those mistakes under your feet and use them as stepping stones, I would encourage you to give them to God where they will be cast "[a]s far as the east is from the west" (Psalm 103:12). You see, some people will never let you forget a mistake. These folks feel it is their job, their responsibility, to remind you at every opportunity about every mistake, big and small, that you've made. They'll beat you over the head with it thirty years later.

But God will wipe the slate clean every time. And in the whole scheme of life, it doesn't matter one iota what anybody else thinks because it's between you and God and that's all that really matters, period.

So go ahead, unload those mistakes you've been carrying around with you. Hand them to the Creator of the universe, do a happy dance around them, and then lay them at your feet and use them as a pathway to a new beginning!

God's blessings to you on this day! Have a blessed day!

**August 3—*Believe in yourself! Have faith in your abilities! Without a humble, but reasonable confidence in your powers you cannot be successful or happy.*—Norman Vincent Peale**

Regardless what we are attempting to accomplish—particularly a life-changer—first days are never, ever easy!

A first day at the gym, starting a diet, at a new job, attempting to quit smoking, or leaving an addiction behind can be a daunting task; it can lead many people to throw up their hands in submission and simply quit. This is why gyms and fitness centers are packed with people the first week in January and not so busy in mid-March. Many folks want instant results for a minimal amount of work and effort, and then get frustrated and bail when they don't transform from being a couch potato to a bodybuilder in three days! And this quote doesn't just pertain to a physical transformation but also a spiritual walk.

That's where today's quote comes in to play. Success is not going to happen overnight; it's not going to be an instantaneous happening. Instead, as today's offering illustrates, success is the sum of small efforts, incremental steps that we do over and over again, day in and day out. Scientific studies show that it takes a minimum of three weeks to form a new habit. That's a minimum of three weeks of small efforts repeated over and over again, day in and day out.

So, on those long and sometimes monotonous days when you think your small efforts have little or no meaning, when you feel like you are fighting a battle you can't win, remember this quote, remember the sum of small efforts repeated over and over again, day in and day out . . . and keep on pushing forward!

God's blessings to you on this day! Have a blessed day!

**August 4—*You can have results or excuses–not both.*—Arnold Schwarzenegger**

I recently heard a speaker talk about our ability to find excuses to get out of doing things we don't want to do. His comment was that every aspect of life—every single thing we do on a daily basis—boils down to either finding a way to do something or finding an excuse not to do it at all. He ended using a quote similar to today's offering; his final comment was that we had to work daily to be stronger than our excuses!

I wish that I would have never heard his comments, because now they ring in my ears daily. I can't tell you the times that I have thought about a task in front of me and heard those comments in my head. Of course, his comments and today's quote are 100 percent accurate. Plug in anything you do in life—church, gym, a closer relationship with God, visiting a friend, getting up when the alarm goes off instead of hitting the snooze, doing a little extra at work, etc.—and every single time it comes down to finding a way to get things done or finding an excuse not to do it at all. Every. Time. No. Exceptions.

The key to today's offering is that applying this simple philosophy to every part of our daily routine would be a positive, life-changing experience! It's not easy, but it's worth repeating again: You can have results in your life, and we all want results, or you can have excuses. You can't have both. My simple prayer today is that we all find a way to be stronger than our excuses.

God's blessings to you on this day! Have a blessed day!

**August 5—*Anger is an acid that can do more harm to the vessel in which it is stored than to anything on which it is poured.* —Mark Twain**

There are people, and we all know them, who have been mad at something or somebody for so long that they've actually forgotten what they're mad about. They just know they're mad and angry, they wake up that way every single day, and they're going to stay that way.

What these folks haven't figured out yet is that hanging on to anger and refusing to let go of a grudge is living in the past, which makes enjoying the present and the future impossible. But the key point is that holding anger and refusing to let go of a grudge does harm to themselves, not the people who are the target of their animosity.

I recently read a quote by an anonymous writer that details that exact point and fits well with the great words of Twain: "Anger doesn't solve anything. It builds nothing, but it can destroy everything." Don't forget, for every minute you stay angry, you give up sixty seconds of peace of mind.

Let me sum up today's effort in three simple words: Let . . . anger . . . go! My prayer today is that you let go of anger, resentment, and grudges, and in the process set a prisoner free—yourself.

God's blessings to you on this day! Have a blessed day!

### August 6—*Disappointments are inevitable—misery is optional!* —Joel Osteen

Today's quote, only six words, packs a punch and contains a great measure of truth.

One of the mysteries of life is why bad things happen to good people. I see it happen daily, and it always remains a head-scratcher for me when wonderful people experience loss or go through a difficult time. Until I have a chance to ask God that question, the only explanation I have is to borrow a line I heard my late mother say often: "It rains on the just and the unjust."

I recall talking one time to a lady who lost her youngest son in a terrible and tragic accident. He was an excellent student, a gifted athlete, and a model citizen. He was only eighteen years old when he died. She told me that she quit going to church, abandoned her faith, and lived a life of anguish after his death, questioning God daily why her good son had died and bad people remained alive. I recall her telling me that her life sank to a level of misery that she did not know existed.

This story has a good and positive ending. The lady sought help, and with counseling and God's grace she was able to recover and even help people who had experienced the same kind of loss she had. Today's one-sentence quote holds true for anything—big or small—out of your control that happens to you. It's your choice whether or not you are reduced by those things. I used a quote in the past from an unknown author that says: "Every test in our life makes us bitter or better, and every problem comes to break us or makes us. The choice is up to you and you only, whether you become victim or victor."

The example I used, and virtually every other big or small problem in life, comes down to choice—does a test or a problem become an obstacle or an opportunity? In life you have three choices—give in, give up, or give it all you've got. Don't be a victim, be a victor! Don't give in, don't give up, and remember that disappointments are inevitable but misery really is optional.

God's blessings to you on this day! Have a blessed day!

## August 7—*Getting knocked down in life is a given. Getting up and moving forward is a choice.*—Zig Ziglar

At one point or another, life knocks everybody down. As today's quote says, it's "a given." It's what we do after getting knocked on our butts that speaks to our character. You see, there are people who get knocked around and beat up by life and then use that as reason to simply give up, give in, and quit trying. Others use life's setbacks as motivation and fuel to drive them to get up, dust themselves off, square their shoulders, and march forward.

The beauty of life is that we don't even have to wait for the black eye that life gave us to heal before we can start again. I recall a quote that I used in the past that says: "Every second brings a fresh beginning, every hour holds a new promise, every night our dreams can bring new hope, and every day is what we choose to make it."

One of the beautiful aspects of life is that we don't have to wait for a new calendar, a new week, a new month, or a new year because we have the ability to start from any second, any minute, or any hour of any day we choose and start a brand-new beginning.

Remember, you can't go back and make a new start, but within you and with God's help, there is the ability to make a brand-spanking-new ending! Today . . . today is called the present, and rightfully so, because it's a present from God. It's a present that contains another chance, a new opportunity, and the hope to be a better person. The second your eyes open every morning, that present is waiting on you.

Remember, every day is what we choose to make it. The choice is yours and totally yours—what kind of day will you make?

God's blessings to you this day! Have a blessed day!

**August 8—*To achieve anything, you have to start where you are, use what you have, and do all you can. Remember, it is better to do something imperfectly than to do nothing flawlessly.*—common expression**

Either one of the sentences in today's quote could easily stand alone, but when you add them together it provides a dynamite reminder that taking that first step of getting started on your goal—regardless of what it is—is off-the-charts important.

And of course, taking that first step relates to every single situation in life. The first step is always the hardest, but as we all know, every journey, regardless how long, begins with a single step. Every step after the first one will be easier, but you have to take that first step.

Remember, we fail at 100 percent of the things we don't try. The answer is "no" to all the questions we never ask, and the saddest summary of a life contains three descriptions: could have, might have, should have. It's not what you are that holds you back; it's what you think you're not.

My prayer today is that whatever direction you're heading in life, God will guide your journey and help you make that first step.

God's blessings to you on this day! Have a blessed day!

**August 9—*Things turn out best for those who make the best out of the way things turn out.*—John Wooden**

Sometimes, no matter how much we try, how much we cry, how hard we work, or how much we pray, things just don't turn out the way we want. In a nutshell, that's life. But as this great quote points out, it's what we do and how we react in these difficult, disappointing, and trying times that defines the situation and our character.

My mother had a saying for seemingly every situation in life and I have heard her say countless times, "Sometimes you have to look really hard, but there's always a way to make the best out of a bad situation." She always quickly added that the best way to handle any bad situation was to "let go . . . and let God." Looking back, clearly those are words of wisdom and words to live by daily.

My prayer is that regardless of what you are facing—big, small, or in between—you will trust God to make the best out of a bad situation. Just as today's offering points out, things turn out best for those who make the best out of the way things turn out.

God's blessings to you on this day! Have a blessed day!

## August 10—*Life is full of give and take. Give thanks, and take nothing for granted.*—common expression

Give and take—we hear those words used a lot together, but not in the context they're used in this quote. Isn't it amazing that in two short sentences—fourteen total words—this quote provides a guide to help us down the road of life?

Let me begin today's offering by asking a question: What if you woke up today with only the things that you thanked God for yesterday? That's a question that should cause all of us to do some soul-searching. And of course, that's a question that we should ask ourselves every single day.

Perhaps the best way to know the answer to that question is to give thanks to God every day for all things. And as today's quote reminds us, after giving thanks, be sure to take nothing for granted. Remember, your family is gold, your time is priceless, and your health is wealth!

In my daily offerings I share a lot of quotes and write about the importance of attitude. I have often pointed out that our attitude is the one thing we are in control of every single day. I'm convinced that an attitude of gratitude is the most important and by far the most life-changing we can acquire. I should point out that an attitude of gratitude does not change what you see daily—it just cleans the windshield you look through each day so that you can better see the countless blessings God gives us each day!

Give and take—give thanks and take nothing for granted. Those are some words to tuck away, remember, and live by!

God's blessings to you on this day! Have a blessed day!

## August 11—*Life changes without our permission. It's our attitude that determines the ride.*—common expression

These two short sentences pack a powerful punch!

Take a look around on any given day and you realize that the first sentence is exactly right, because life can change dramatically from one minute to the next and it certainly changes without our permission and without warning. That means it's very important to take nothing and nobody for granted—your family is priceless, your time is gold, and your health is wealth.

But it's the second sentence that holds the key because our attitude really does determine the ride, especially when life changes in a way that tests us. I used a quote recently by an unknown writer: "There is little difference in people, but that little difference makes a big difference. The little difference is attitude and the big difference is whether it's positive or negative."

No matter how hard we try, there are situations in our lives that we simply cannot control. We can't change the fact that some people will act a certain way, that we will cross paths with negative people, and that there are days when we have ten thumbs, the alarm doesn't go off, we stub our toe on the coffee table, and everything that can go wrong seems to go wrong.

However, the one thing we can control every single day is our attitude and the way we react. I don't believe there is anything more important than attitude. While a lot of folks worry about the clothes they put on each morning, many would be better off to concentrate more on the attitude they "dress" themselves in each day. A home, a business, a church, a work environment, and our relationship with every single person—attitude is the make-or-break difference in all those.

We have the ability within us every single day to decide what our attitude will be that day. We are all in charge of our attitude . . . put on a good one today!

God's blessings to you on this day! Have a blessed day!

**August 12—*You are free to make whatever choice you want, but you are not free from the consequences of those choices.*—common expression**

Certainly today's quote refers to every single choice that we make in life being attached to a consequence. But when I read this, the first thing that came to my mind—and maybe the most important choice we make daily—is the words we use.

There are two things in life that can't be taken back, can't be recalled—time and words. While time is extremely important I believe it pales in comparison to words. I see every day the power that words have, both good and bad, positive and negative. Something that is sometimes missed here in the twenty-first century is that words have consequences—big, big consequences!

Say a kind and caring word to somebody and you can make their day, or make a hateful and mean-spirited comment and you can ruin their day. Words are powerful and everlasting. Words can heal and unite or damage and divide.

Choose your words wisely, chew on your words if necessary, roll them around in your mind, or bite your tongue until it bleeds . . . but don't speak in anger. We've all heard the phrase, "You can't un-ring the bell." The same holds true with what you say, because you also can't "un-say" words. Once those angry, hurtful words are said, just like time you can't recall them; you can't bring them back. And the consequences of those hurtful words could last a lifetime.

God's blessings to you on this day! Have a blessed day!

**August 13**—*Life is like standing by a flowing river. It's up to us whether we take a bucketful or a spoonful.*—**common expression**

I am a visual person, so being able to compare our life to a flowing river provides a great illustration for me to imagine. And certainly, both life and the river are passing us by, so the second sentence—"It's up to us whether we take a bucketful or a spoonful"—is spot-on accurate.

Think about the many different situations you will encounter in your life, and then think about whether you've taken a bucketful of life or only a spoonful. There are so many things we can do to expand our horizons and step out of our comfort zone with a bucket in our hand. Something as simple as reaching out to an old friend, being kind in a difficult situation, saying a pleasant "good morning" to a stranger, encouraging someone going through a rough time, or simply holding a door for somebody you don't know might be the only positive interaction that person has on this day. Remember, it was Mother Teresa who said, "Kind words can be easy to speak but their echoes are truly endless."

I'm going to throw in a second quote this morning that fits well: "Today will never come again. Be a blessing. Be a friend. Be kind. Encourage someone. Take time to care. Let your words heal and not wound. Take a bucketful." I added that last sentence . . . but you get the point!

We get one chance to grab our bucketful on this day—just one chance, that's it. And the plain fact that today will never come again puts even more importance and significance on taking a bucketful of life versus only a spoonful. Remember, what you sow, you reap. What you give, you get.

And because life truly is an endless echo, our actions—good and bad, big and small—will reverberate over and over and over again. Again, it's up to us whether we take a bucketful or a spoonful! I don't know about you, but I think I'm going to grab a couple buckets of water!

God's blessing to you on this day! Have a blessed day!

**August 14—*Comparison is the best way to judge our progress . . . but not with others. Compare yesterday to today!*—anonymous**

Rehashing, rereading, or reliving yesterday will not change one thing that happened, while worrying, fretting, and being anxious will not alter what happens tomorrow. So that just leaves today, the present, as your gift to enjoy.

I believe social media and Facebook have helped make the comparison problem even worse. We see other people's highlight reel and compare it to our everyday, sometimes boring lives. We watch others and somehow believe that everybody but us has a perfect life, with a perfect job, perfect children, a house that is always clean, and meals that are always healthy, nutritious, and on time. Most of us know "that life" doesn't exist for anybody . . . except on television and Facebook!

And sadly, when problems, trials, and difficulties happen, or when "life" happens to us, any variance away from our dream of "living happily ever after" causes many people to feel that they failed. Then the situation is compounded when they start comparing their life to others.

The key point in today's offering is to always, always remember that comparison is the thief of joy—don't let it steal yours!

God's blessings on you this day! Have a blessed day!

**August 15—*Good, better, best, never let it rest, until your good is better and your better is best.*—common expression**

Words are powerful and everlasting, and in some instances can provide a lifetime of motivation.

Read today's quote again and then consider this: I recently read a story where Tim Duncan, a former NBA star, said a coach in grade school had used this quote to motivate him when he was young. The player heard this every practice, every game, and every day. He said he heard it so often that it was engrained in his mind.

After he reached the professional level and began playing against the best basketball players on the planet, he said he still applied it to his playing days and to his game. The phrase he heard as a little boy provided motivation for him decades later.

Here's a simple question in today's offering: What if we all applied that little catchy sentence to our lives? Think about this and then ponder what the world would be like if we applied "good, better, best, never let it rest, until your good is better and your better is best" to everything we attempted to do, every day? Take a moment today and think about that. My prayer today is that your good becomes better and your better becomes best.

God's blessings to you on this day! Have a blessed and a "best" day!

### August 16—*What if I fail? But, oh my darling . . . what if you fly?*— Erin Hanson

This quote is cute and catchy, but it also holds an immeasurable amount of truth. Let's take a minute and look closely at the simple question asked in today's offering, and also at the remarkable answer.

Every person—I don't care who they are or how much self-confidence they seem to show—has doubts and fears failure. Again, nobody, not one person on the face of the earth, is excluded from that list. And everybody, at some point in their lives, has let the enemy that sometimes resides between their ears convince them to not even try because failure is certain.

I first saw this quote awhile back and I can't count the times that I've thought of it when making a decision—what if I fail . . . but what if I fly? Regardless if it's a big decision or small decision, it's a great question to ask yourself.

As a footnote to today's two-sentence gem: Don't forget that the saddest summary of a life contains three descriptions: could have, should have, and might have.

God's blessings to you on this day! Have a blessed day!

**August 17—***Your past has given you the strength, wisdom, and compassion you have today, so get past your past and celebrate it.*—**anonymous**

The past—that's an entire can of worms in itself, isn't it? We all have one, and for some it's been a little bumpier ride than for others. Some people become so consumed with the past that they forget about the present.

The past is the past, and what lies behind us is exactly where it should stay—behind us.

Remember, there is no way to start a new chapter of your life if you keep rereading the last one. It's OK to glance back, but that's not the direction you're going. As far as the future and what lies before us, that chapter has not been written yet. It does absolutely no good to worry and fret about what might happen. Worrying about the future is like carrying an umbrella with you everywhere you go, on the chance that it might rain.

You know, no one can go back and make a brand-new start; it just isn't possible. But anyone can start from this day, even from this very minute, and make a brand-new ending. Don't let the past defeat you; let it prepare you. And like today's offering reminds us, use your past to your advantage. Take the strength, wisdom, and compassion you gained from your past experiences and use it to make your future better.

God's blessings to you on this day! Have a blessed day!

**August 18—***The reason why people give up so fast is because they tend to look at how far they still have to go, instead of how far they've already gone.*—**common expression**

There are a lot of quotes—and I've shared many of them—that talk about not looking back, not getting caught up with the past. While I still agree with those and practice them in my own life, I think today's quote is a great example that it's OK to glance back when you're measuring what you've accomplished and how far you've progressed. In many instances this provides a great measuring stick of your success, and certainly that's great motivation to continue on toward your goal.

Regardless if it's a renewed walk with God, a diet, an exercise program, or a new relationship, go ahead and take a peek back at where you were so you can measure the great strides you've made in reaching your goal. But only take a peek, a quick glance back, and then it's eyes straight ahead on that big windshield of life in front of you.

Remember, two steps forward and a baby step back is still progress toward your goal.

God's blessings to you on this day! Have a blessed day!

**August 19—*It is better to do something imperfectly than to do nothing flawlessly.*—common expression**

I can recall times in life when I had a list of tasks to do that seemed so overwhelming that I didn't know how or where to start—so I didn't. In other words (just like the quote says) instead of doing something imperfectly I did nothing flawlessly. Can you relate?

When you look at the tasks in front of you every single day, it really comes down to two things—if it's really important to you you'll find a way, and if it's not you'll find an excuse. In every single aspect of our life—our relationship with God, family, friends, work, exercise, etc., today's quote should be our measuring stick. Do we find a way to do something—sometimes imperfectly—or do we make an excuse and flawlessly do absolutely nothing?

Don't be afraid to fail—be afraid not to try!

God's blessings to you on this day! Have a blessed day!

**August 20**—*It's not your job to like me . . . it's mine.*—**common expression**

Many people spend every waking minute of every day consumed with what others think of them. I read a cute little ditty recently that stated: "You wouldn't care so much what other people think of you, if you knew how little they did." Yet many people—I would estimate a majority of people—base everything in their life on the opinion of others. Every action, every decision, every word, and even the items we purchase are geared toward others.

Let me drop a nugget on you in this offering that should be your top priority every day: Your worth is found in God, not the opinion of others. You are a child of the Creator of the universe, a chosen vessel of Christ the King; and every sin, mistake, and miscue you have made (or will ever make) has been paid for on an old rugged cross! Based on that, the opinion of others is somewhat trivial, don't you agree?

One of the greatest lessons I've learned in life is that we are never going to measure up in the eyes of man . . . never, ever! In the polarized society we live in here in the twenty-first century, it's a near-certainty that what you think, what you do, and what you say will offend somebody. So our goal every day should be to please God with our actions, and happily ignore the notion of what others might think of us. I think it's worth repeating the one-sentence pearl of wisdom I used earlier: "You wouldn't care so much what other people think if you knew how little they did."

God's blessings to you on this day! Have a blessed day!

**August 21**—*You don't inspire others by being perfect. You inspire them by how you deal with your imperfections.*—**Lewis Howes**

Everybody—and I mean every single person that has lived—has failed at one time or another. Failure is inevitable; it's just part of life. It's what you do when those failures come that matters the most. Do you let it defeat you, or do you use it as a stepping stone and a learning experience and push on?

Many times, failing or losing reveals much more about a person's character than winning. Nobody goes through life without some adversity—some seem to have more than their share—but it's how you handle the adversity that reveals your character. It either defeats you, or it defines you. Some people simply hunker down and quit; others say, "Watch this," and then pull themselves back up, square their shoulders, hold their head up, and fight on.

It seems that a constant rule for people who have enjoyed success is that they simply refuse to give up. Somehow these people use setbacks, failures, obstacles, the doubts and negativity of others, and the word "no" as motivation to reach their goals. Always remember that it's not a failure to get knocked down—failure comes when we refuse to get back up.

God's blessings to you on this day! Have a blessed day!

## August 22—*Life is full of choices . . . remove your shoes or mop the floor.*—common expression

What a great illustration to show that we are free to make any choice we want, but that we are not free from the consequences of that choice. In life, you can't go back and get a "do-over" and a brand-new start, but anyone can start from this day, this very minute, and make a brand-new ending. Hindsight is always 20/20. Looking back, it would have been much easier to remove your shoes, but if you didn't and you have to go back and mop the floor, make it shine.

There's a quote I've used in the past: "The greater your storm, the brighter your rainbow." I recently read a story that pointed out that a rainbow is a promise to everybody who sees it—it's a promise of sunshine after rain, calm after storms, joy after sadness, peace after pain, love after loss, morning after night, a bright beginning after a painful ending—and, to go along with today's offering, a bright and shining floor after mopping.

My prayer today is for strength, endurance, and an extra measure of love for all those who made a wrong choice and are now mopping the floor.

God's blessings to you on this day! Have a blessed day!

**August 23—*The three C's of life: Choices, chances, and changes. Sometimes you must make a choice to take a chance or your life will never change.*—Zig Ziglar**

These three C-words—choices, chances, and changes—all carry a lot of weight in our daily life, but to me the most important of those three is "choices." Let me explain why. There's a familiar quote that I've used in the past: "Every positive change in your life begins with a clear, unequivocal decision that you are going to either do something or stop doing something."

So, until that important choice is made, there is no chance to take, and no change can happen. But after the choice is made, the next step is to take a chance in order to bring about change. I believe the three C-words have to go in this exact order, to be successful. Remember, if you want something you've never had you have to make the choice to do something you've never done.

My prayer is that regardless of whether you're trying to achieve great things or accomplish small things today, this week, or in the future, you will have the strength, stamina, and determination to make the choice to take the chance to let good change happen in your life!

God's blessings to you on this day! Have a blessed day!

**August 24—*I believe I am here for a reason and my purpose is far greater than my challenges.*—common expression**

It's often said that if you don't know your purpose in life, simply find your passion and the two will collide. I recently read a quote that said, "Passion plus purpose equals profession." I like that a lot.

It seems like many of the quotes and verses I use in my daily offerings refer to purpose. Maybe that's because I love the word; I love to write about it, talk about it, and I love to try and fulfill—with God's help and grace—what I believe is my purpose. I am a strong believer that everybody has a purpose in life and I encourage you—no, let me rephrase that, I challenge you—to find yours. It changes the way you look at life.

At this point in my life I find it very exciting to be challenged, motivated, and enthused about that one word: purpose. I ran across a short, one-sentence quote recently that summed up my feelings exactly: "I'm on the hunt for who I've not yet become." Maybe I will always be looking for who I've not yet become, but that's OK, because I like the direction the hunt is taking me.

My prayer today is that we all join the hunt to become the best people we can be and the people we've not yet become! Find the passion that lights your way, and your purpose will be there waiting for you!

God's blessings to you this day! Have a blessed day!

### August 25—*I'd rather have a life of "oh-wells" than a life of "what-ifs."*—common expression

I have often said that I would rather look back and say, "I tried that and it turned out poorly, or even was an outright failure" than to look back many years later and say, "I wish I would have tried that."

To me, looking back with regret on missed opportunities is a far tougher pill to swallow than trying, giving your absolute best shot, and failing miserably. And the beauty of this quote is that it can be applied to any aspect in your life—big, small, or in between—and at any time in your life. You are never too old to set new goals and dream new dreams!

An anonymous quote that I have used before ties in well with this: "No one can go back and make a brand-new start, but anyone can start from this day, this minute, and make a brand-new ending."

Every person—I don't care who they are or how much self-confidence they seem to show—has doubts and fears failure. Again, nobody, not one person on the face of the earth is excluded from that list. And everybody at some point in their life has let the enemy that sometimes resides between their ears convince them to not even try because failure is certain. Don't be a "what-if" person! Set goals, go after your dreams—and then, regardless of the outcome, look back with pride at your effort.

God's blessings to you on this day! Have a blessed day!

## August 26—*When it rains, look for rainbows. When it's dark, look for stars.*—common expression

I could add one more short sentence to today's offering that would make it complete and make it perfect: In every situation—rain, dark nights, and everything in between—put your trust in God.

Certainly, we all enjoy sun-drenched, golden days when there is nary a cloud in the sky and all seems right with the world. That's a great scene for a movie, but those of us who live in the real world on a daily basis understand the folly that life is always going to be filled with days when the sun is on our face and the wind is at our back.

As we roll through the seasons of our life, you come to understand that it was those tough days when it rained sideways in sheets, and those dark nights when there was not a star in the sky, that shapes our character and defines our attitude about life—and our understanding that God loves us and never leaves us.

One of my favorite Bible verses is Joshua 1:9, which states: "Be strong and of good courage; do not be afraid, nor be dismayed, for the LORD your God will be with you wherever you go." Let me paraphrase just a little by adding that "wherever you may go" means rainy days and dark nights!

God's blessings to you on this day! Have a blessed day!

**August 27—*Don't be discouraged if you fail. It's often the last key on the ring that opens the door.*—common expression**

Today's quote points out one of the uncanny and true things about life. Just as it is always the last key that unlocks the door, it's also sometimes the second, third, fourth, or umpteenth time we try that we finally succeed.

My parents were good, hard-working, determined people who spiced up their vocabulary and life lessons with old-fashioned sayings. They seemed to have one for any situation. It seems I find myself repeating many of those sayings on a daily basis.

I have heard my dad say countless times, "You've got to pull yourself up by your bootstraps," "You've got to put your shoulder to the wheel," or "Get knocked down seven times . . . you get up eight"—you get the picture. Regardless of the situation, you always give it all you've got. That was a mindset learned early, repeated often, and I'm thankful for that today. I have said often that the two most valuable things my dad gave me in life was a strong belief in God and an equally strong work ethic. Both of those things will carry you a long way in life. My prayer is that regardless of your situation—good, bad, happy, sad, or anywhere in between—you give it all you've got. In many, many instances in life, it's the only option you have.

God's blessings to you on this day! Have a blessed day!

**August 28—*Being defeated is just a temporary condition. Giving up and quitting is what makes it permanent.*—Marilyn Vos Savant**

Everybody, throughout history, has tasted defeat and experienced setbacks—that's just a part of life. Nobody gets a pass and skates through life without dealing with some difficult times. It's what we do with those defeats and difficult times that either defines us or defeats us.

Failure is not falling down; failure only happens when you refuse to get back up. If you spend any time reading and studying people who are successful, you'll find that the common denominator on their road to success is failure. Every person who trudges through life experiences failure; it's what you do with those failures that make the difference. Failure is a temporary condition—giving up is what makes it permanent. Don't be afraid to fail—be afraid not to try!

Remember, today's struggles will develop tomorrow's strength—don't ever give up.

God's blessings to you on this day! Have a blessed day!

## August 29—*Sometimes you will never know the true value of a moment or a person until that moment or that person becomes a memory.*—common expression

I agree with this quote completely, but there's one word that I would change. I don't think it's "sometimes" that we don't know the true value of a moment or a person, I think it's "often."

In the hustle and bustle of daily life we all take people and moments—very special people and moments—for granted. It's not intentional and it doesn't mean we don't care; it's just that we're all going a hundred miles an hour in different directions trying to take care of the daily challenges of life.

And sadly, life doesn't come equipped with flashing lights or ringing bells to remind us to cherish a moment or a loved one as long as we possibly can. I guess the easiest way to sum up today's effort is to say: "We all need to slow down, take a good look around us . . . and then stop and smell the roses."

God's blessings to you on this day! Have a blessed, rose-smelling day!

## August 30—*Shake it off . . . and take a step up.*—Curt Reed

One day a farmer's donkey fell down into a well. The animal cried mournfully for hours as the farmer tried to figure out what to do. Finally, he decided the animal was old, and the well needed to be covered up anyway; it just wasn't worth it to retrieve the donkey.

He asked all his neighbors to come over and help him. They all grabbed a shovel and began the task of shoveling dirt into the well. Immediately the donkey realized what was happening and began to cry again. Then, to everyone's amazement he quieted down.

A few shovel-loads later, the farmer finally looked down into the well. He was astonished at what he saw. With each shovel of dirt that hit his back, the donkey was doing something amazing. He would shake the dirt off his back and then take a step up on the dirt that was being tossed on him. As the farmer's neighbors continued to shovel dirt on top of the animal, he would shake it off and take a step up. Pretty soon, everyone was amazed as the donkey stepped up over the edge of the well and happily trotted off!

The moral of today's offering is simple: Life is going to shovel dirt on you, lots of dirt, all kinds of dirt. The trick to getting out of the well is to shake it off and take a step up. Each of our troubles is a stepping-stone. We can get out of the deepest wells just by not stopping, never giving up! Shake it off and take a step up.

God's blessings to you on this day! Have a blessed day.

**August 31—***Every second brings a fresh beginning, every minute holds a new promise, every hour holds new hope, and every day is what we choose to make it.***—common expression**

Most people, myself included, are procrastinators about change. Even if we're stuck in a rut, sometimes it's just easier to stay in that rut than to take that difficult first step to change. Even though in many instances it's changes we know we need to make, it's just so much easier to say we'll wait until Monday, or until the first of the month, or maybe even make it a New Year's resolution

I used a quote recently that I think goes well with today's offering: "No one can go back and make a brand-new beginning, but every person can start from this day, this minute, this second, and make a brand-new ending!"

Remember, your present circumstances do not determine where you go—they only determine where you start. It's worth repeating: "Every second brings a fresh beginning, every minute holds a new promise, every hour holds new hope, and every day is what we choose to make it."

God's blessings to you on this day! Have a blessed day!

**September 1—*Stay strong! Your test will become your testimony and your mess will become your message.*—common expression**

I love this quote because it speaks in the present about the ability to overcome and conquer the past. One of the certainties of life is that we are all going to face a "test" and we're all going to deal with a "mess." That's just life . . . nobody gets a pass!

But, it's not your test or your mess that defines you; instead it's how many times you get back up after you face a test or a mess. It's how many times you stand up, square your shoulders, shake yourself off, and keep moving forward. It's how many times you ignore the words of your detractors and fight to make yourself a better person today than you were yesterday.

I am a big believer that no matter what misfortune comes our way, we have within us—and with God's help—the ability to turn it into something of value to help others and become a stronger, better person. Or, as today's quote says, if we stay strong we can "turn our test into our testimony and our mess into our message." The two key words in today's offering are "stay strong"—something we must be vigilant about each and every day!

God's blessings to you on this day! Have a blessed day!

**September 2—*Your talent is God's gift to you. What you do with it is your gift back to God.*—Leo Buscaglia**

I am convinced that everybody has a talent—a God-given talent. Some people use their talent in a positive, purposeful way; some toss it aside; some never try to find it; and many never open the "gift" they've been given.

You might be saying: "I'm not sure what my talent or purpose is in life." For those who want to use that excuse, consider this: Think about what a great world it would be if we all started each and every day with the simple purpose of being kind to each other, smiling more, complaining less (or not at all), being helpful, being positive, and just trying to be a better person than we were yesterday. There's a great place to start.

When I read today's offering for the first time it triggered a memory of another quote about God-given talent by the late comedian/author Erma Bombeck: "When I stand before God at the end of my life I would hope that I would not have a bit of talent left, and I could say, 'I used everything you gave me.'"

My prayer is that you find your talent, your purpose, your gift . . . and then give it back over and over again!

God's blessings to you on this day! Have a blessed day!

**September 3—*The tallest oak in the forest was once just a little nut that held its ground.*—common expression**

Have you ever embarked on a new goal or project and within minutes of starting thought, "I can't do this . . . there's no way I can finish or even go on"? If we're honest, we've all been in that spot. And when that happens, dreams die, goals get pushed to the side, and in many instances we stay stuck in the same rut.

Let me share with you an experience that happened to me. I have always battled my weight, and being active, walking, and exercising was always a huge help to me to try and keep my waistline in check. Last year I started a new job and quit exercising, and ate more than I needed of the wrong type foods at the wrong time of the day. Again, many of you can relate to that quandary!

About six months ago I decided to begin an exercise regimen and diet at the same time. Even getting to the gym was a huge challenge! I didn't feel comfortable around people who were already in good shape, and the idea of starting all over again weighed heavy on my mind. But I trudged forward, swallowed my pride, and started again. Those early days when I had to literally make myself enter the gym I motivated myself with a familiar quote I've used often: "Success is the result of small efforts repeated over and over again, day in and day out."

And during the past several months I have used those small daily efforts to lose more than fifty pounds and establish a five- and six-day-per-week workout routine. Again, small efforts repeated over and over again lead to success! My prayer today is for strength and determination if you are in a fight with yourself about taking that first small step. As the voice of experience, that first step will be the most difficult, so that makes it all downhill after that.

God's blessings to you on this day! Have a blessed day!

## September 4—*Lord, prop us up on the leanin' side.*—anonymous

I heard a story about an old farmer who was the deacon of his church, and was often asked to offer a prayer at the close of Sunday services. Without fail the old farmer always prayed, "Lord, prop us up on the leanin' side."

One day, a young man asked the old farmer what exactly that prayer meant. The old deacon said: "I've got an old barn out back. It's been there a long time and it's withstood a lot of weather, it's gone through a lot of storms, and it's stood for many years. It's still standing but one day I noticed it was leaning to one side a bit . . . so I went and got timbers and propped it up on its leaning side so that it wouldn't fall."

The farmer continued: "I got to thinking how much I was like that old barn. I've been around a long time, I've withstood a lot of hard times and I'm still standing, too. But I find myself leaning to one side from time to time, so I ask the Lord to prop us up on the leaning side—because we all get to leaning once in a while. Sometimes we lean toward anger, we lean toward bitterness, we lean toward hatred, toward things we shouldn't—and it's then we should say, 'Lord prop us up on the leaning side so we can stand straight and tall.'"

My prayer today is that the Lord will prop us all up on our leaning side.

God's blessings to you this day! Have a blessed day!

**September 5**—*Every day is a new beginning, treat it that way. Stay away from what might have been and move on. Don't let negative words or actions of others affect your smile. Decide that today is going to be a good day.*—**anonymous**

Four short sentences make up today's quote, but my goodness, what a punch those four little sentences pack. Each one would certainly stand alone by itself, to give us all something to ponder. Let's spend a moment in today's offering breaking down these four gems.

Certainly each day is a new beginning. I still think it's remarkable that we get the chance every single morning to wipe the slate clean and start all over again. Thank you, Jesus, for the opportunity to start brand-new each day! The second sentence is a great reminder to keep our eyes straight ahead and not revisit yesterday's troubles today. If we start packing the baggage from a bad day for the next day we will soon have a trunkful of bad days, pessimistic people, and sour attitudes dragging behind us. I can't stress enough how we have to stay away from the past and what might have been—remember, eyes on the big picture in front of you.

The third sentence is yet another reminder that we have to . . . it's imperative . . . limit our time spent with negative people. Remember, these folks have a problem for every solution! The last sentence is, in my estimation, the most important one because we truly do have the ability and the power within us to make every day a good day, period! Remember the wise words of Abraham Lincoln: "Most people are about as happy as they make up their mind to be."

Today's offering provides us with a solid, spot-on, four-point battle plan to arm ourselves every single day. Tuck this one away—it's pure gold!

God's blessings to you on this day! Have a blessed day!

**September 6—***Change is choice. You can stay in your comfort zone or you can take the first step toward a new beginning!***—anonymous**

The single word that jumps out in this quote is "choice" because we really do have the option to choose what direction life's tests and problems take us. We've all seen people face what looked like an impossible situation, and then make the choice to either become the victim or the victor. Again, it came down to choice—does a test or a problem become an obstacle or an opportunity?

How many times have you seen a person go through a bad experience, and then let that particular event define them and become their reason to frown and have a bitter, sour attitude about every aspect of life?

On the flip side, we see people who go through the same type of struggles and use a difficult experience for motivation to become stronger, better people, to help others and to achieve their goals.

Many times, failing reveals more about a person's character than winning. Nobody goes through life without some adversity—some seem to have more than their share—but it's how you handle the adversity that reveals your character. The choice is ours today and every day. Will you take that first step to a new beginning?

God's blessing to you on this day! Have a blessed day!

**September 7—*One of the most prevalent verses in the Bible is "fear not." That's another great reminder from God to live each day worry-free.*—anonymous**

I read through today's quote and it immediately triggered a recollection of a verse I think about when we are faced with fear. It's my go-to verse and one that I am sure you've heard often. Isaiah 41:10 says: "Fear not, for I am with you; be not dismayed, for I am your God. I will strengthen you, yes, I will help you, I will uphold you with my righteous right hand."

I know most have heard this verse before, but have you ever slowed down and let it really sink in and resonate? I read it slowly, word by word, and it was then that the promises and the messages of hope jumped off the page at me: Fear not . . . I am with you . . . be not dismayed . . . I am your God . . . I will strengthen you . . . I will help you . . . I will hold you up with my righteous right hand.

In only two short sentences there are eight promises for us to use and embrace, to face any and every situation that comes our way. These two sentences provide a full-proof, full-service battle plan to conquer fear in our life!

And maybe, along with all these wonderful promises and messages of hope, another lesson in this verse is for all of us to slow down, don't be afraid, and understand that God is in control. My prayer is that perhaps when you feel the stress of everyday life closing in, you will remember the promises of Isaiah 41:10.

God's blessings to you on this day! Have a blessed day!

**September 8—*Today be thankful and think how blessed you are. Your family is priceless, your time is gold, and your health is wealth.*—Zig Ziglar**

What are you thankful for today? You might want to grab a pen and notebook, because if you answer honestly about family, friends, and health, and then add in the freedom, beauty, wonders, excitement, physical, and mental ability . . . and on and on . . . that make up your life, it will take you a while.

What are you thankful for today? Before you give me the standard answers—some of which are mentioned in today's quote—think about the question and start from the moment you opened your eyes this morning, to the ability to think about what your plans are today (probably still in bed), to your feet hitting the floor to take a first step, to a cup of coffee (or the caffeine of your choice), to the quietness and beauty of an early morning. As you move on down your list it's easy to see that all our lives are made up of countless miracles stacked on top of each other. Our blessings, our "thankful list," are endless!

As an exclamation point to today's offering, consider this quote that sums up today's thought nicely: "A thankful heart is not only the greatest virtue, but the parent of all other virtues."

My prayer today is that we all develop and focus on a daily attitude of gratitude so that we can truly see the endless list of God's blessings and handiwork in each of our lives!

God's blessings to you on this day! Have a blessed day!

**September 9**—*The greatest danger for most of is not that our aim is too high and we miss, but that it's too low and we reach it.*— **Michelangelo**

I am a big believer in goals and believe that, regardless of age, we should all set goals because they provide us with a roadmap and a plan about what we hope to accomplish with our lives. How do you know where you are going, or where you want to end up, without establishing goals?

But let me stress that in no circumstances should goals be easy! In fact, to ratchet that point up a little more, goals should be uncomfortable and nearly unattainable. Goals, with God's help, should make us try to reach new heights in our lives. Any time I hear about reaching for more in life I always recall the brilliant words of educator Benjamin E. Mays:

It must be borne in mind that the tragedy of life doesn't lie in not reaching your goal. It lies in having no goal to reach. It is not a calamity to die with dreams unfulfilled, but it is a calamity not to have a purpose in life and not to dream. It is not a disgrace not to reach the stars, but it is a disgrace not to have any stars to reach. Failure is not a sin, but low aim and lack of purpose is.[3]

Set goals—many goals. Reach for the stars, aim high, and remember that failure is not a sin, but low aim and lack of purpose is. My prayer today is that where your goals, dreams, and purpose are concerned your aim is high!

God's blessings to you on this day! Have a blessed day!

## September 10—*The road to success runs uphill.*—Willie Davis

For the most part, daily life is lived walking uphill . . . so focus on the climb! And that uphill fight will not be lost because you didn't wear good shoes; instead, it will be lost by the battle that takes place in your mind.

You see, while you're trudging along uphill, those enemies that reside in your head—doubt and fear—will convince you that you can't win, can't succeed, and can't reach your goals. These dream-crushers will do this by convincing you that you are not good enough, smart enough, gifted enough, nor talented enough.

Every person—I don't care who they are or how much self-confidence they seem to show—has doubts and fears failure. Again, nobody, not one person on the face of the earth is excluded from that list. And everybody at some point in their uphill walk through life has let the enemies that sometimes reside between their ears—doubt and fear—convince them to not even try because failure is certain. That voice keeps people from reaching out to God and it

---

[3] John Herbert Roper, *The Magnificent Mays* (Columbia: The University of South Carolina Press, 2012), September 9 devotional.

keeps people in dead-end jobs, harmful relationships, and dozens of other life-traps.

Remember, you cannot climb uphill while thinking downhill thoughts. Keep climbing your daily uphill walk and you will have a great view from the top of that mountain called life! My prayer today is for a little extra spring in the step for all those with a steep hill to climb!

God's blessings to you on this day! Have a blessed day!

## September 11—*Make sure your worst enemy doesn't live between your own two ears.*—Laird Hamilton

How many times in your life have you uttered the phrase, "I talked myself out of doing that"? Or, how many times have you looked back years later and said, "I wish I would have done that"? Regardless if it involves a job, a relationship, going to church, starting a diet, going to the gym, or countless other things, the enemies between our ears—commonly known as doubt and fear—wins a lot of decisions. And of course that means we lose, because fear and doubt are dream-killers, life-changers, and career-crushers.

Keep in mind that courage is not the absence of fear—everybody has fears. But instead, courage is the triumph over fear. In the words of legendary actor John Wayne, "Courage is being scared to death and saddling up anyway." My prayer today is that you challenge the enemy between your ears and saddle up anyway!

God's blessings to you on this day! Have a blessed and fearless day!

## September 12—*Life is a journey that must be traveled no matter how bad the road or accommodations.*—Oliver Goldsmith

As I get older, I realize that it's not the times when we're cruising down the wide-open road with great visibility that define us. Instead, it's those bad roads, sharp curves, and hairpin turns when the road is slippery, and it's really difficult to see that shape our character. Sometimes you have to slow down to a crawl to navigate these rough patches of life's highway, and sometimes you have to stop completely to get your bearings.

Every person has faced a few bad roads in life. We've all been there, cruising along the straight highway of life, and then out of nowhere comes that rough patch, that sharp curve that is difficult and seemingly impossible to navigate. It could involve family, a relationship, finances, loss of employment, health issues, and countless other life-related issues that bog us down.

Other times, when you can't stop and you have to keep moving, you have to turn loose of the steering wheel completely—let go and let God! One of my favorite verses states: "Trust in the LORD with all your heart, and lean not on your own understanding; in all your ways acknowledge Him, and He shall direct your paths" (Proverbs 3:5–6). Let me paraphrase that last sentence: "In all your ways acknowledge him and he shall direct your paths . . . particularly when the road and accommodations are bad!"

God's blessings to you on this day! Have a blessed day!

## September 13—*When you have exhausted all possibilities, remember this: you haven't.*—Thomas Edison

This quote reminds me of another one I've used in the past: If Plan A fails, remember, there are twenty-five more letters in the alphabet. Today's quote takes that even further and basically says, if you exhaust the alphabet, start over with 1A, and then 2A, and keep going. In other words, the opportunities to find a solution to your problem are infinite.

I loved this quote the second I read it because it promotes a "don't give up, don't give in" mentality. Or, as my mother used to say, where there's a will, there's a way—which means that with "will" we can find a "way" to correct any problem or situation. But sometimes putting the will and the way together is not quite as easy as that little seven-word proverb states. There are those who have the will but are so far off track they can't find their way, and there are others who know the way but can't muster up the will to get back on course.

I have found that sometimes, when we run out of letters in the alphabet trying to come up with a plan to solve a problem, the best solution—and probably what should have been our first solution—is to simply "let go . . . and let God." My prayer today is that God would pour out an extra special blessing of strength and courage on all those who have lost their will and provide a clear and straight path for those who can't find their way. And never forget, "When you think you've exhausted all possibilities . . . you haven't."

God's blessings to you on this day! Have a blessed day!

**September 14—Hope . . . *is wishing something would happen. Faith . . . is believing something will happen. Courage . . . is making something happen.*—common expression**

The very first thing that came to my mind when I read this quote is that these three little words—hope, faith, and courage—are the key ingredients in virtually any single thing we attempt to do throughout life. And the main thing is, all three must be applied to see change or to make something happen.

We can all hope for something to happen, but until we apply the faith to really believe and the courage to take that first difficult step, it will always remain a hope . . . just a hope. But when faith is applied—an unwavering belief that God is directing your path—and then a sprinkle of courage to take that first step is added, it's a recipe for change and a blueprint for success.

And the beauty of this quote, through my eyes, is that sometimes we can still make great things happen with a scared-to-death courage, enough to take a baby step. Then we can apply a dash of hope and mustard seed-sized faith and still see positive results. Think about it like this: Hope (and pray) for the change in your life, keep your faith strong, then take a tiny step forward and give it to God—that's hope, faith, and courage all wrapped up in one package.

God's blessings to you on this day! Have a blessed day of hope, faith, and courage.

**September 15—*The past is where you learned the lesson. The future is where you apply the lesson. Don't stop in the middle.*—anonymous**

Some people are fighting a daily battle against an unbeatable opponent: the past. These folks are waging war against things that happened ten, twenty, thirty years ago. It's a battle that nobody can win!

Sadly, some people never complete the three sentences that make up today's offering. Many folks learn the lesson, and then stop in the middle and never get the chance to apply the lesson to their lives.

Today's offering is a great reminder that in order to change, we have to move forward and complete the process involving the past and the future. You are not defined by your past, and you don't reside there. The past is a place of reference, not a place of residence. Instead, you are prepared by your past—prepared to keep your eyes on that big windshield in front of you, to plan your future with purpose, and to frame your life with faith in God. Remember, we all have a blank 365-page book in front of us, and today is the first chapter. The key thing is that you are the author of that book; you can write the story to illustrate those lessons you learned in the past. And as you write your story, remember that the past is where you learned the lesson, and the future is where you apply the lesson! And just like the quote says, don't stop in the middle!

God's blessings to you on this day! Have a blessed day!

**September 16—*Caution: Rough road ahead.*—common expression**

I was recently driving on a two-lane highway, and alongside the road was a portable flashing sign that read, "Caution: Rough road ahead." As I drove past the sign, and noticed more signs ahead with the continued warning, I immediately thought of our travels down life's highway.

"Wouldn't it be nice," I thought, "if there was a flashing sign to warn us of the troubles and rough roads that are ahead of us in life?" But, that's not how life works, is it? Many times in life we find ourselves in the middle of a rough stretch of road before we know it—a road full of potholes and ruts caused by health issues, the loss of a loved one, relationship problems, family issues, and financial concerns.

The words "fear not" are in the Bible many, many times. Think about that, and use it as a daily reminder and a flashing sign from God that he will provide strength and courage to help us when the road of life turns rough and difficult to travel. While there are no visible flashing signs along life's highway to warn us of rough roads ahead, it should provide immeasurable comfort for all of us to know that we do not fear those bumpy, unpaved roads because Jesus has the steering wheel.

Life changes without our permission. Take a look around on any given day and you realize that life can change dramatically from one minute to the next. That means it's very important to take nothing and nobody for granted—your family is priceless, your time is gold, and your health is wealth.

God's blessings to you on this day! Have a blessed day!

## September 17—*Your attitude belongs to you, and it's your choice if you want to have a good one.*—Joyce Meyer

I don't believe there is anything more important than attitude. While a lot of folks worry about the clothes they put on each morning, many would be better off to concentrate more on the attitude they "dress" themselves in each day. A home, a business, a work environment, and our relationship with every single person—attitude is the make-or-break difference in all of them.

All of us, every single person, have days when we swing and miss and strike out—sometimes multiple times in one day. But the beauty of life is that the very next day we have another chance to step up to the plate (of life), dig back in, and swing for the fence.

Every single morning when our feet hit the floor we have the option of how the day will go—and this option is based solely on our attitude. Isn't that remarkable that we can wipe the slate clean every day, no matter what happened yesterday, and try again? Certainly we will face struggles and problems almost every day, but again we have the option, with God's help, of how we handle them.

Remember, disappointments, struggles, and problems are inevitable, but letting them defeat you is optional. So, this morning and every morning when you get spiffed up to face the day, make the big difference to the little difference and add a positive attitude to your daily wardrobe.

God's blessings to you on this day! Have a blessed day!


## September 18—*Don't judge by appearance; a rich heart might be under a poor coat.*—Scottish proverb

When I read this quote, I was reminded of a life lesson my mother taught me many, many years ago. Like most teenagers in the late 1960s, I had long hair. One Sunday morning at the end of church, as folks were on their way out of the building, the minister walked up beside me and said, "It's about time you got a haircut, isn't it?" My mother Geraldine, who was not one to mince words, turned on a dime, leveled a stare at him with those steely blue eyes, and said, "I try to look at his heart and not his hair, Reverend . . . and I'd suggest you do the same thing." As she turned to walk away she finished him off by adding, "That might make a good sermon topic for you sometime."

Even though we've heard the phrase "don't judge a book by its cover" countless times, we all tend to form an instant judgment based on appearance. Recently, I was leaving a local convenience store and a young girl, probably seventeen or eighteen years old, was pushing a baby in a stroller. She had purple hair and more than a few visible tattoos. In my mind, I immediately went on a judgmental rant about her appearance . . . and the baby was another story. In a matter of seconds, it was like God checked me and stopped me in my tracks and I instantly thought, "Who am I—a person who has made a gazillion mistakes and is saved by the grace of God—to judge anybody?" I quickly replaced my judgment with a prayer for the young girl and her baby.

Geraldine was right nearly fifty years ago and she's still right today. Try to look at the heart and not the hair . . . or the tattoos . . . or the piercings . . . or the opinions . . . or the philosophical, religious, and political differences . . . or the poor coat. Again, try to look at the heart!

God's blessings to you on this day! Have a blessed day!

## September 19—*Our reaction to any situation literally has the power to change the situation itself.*—anonymous

I read this quote through once, and then slowed down and read it slowly through again. After I wrapped my mind around this one-sentence, fourteen-word gem, I thought about the plain, old, unvarnished truth in this quote and realized that in all the quotes I've used, this might be one of the most powerful.

Think about it like this: On any given day we have no control over other people we deal with—over family issues, coworkers, traffic, and what kind of a mood some people happen to be in on that particular day. In short, life can change dramatically from one moment to the next, and it certainly changes without our permission. However, the key to today's offering is found in the first two words: our reaction. While we have no control over many things, we have total control over our reaction. And just like the quote says, our reaction—let me say it again, *our* reaction—to any situation literally has the power to change the situation itself.

We don't control the outcomes, but we do control our reactions to them. And certainly sometimes it's better to not react at all. I often use the wonderful quote by Dr. Charles Swindoll, who said that life is 10 percent what happens to you and 90 percent how you react to it. And just like today's quote says, we all have within us the power to change that 90 percent simply by the way we react. That's powerful stuff—that's a life-changer!

God's blessings to you on this day! Have a blessed day!

### September 20—*Don't let anyone dull your sparkle.*—common expression

When I ran across this quote—just six little words—I loved it immediately. You see, it took some time but I've learned that there are people who I believe roll out of bed with the sole intention of trying to dull somebody's sparkle that day.

We all deal with and encounter daily those people who walk around with a black cloud over their heads. You know the ones I'm talking about—everything is bad, nothing is good, and the world is out to get them. It might be a beautiful day today, but they will remind you that it is supposed to rain in a few days!

But the key thing—something it took me a long time to learn—is that these people cannot dull your sparkle without your consent. In short, never, ever let yourself be defined by somebody's comment, opinion, or ignorance. Remember, your value doesn't decrease based on somebody's inability to see the good and the worth in you. My prayer today is that we all develop a strong defense when we cross paths with a "sparkle-stealer."

So, get out there today and sparkle!

God's blessings to you on this day! Have a blessed and a "sparkly" day!

### September 21—*Don't be pushed by your problems; be led by your dreams.*—Ralph Waldo Emerson

In a nutshell, life is full of trouble and problems that we are going to encounter along the daily path we walk. From a car that won't start, to a leaky roof, to relationship issues or major illness, we all face problems from time to time. The point of today's offering is how we face those problems. Are we pushed by our problems, or led by our dreams?

We can't do anything about the winds of trouble that will blow through our lives, but we can learn to adjust the sail. There are always going to be troubling and difficult winds that blow in life in the form of trouble, mistakes, missteps, contrary people, sickness, hardships, and problems. That's just a given, and for some it seems those ill winds howl more often. The key is to learn how adjust the sail—with God's help—so that we can navigate those "winds" that will either make us or break us.

Many people experience a failure (or failures) in life, and then use that as a standby excuse to never try again. It's been said that hardships and failure often prepare ordinary people for an extraordinary destiny. I truly believe that, because it seems that a constant rule for people who have enjoyed success is that they simply refuse to give up. Somehow these people use setbacks, failures, obstacles, the doubts and negativity of others, and the word "no" as motivation to reach their goals. They learn to adjust their sail so they are not pushed by their problems and instead they are led by their dreams.

God's blessings to you on this day! Have a blessed day!

**September 22—*Success is not measured by what you do compared to what others do. It is measured by what you do with the ability God gave you.*—Nicky Gumbel**

All of us, at one time or another, have been guilty of measuring success by comparing ourselves to others, instead of based on the ability God has given us. And when this happens, we will inevitably always fall short.

I think the increase in social media has made this even worse as many people compare their sometimes mundane lives to the highlight reels that some people portray on Facebook and Twitter. While some people might try to make you believe otherwise, nobody has a perfect day every day and nobody travels down the road of life without experiencing a few bumps and potholes. That's just life . . . period.

When I first came across today's offering I was reminded of a quote I heard many years ago by the late humorist, columnist, and author Erma Bombeck: "When I stand before God at the end of my life I would hope that I would not have a single bit of talent left, and could say, 'I used everything you gave me.'" That sage bit of wisdom by Bombeck should be the goal for all of us, every single day!

God's blessings to you on this day! Have a blessed day!

### September 23—*Every person is gifted, but some never open the present.*—common expression

How often in life have you heard it said: that person failed to reach his or her goal? I don't believe the word "fail" can't be used to describe any person working hard to try and achieve a goal. There is no failure in not reaching your goal, but the failure lies in having no goal to reach.

As is often the case. it seems, this quote reminds me of another quote I used awhile back: "Those who do something and fail are infinitely better than those who do nothing and succeed." Remember, it's not a failure to reach for the stars and miss, but it is a failure not to have any stars to reach for.

I think this offering is so important to so many people. You see, life is like riding a bicycle: If you stop moving, you'll lose your balance. So, if you're twenty-three or ninety-three, set goals, trust God, dream dreams, trust God, strive to be better than you were yesterday, and keep your balance by moving forward! And most importantly, keep on trusting God!

My prayer to go along with today's offering is that, regardless of whether you're trying to achieve great things or accomplish small things, we will all have the energy, strength, stamina, and determination to set new goals and dream new dreams! My prayer today is that we all aim high and reach for the stars!

God's blessings to you on this day! Have a blessed day!

**September 24—*Don't waste words on people who deserve your silence. Sometimes the most powerful thing you can say is nothing at all.*—Mandy Hale**

Have you ever considered how much energy and time is wasted on a daily basis by people trying to respond to something negative that was said to them? Sadly, there is a group of people who roll out of bed every morning with a chip on their shoulder and itching for a confrontation. These are the naysayers of life who love to toss a "zinger" at somebody in hopes of getting a response. Most of the time these folks have a favorite few people they like to pick on, and toss a few "verbal bombs."

Today's quote, in only two short sentences, addresses perfectly how we should respond when confronted by one of these two-legged barking dogs. A sure sign of maturity and growth on our part is coming to the realization how many things don't require our comment.

There's an old adage that says, "It takes two to tango." Well, it also takes two to have a verbal confrontation, and if we all learn not to waste our words on people who deserve silence, there's won't be a tango. Also, keep in mind that when we retaliate after something is said to us, we give up control of our emotions in that particular situation. So, by saying nothing at all, we are giving the most powerful answer we can, and we are also maintaining control of the situation. That's a double-whammy!

God's blessings to you on this day! Have a blessed day!

**September 25—*Your life does not get better by chance . . . it gets better by change.*—Jim Rohn**

One of the great mysteries of all time takes place daily as countless people get up and live in the same difficult, abusive, harmful, hurtful situation but continue to insist that things will somehow magically get better. This mindset has to be one of the true wonders of the world! I probably should also point out that the definition of insanity is to keep repeating the same harmful things day after day while expecting a different result.'

As this single sentence quote aptly points out, our lives do not—and let me add, cannot and will not—get better by chance, only by change. And as many of us know, change is hard. I recently read a story that made an excellent point worth repeating: Many people resist change because they focus all their attention on what they have to give up instead of what they have to gain.

There's an old adage that says, "A journey of a thousand miles begins with a single step." But really, that phrase can be used with anything we do in life that involves change, from small everyday tasks to life-changing decisions. As today's offering points out, that first step is difficult, because we all underestimate our capacity for change.

I speak from experience and not something I read when I say that everything we do in life— and I mean every single thing—has to have a first step involved. And of course, that first step is the hardest one; there is never, ever a right time, a perfect time.

Another quote that fits in well here states, "To achieve great things or to accomplish small things the formula is the same—start where you are, use what you have, do all you can, and trust in God." I love this quote because it's in the present and there is no procrastination—start where you are, use what you have, do all you can, and . . . most importantly . . . trust in God. That means right now!

God's blessings to you on this day! Have a blessed day!

**September 26—*Stop thinking about what could go wrong, and instead start thinking about what could go right.*—Tony Robbins**

Many people begin each morning with a defeatist attitude by compiling in their mind a list of all the things that could wrong that day. That's admitting defeat before you try, giving up without a whimper, and tossing in the towel before you begin!

As today's quote points out, we all need to stop thinking what could go wrong and focus on what could go right. Instead of stating what we believe—"God is our refuge and strength, a very present help in trouble" (Psalm 46:1) or "I can do all things through Christ who strengthens me" (Philippians 4:13)—we cling to a feeling, an emotion, and a negative belief.

One of the beautiful aspects of life is that we don't have to wait for a new calendar, a new week, a new month, or a new year because we have the ability from any second, any minute, or any hour of any day to choose and start a brand-new beginning. Every day is what we choose to make it. Let those nine words sink in. We have that ability every morning to put on a positive attitude, to make the day and shape the day any way we want.

Remember, you can't go back and make a new start, but within you and with God's help, there is the ability to make a brand-spanking-new ending! Today . . . today is called the present, and rightfully so, because it's a present from God. It's a present that contains another chance, a new opportunity, and the hope to be a better person. The second your eyes open every morning that present is waiting on you.

Remember those nine words again—"every day is what we choose to make it." So, the choice is yours and totally yours—what kind of day will you make?

God's blessings to you on this day! Have a blessed day!

**September 27—*Inner peace begins the exact moment you make the choice not to allow another person or event to control your emotions.*—anonymous**

This one sentence quote is powerful stuff and 100 percent accurate! But there is one word that stands out to me, and it should also jump out at you. Let me challenge you to read it again and pick out what you feel is the single word that is the difference-maker that ties the meaning of this quote together.

That one word is "choice." You, see we have the ability every single day to determine our boundaries and establish that we are not going to allow people and events to dictate what we think and what we feel.

Think about it like this: On any given day we have no control over other people we deal with, over family issues, coworkers, traffic, and what kind of a mood some people happen to be in on that particular day. In short, life can change dramatically from one moment to the next and it certainly changes without our permission. Once again, let me point out the word "choice." While we have no control over many things, we have total control over our choice not to allow people and events to control us. Our daily choice concerning any situation literally has the power to change the situation itself.

The key point in today's offering is that we don't control the outcomes, but we do control our reactions to them. And certainly, sometimes the best reaction is no reaction and the strongest response is no response. My prayer today is that we all make that important choice to not allow people and events control our emotions!

God's blessings to you on this day! Have a blessed day!

## September 28—*Silence is the most powerful scream.*—common expression

While it seems so simple, I didn't learn until just a few years ago that I do not have to respond to everything that is said to me. And what a revelation that was to me when I finally realized—after years of trying to get even and get the last (and louder) word—that no answer, no reply, no comeback, no zinger, and no verbal bomb from me was necessary. Trust me on this. If you haven't tried this, it's worth your time and it feels so much better to simply say nothing, rather than to get into a heated war of words—words that cannot be taken back. Remember, hurtful words can be forgiven, but never forgotten.

In fact, one of the greatest lessons I've learned in life is that no answer is most always the strongest and loudest answer you can give. Or, as my late mother used to say, "Sometimes it's better to chew on your words before you spit them out."

And of course, here in the twenty-first century, that also holds true for social media where some people clearly need a speed bump between their keyboard and their brain. Lately I have started asking myself the question: In the whole scheme of life, is replying to somebody's antagonistic/wrong/disrespectful comment going to change anything? The answer is, of course, always no.

God's blessings to you on this day! Have a blessed day!

## September 29—*Maturity comes when you stop making excuses and start making changes.*—anonymous

I read this quote, and then applied that simple sentence to my own life. I encourage you to do the same. If you're honest with yourself, you have to admit that it is 100 percent accurate—if we're going to see needed change in our life, we have to stop making excuses.

I know I quote my parents and their old-fashioned phrases a lot, but when I thought about the truth behind this quote, I remembered hearing my mom say countless times: Where there's a will there's a way. In essence, this quote says the same thing: If you have the will (and it's important), you will find a way to get it done.

In every aspect of our life—our relationship with God, family, friends, work, exercise, etc.—this quote should be our measuring stick. Do we find a way or make an excuse? I hope the next time that any of us are conjuring up an excuse why we can't do this or that, this quote will be a giant flashing light reminding us that change will only happen when excuses stop!

My prayer is that whatever you're facing today, this week, this month, or this year, you find a will and then you find a way.

God's blessings to you on this day! Have a blessed day!

**September 30**—*Never allow yourself to be defined by somebody else's opinion.*—common expression

When I read this, I thought of a quote I used some time back: "If you want to improve your self-worth, stop giving other people the calculator."

You see, it took some time, but I've learned that there are people who roll out of bed every morning with the intention of spreading as much negativity as possible. And then once that negative seed is planted, that voice that lives between our ears takes over and says you're not good enough, smart enough, talented enough—you fill in the word in front of "enough"—to reach your goals and accomplish your dreams. That voice—it's called doubt and fear—keeps people in dead-end jobs, harmful relationships, and a dozen other life-traps.

This is why you can never, ever give the calculator to somebody else. Keep it in your hand, always. Then you have to be strong, not listen to the enemy between your ears, and not let a negative comment from a person who eats razor blades for breakfast dampen your enthusiasm or crush your spirit.

The key thing is that the detractors and naysayers can't defeat you without your consent. So, never, ever let yourself be defined by somebody's comment, opinion, or ignorance. Remember, your value doesn't decrease based on somebody's inability to see the good and the worth in you. You hold the calculator that determines your self-worth. It belongs to you and only you!

God's blessings to you on this day! Have a blessed day and keep a tight grip on your calculator!

**October 1**—*Life is an open book full of blank pages. You write the story as you go.*—anonymous

Today's quote is spot-on accurate, but there are three small but very important words in it that some folks just don't count on: "as you go."

You see, some folks make the mistake of believing that they can write the pages of their lives and then just live them out. Sorry, it doesn't work that way. Yes, those pages in your life-book are blank and waiting to be filled in . . . but every word, every paragraph, every page, and every chapter can only be written based on those three little words: as you go.

There are times when things are going well and we think we could fill in those blank pages and write a few chapters ahead, but then we find ourselves in the middle of a life-related storm caused by health issues, the loss of a loved one, relationship issues, family problems, or financial concerns. The list is endless. One minute we're cruising down life's highway and the road in front of us is clear and dry, and the next instant we're caught in a downpour, visibility is poor, and we're just trying to hold on tightly.

The key point in today's offering is simple, and those three little words—as you go—hold the key. While you have to write your story as you go, I want to emphasize and encourage you that . . . as . . . you . . . go . . . place your complete trust in God to direct your paths, your decisions, and your words. My prayer today is that you can look back years from now and be happy, satisfied, and proud of the way you filled those "as you go" blank pages.

God's blessings to you today! Have a blessed day!

**October 2**—*If you always do what you always did, you will always get what you always got.*—Anthony Robbins

I read this quote and recalled a story that happened when I worked in the coal mine. We were getting ready to move a piece of machinery and an older worker explained how we were going to do it. A young miner spoke up and asked, "Wouldn't it be easier and quicker if we . . ."

and then he explained what he thought we should do. The older miner spoke up, and what he said goes hand-in-hand with today's offering: "It might be easier and quicker to do it that way . . . but we've been doing it this way for thirty years and that's how we're going to keep on doing it."

In every aspect of a person's life—spiritual, physical, emotional, work, relationships, etc.—if you do what you've always done, you shouldn't be surprised that the end result is always the same. And sadly, many, many people are caught in harmful situations doing the same thing over and over again, while believing that things will somehow change.

Yet people are surprised, sometimes shocked that nothing ever changes. To me, that mentality represents one of the true wonders of life. To add to this, keep in mind that the definition of "insanity" is to keep doing the same thing over and over and over again and expect a different result.

In life, change is inevitable, while progress is optional. Don't forget that if nothing ever changed there would be no butterflies.

God's blessings to you on this day! Have a blessed day!

## October 3—*Each morning we are born again. What we do with today matters most.*—anonymous

In a nutshell, those two short sentences really do sum up how we should approach life. They provide a blueprint, a guide on how to handle those three very important and sometimes tricky areas—the past, present, and future.

First, I think it is so important to emphasize that those three areas—past, present, and future—certainly don't and shouldn't carry the same weight. In fact, these three areas are not even close to being equal. You see, I believe we should learn from yesterday but certainly not fix our gaze on yesterday, and we should hope for tomorrow but not dwell on tomorrow. A glance back and a peek forward are all right, but our main focus and attention should be on today. There is an old adage that I think of and use often that goes well right here: "Yesterday is history, tomorrow is a mystery, but today is a gift. That's why it's called the present."

And today, well, as Lamentations 3:22–23 (ESV) says, "The steadfast love of the LORD never ceases; his mercies never come to an end; they are new every morning." Let me paraphrase that just a little: I am renewed every morning because this is the day the Lord has made for me and his love and mercy never stops or ceases. We are doing a great disservice to our Creator if we do not rejoice and be glad and thankful for this day—this wonderful present —that we have been given.

God's blessings to you on this day! Have a blessed day!

## October 4—*Never let success get to your head and never let failure get to your heart.* —common expression

Life is full of failures, some big and some small, and some private and some very public. While we only see the highlight reel on some folks' lives, keep in mind that everybody—let me say that again, everybody—fails at one time or another in life.

But it's what we do with those failures that define us. In reality there are only two choices regarding failure—you can curl up in a ball and quit, or you can square your shoulders, pick yourself back up, and try again. That's it—those are your choices when you fail. With a healthy dose of stubbornness and a bigger dose of God's help, I have always chosen the latter. I hope you do, too.

I recently read a quote by an unknown writer about failure and it's worth repeating: "Failure is something we can avoid only by saying nothing, doing nothing, and being nothing. Failure is not an undertaker, defeat, or a dead end. Instead, failure should be looked on as our teacher, a small delay, and a slight detour on our way to success."

Perhaps Winston Churchill summed up failure best: "Success is moving from failure to failure without loss of enthusiasm." You have to love a quote about failure that begins by defining success! My prayer is that we do not let failure, big or small or public or private, be a stopping point in our life. Instead, make it a new enthusiastic beginning, a starting point!

God's blessings to you on this day! Have a blessed day!

**October 5—*The best preparation for tomorrow is doing your absolute best today.*—H. Jackson Brown, Jr.**

Think about this for just a moment: Every single morning, when our feet hit the floor, we have the option of how the day will go. It's in our hands every day what that brand-spanking-new day—a day that God created just for us—will be. And this is based solely on one thing and one thing only: our attitude. Isn't that remarkable that we can wipe the slate clean every day, no matter what happened yesterday or the day before or last week, and try again?

Certainly we will face struggles and problems almost every day, but again we have the option, with God's help, of how we handle them. Just like the quote I shared some time back, life is 10 percent what happens to us and 90 percent how we react to it. Again, our attitude will be the determining factor in how we deal with the 90 percent!

Remember, disappointments, struggles, and problems are inevitable, but how we react is optional. You're the captain of your ship, you're the author of your book, and you're in control of your attitude. My prayer is that you take advantage today of yet another chance and another new beginning that God has given to each of us.

God's blessings to you on this day! Have a blessed day!

**October 6—*Getting knocked down in life is a given. Getting back up and moving forward is a choice.*—Zig Ziglar**

Every person—young and old, rich and poor, and every description in between—at some point in their life gets knocked down. As the quote says, it's "a given."

Issues involving work, finances, relationships, family, and health are only a few of the ways that life can knock us down. But, in most instances these defeats are only a temporary condition. Giving up and refusing to move forward is what makes them permanent. The true character of a person is measured when they get back up and move forward. Even if it's baby steps to begin with that's OK . . . two steps forward and one step back is still moving forward and making progress!

There's an old and popular saying that says, "Get knocked down seven times . . . get back up eight." So, sometimes we get knocked down by life more than once, but each time we have to get back up, dust ourselves off, and with God's help, keep pushing forward. You might be knocked down right now, but stay focused. Your present circumstances don't determine where you can go; they merely determine where you start.

God's blessings to you on this day! Have a blessed day!

## October 7—*Making a big life change is pretty scary. But do you know what is even scarier? Regret.*—common expression

I recently spoke with a young man who was considering a major life change that would involve moving his young family halfway across the country. He had a well-paying job locked down, and had weighed the pros and cons of moving young children to another state. His question to me was more about looking for approval that he was making the right choice. My advice to him was simple: Pray about it—and then follow your heart—but there is no guarantee attached to any life decision we make. He seemed disappointed with my answer, but again, there are no guarantees in many life decisions.

His situation is one that many people, particularly young people, find themselves in often. They're faced with a tough decision and want somebody to provide them with a "guarantee" that their choice is the right one. I hate to be the bearer of bad news, but life doesn't work that way.

Oftentimes in life we are faced with decisions involving jobs, relationships, education, and a long list of other things. The only way we will ever know if we made the right decision is to make it, and then move ahead. The answer concerning good decision versus bad decision will show up down the road because, as many of us know, for every action in life, good and bad, there is a consequence.

There is a key word in today's offering that stands out, and that word should have a lot to do with our decision: "regret." If regret is scarier to you than a big life change, then your decision has been made.

God's blessings to you on this day! Have a blessed day!

## October 8—*If you can't be positive, then at least be quiet.*—Joel Osteen

I've mentioned often that my mother always had an old-fashioned saying for every situation in life. As a kid I heard her say a thousand times, "If you can't say anything good about somebody don't say anything at all . . . or say you heard they are a good whistler." While I heard that old adage many, many years ago, I still run across people almost daily and think (as I smile to myself) "I bet they're a good whistler."

It seems the older I get, the less I want to be around negative, pessimistic people who can turn a sunny day into a thunderstorm just by showing up. So, to add a little more to today's quote, if you can't be positive, kind, nice, pleasant, cheerful, or cordial, then at least be quiet. Some people bring joy wherever they go while others bring joy whenever they go. Don't be a "whenever" person! My prayer is that we all strive to see the many blessings and the positive things in our life—because there are many!

God's blessings to you on this day! Have a blessed day!

**October 9**—*Every second brings a fresh beginning, every hour holds a new promise, every night our dreams can bring new hope, and every day is what we choose to make it.*—**common expression**

I recently saw a story encouraging people to start preparing for their New Year's resolutions . . . in early October. I think planning ahead is great, and I know that January 1 represents a new year and a clean slate, and I'm fully aware that people make resolutions to improve and be better at this and that. But, one of the beauties of life, as today's offering points out, is that we don't have to wait for a new calendar, a new week, a new month, or a new year because we have the ability within us to start from any second or any hour of any day we choose and start a brand-new beginning.

I particularly love the final nine words of today's quote: "every day is what we choose to make it." We have that ability every morning, by putting on a positive attitude, to make the day and shape the day any way we want. Make a day . . . and shape a day —I just love the thought of that! We can build our day and we can mold and shape our day any way we want! What an amazing opportunity we have every morning! Remember, the choice is yours and yours alone every single day! You can't go back and make a new start, but within you and with God's help, there is the ability to make a brand-spanking new ending!

God's blessings to you this day! Have a blessed day!

**October 10**—*Here is the test to find out if your mission in life is finished: If you're alive, it isn't.*—**common expression**

I recently had a conversation with a young man in his late twenties—a conversation that is a great reminder that it's never too late to embark on a new journey. He told me that he had started college, changed his mind, and got a job that he was certain he didn't want to spend the rest of his life doing. While I remained serious with him, his last comment made me chuckle to myself.

"I feel like I've let a lot of years get away from me," he told me with some disappointment in his voice.

I saw the conversation as a great opportunity to practice what I preached, and also to give a young man a life lesson about age and starting a new path in life. I told him that I worked in the coal industry for twenty years and then lost my job when the coal mine shut down. I told him I started college for the first time at age thirty-nine and later carved out a dual career as a radio broadcaster and newspaper reporter/columnist, a career that spanned twenty-five years. And then at the age of sixty-three I decided to run for public office and won—and launched another career!

"Every person, regardless of age, needs goals and dreams and ambition to do things or you quit growing and learning," I told him. "As long as you're moving forward I'd say you're right where you're supposed to be."

I think this offering is so important to so many people. You see, life is like riding a bicycle—if you stop moving, you'll lose your balance. So whether you're twenty-three or ninety-three, set goals, trust God, dream dreams, trust God some more, strive to be better than you were yesterday, and keep your balance by moving forward! And most importantly, keep on trusting God!

My prayer, to go along with today's offering, is that regardless of whether you're trying to achieve great things or accomplish small things, you will have the energy, strength, stamina, and determination to set new goals and dream new dreams!

God's blessings to you on this day! Have a blessed day!

**October 11—*The only people with whom you should try to get even, are those who have helped you.*—John E. Southard**

Have you ever considered how much negative energy is used by some people trying to get even with each other? You know the old scenario: One person tries to one-up somebody and then that person retaliates, and a never-ending cycle of negativity and hatred goes around and around. Sometimes this get-even merry-go-round lasts for decades!

Don't get caught in that negative get-even cycle of trying to inflict more harm or get in the last word. I recently read an anonymous quote that stated: "Inner peace begins the exact moment you choose not to allow another person or event to control your emotions." Remember, sometimes the easiest way to solve a problem is to stop participating in the problem. The strongest reaction is no reaction.

Instead of spending negative energy trying to even the score with those who might have wronged you, pour every ounce of positive energy into getting even with those who have helped you, prayed for you, defended you, stood by you, and loved you. Those are the people to make the effort to get even with—and of course you do that by returning the help, prayers, love, and understanding they have shown you.

God's blessings to you on this day! Have a blessed day!

## October 12—*Leave a little sparkle wherever you go.*—common expression

This quote reminded me of a story I read recently about our daily interactions with people—interactions that might seem meaningless and inconsequential to most people. The story pointed out that in some instances a casual "hi" or "good morning" might very well be the only interaction that some people have all day with anybody. So, what might seem like nothing to one person could mean the world to somebody else.

A quote I read recently sums this point up nicely. The seven-word gem stated: "Leave a little sparkle everywhere you go." Just think what a different world it would be if everybody would leave a little—just a little—sparkle wherever they go. You might be saying, "I don't have any sparkle, and I'm not even sure what that means." Well, everybody has "sparkle" . . . and I mean everybody. Every person has within them the ability to be kind, considerate, thoughtful, compassionate, and understanding. Everyone can offer a smile, a handshake, a hug, a pat on the back, a word of encouragement, or a random act of kindness. And that list doesn't scratch the surface of "sparkle" that we can leave wherever we go.

So get out there today and leave a trail of "sparkle" behind you, and do your part to make everybody feel like somebody! Remember, your true character is most accurately measured by how you treat those who can do nothing for you.

God's blessings to you on this day! Have a blessed day!

**October 13—*Don't think there are no second chances. Life always offers you a second chance. It's called tomorrow.*—Nicholas Sparks**

While today's quote is spot-on accurate, it also contains a "catch." You see, if you had a bad day yesterday, then today is that tomorrow—your second chance. Spending all your time today complaining about yesterday won't make today or tomorrow any better.

If that previous sentence sounds like a tongue-twister, I want you to read it again slowly—and then remember that every day is a brand-new beginning; every morning starts a new page in your story. You hold the pen in your hand, and you are the captain of the ship. You, and nobody else, have control of your attitude. That fact gives you the strength to shake off a difficult yesterday—or a string of difficult yesterdays—and make this day and the days that follow a new beginning.

Eleanor Roosevelt said: "Yesterday is history, tomorrow is a mystery, and today is a gift—that's why it's called the present."

Today is yesterday's tomorrow, your second chance. Use it wisely!

God's blessings to you on this day! Have a blessed day!

**October 14**—*A negative thinker sees a difficulty in every opportunity. A positive thinker sees an opportunity in every difficulty.*—**Zig Ziglar**

I work hard these days to avoid contact with what I call "the black cloud" people. These are the folks that walk around, like the little guy in the cartoon, with black clouds hanging over their heads. Everywhere they go, it rains. Don't you know people just like that? If you mention that it's a beautiful day, they will promptly tell you that it's supposed to rain and storm in a few days. If you tell them all the things going right in your life, they'll quickly tell you all that could go wrong. If you walk on water, the haters will say it's because you can't swim. In short, anything you mention they'll find a negative or a way to hang a dark cloud over an otherwise sunny day.

There is an old adage that says, "The words you speak become the house you live in." I thought of this when I read today's quote. Just like the clothes we choose every single morning, we also have the ability every single day to make our vocabulary positive or negative. We control what we say, what our topic of conversation is, who we spend time talking with. Will we see a difficulty in every opportunity, or an opportunity in every difficulty? The answer to that question—the house you live in—lies solely with you.

Run from negative people and go out of your way to avoid them. But also be thankful for negative people, because they've shown you exactly who you do not want to be!

God's blessings to you on this day! Have a blessed day!

**October 15**—*Do not go where the path may lead, go instead where there is no path and leave a trail.*—**Ralph Waldo Emerson**

How many times have you had a positive thought about embarking on a new journey in life, a new direction, and immediately doubt and fear took over and your ideas and dreams were tossed to the side? If you're like most people, me included, this has happened often.

Doubt and fear will make you feel you're not good enough, smart enough, gifted enough, or talented enough. This keeps all of us from venturing where there is no path to leave our own trail. Doubt and fear keeps people from reaching out to God, and it keeps people in dead-end jobs, harmful relationships, and dozens of other life-traps. Doubt and fear are the two main culprits behind every dream that perishes!

One of my favorite verses states, "Commit your work to the LORD, and your plans will be established" (Proverbs 16:3, ESV). I believe God will also direct our plans mentioned in that special verse, even if there is no path and we are trying to cut a brand-new trail. My prayer today is for all those trying to navigate where there is no path. Stay strong and don't let those dream-stealers, doubt and fear, set up residence in your head as you forge a new trail in your life!

God's blessings to you on this day! Have a blessed day!

### October 16—*Faith is seeing light with your heart when all your eyes see is darkness.*—anonymous

Faith is an easy thing to talk about, but sometimes a difficult thing to grasp—particularly in trying and uncertain times. I am a visual person so it's a great benefit to picture in my mind a willing and believing heart seeing the bright shining light that is faith, even while your eyes see total darkness.

We all have varying levels of faith, but this one-sentence gem puts all that in perspective. Examples of mustard-seed and childlike faith are wonderful, but there should be great joy for all of us in knowing that regardless what our eyes see, our heart can be filled with the shining light of faith.

Let your faith be bigger than your fear, and remember that faith is not a feeling—it's a decision we make to put our trust in God, even when we can't clearly see the path in front of us. Remember, you don't have to see the entire staircase . . . just the first step!

To all of those facing an uncertain day, a difficult time, or a troubling situation, my prayer is that your fear will be replaced by faith—the bright light of faith that lets us know that our future is in the hands of God.

God's blessings to you on this day! Have a blessed day!

## October 17—*Character consists of what you do on the third and fourth tries.*—James A. Michener

This quote talks about a third and fourth try . . . perhaps I should add the fifth and sixth to that list! Or, if Plan A fails, remember that there are twenty-five more letters in the alphabet.

The premise behind today's quote promotes a "don't give up, don't give in" mentality. Or, as my mother used to say, where there's a will, there's a way—which means that with will we can find a way to correct any problem or situation. I have found that sometimes when we are running short on "will," or when our "way" is too far off course, the best solution is to simply let go . . . and let God.

My prayer today is that God would pour out an extra-special blessing of strength and courage to all those who have lost their will, and provide a clear and straight path for those who can't find their way.

God's blessings to you on this day! Have a blessed day!

## October 18—*The first step in getting somewhere is to decide that you are not going to stay where you are.*—common expression

A journey of a thousand miles, we all know, begins with a single step. Really, that phrase can be used with anything we do in life, from small everyday tasks to life-changing decisions. But as today's offering points out, that first step is difficult because we all underestimate our capacity for change, and because we have to make a decision that we are not going to stay where we are.

I speak from experience and not something I read when I say that everything we do in life, and I mean every single thing, has to have a first step involved. And of course, that first step is the hardest one—there is never, ever a right time, a perfect time. And that word "change" involved with that first step stops many people in their tracks. Many folks are so resistant to change that they would rather stay in a difficult situation than face their fear of change.

Even when we're at the end of that thousand-mile journey—or that life-changing decision—the last step will not be as hard or as difficult as that first one. But while that first step is the hardest one, there is also joy, freedom, and excitement in moving a new direction.

Another quote that fits in well here states, "To achieve great things or to accomplish small things the formula is the same—start where you are, use what you have, do all you can and trust in God." I love this quote because it's in the present and there is no procrastination—"start where you are, use what you have, do all you can and . . . most importantly . . . trust in God." That means right now!

My prayer is that regardless if you're trying to achieve great things or accomplish small things today, this week or in the future you will have the strength, stamina and determination to take that difficult first step . . . and then keep on stepping.

God's blessings to you on this day! Have a blessed day!

### October 19—*Don't judge yourself by the past . . . you don't live there anymore!*—common expression

Through many years of living and talking to people going through a rough patch in their lives, I've learned that most people want to flip a switch and make their lives OK again. I hate to be the bearer of bad news, but that simply is not going to happen.

I've learned that one of the best things that can happen is for these people to set very short-term goals that will lead to a long-term accomplishment. For instance, if it's Monday and you're going through a rough spot in life, look ahead to next Monday and try to stay on course, and then make improvements in your life from one week to the next. Look ahead to the next Monday and the next, and the next, with the big-picture goal to look ahead six months or a year to see how far you've progressed. That same concept holds true for any and all new starts we attempt.

When you're battling through the storms of life, always remember that success and opportunity often comes disguised in the form of misfortune or temporary defeat. My prayer to you today is for strength and determination, if you are trying to forge a brand-new ending!

God's blessings to you on this day! Have a blessed day!

## October 20—*Breathe. It's just a bad day, not a bad life.*—common expression

Let's face it, not everybody is on top of their game every single day. We all have those mornings when nothing seems to go right and we'd really rather not deal with anything or anybody. Turning off your cellphone and going back to bed and pulling the covers over your head seem the best option, some days.

But it's on those days—when you feel overworked, underappreciated, and stressed to the max—that you have to remember that this day is a gift to you from God, and that what you do with it is entirely up to you. Today offers you a new chance, a new beginning, a new start, a new slate, a new opportunity. Most importantly it's a day the Lord has made. Just. For. You.

The key point in today's offering is to encourage you to fight through those bad days—remember, even bad days end at midnight—and then get ready to jump on the next day with both feet. It's another day made just for you. I read a quote recently that has become my nighttime prayer on a bad day: "Courage doesn't always roar. Sometimes courage is a small, quiet voice at the end of a bad day that says—I will try again tomorrow." I promise God, if it's in his plan, that I will definitely be up and trying the next morning.

My prayer for you today is to simply remind you again that a bad day is not a bad life!

God's blessings to you on this day! Have a blessed day!

### October 21—*You are entirely up to you.*—common expression

"Well, if they wouldn't have said that, I wouldn't have said mean things back." "If they hadn't done something bad to me, I wouldn't have retaliated."

Every person, me included, has used those excuses at some point in our life to justify bad behavior. Many years ago I heard a psychologist talk and he used a phrase I will never forget: "situational ethics." He went on to say that many people can make any bad situation in life ethical . . . by blaming somebody else for their actions. He concluded by saying that he has seen this play out in hundreds of ways from a small spat to murder. In reference, go back and read the first two sentences of today's offering again.

Think about it like this: We have no control over other people we deal with, over family issues, coworkers, traffic, and what kind of mood some people happen to be in on that particular day. Life can change dramatically from one moment to the next and it certainly changes without our permission. However, the key to today's offering is found in the very first word: you. While you have no control over many situations, with God's help and guidance you have total control over *you*. And most times, when confronted with a combative situation, the best comment is no comment and the best action is always no action. I love the quote that says, "Instead of spending negative energy to get even with people who have hurt us, we should spend our time trying to get even with the people who have helped us."

In short, we don't control the outcomes, but we do control our reaction to them. It's worth repeating: You are entirely up to you.

God's blessings to you on this day! Have a blessed day!

### October 22—*A smooth sea never made a skilled sailor.*—common expression

In one short sentence this quote sums up life in general. There are going to be troubling and difficult winds that blow and rough choppy waters in life in the form of trouble, mistakes, missteps, sickness, hardships, and problems. That's just a given. For some it seems those ill winds howl more often, which means we have to learn to navigate those sometimes-rough waters.

The key to today's offering is that we can always adjust the sail. It's how we navigate those winds that will make us or break us.

Many people experience a failure (or failures) in life, and then use that as a standby excuse to never try again. It's been said that hardships and failure often prepare ordinary people for an extraordinary destiny. I truly believe that because it seems that a constant rule for people who have enjoyed success is that they simply refuse to give up. Somehow these people use setbacks, failures, obstacles, the doubts and negativity of others, and the word "no" as motivation to reach their goals. They learn that you cannot stop the winds in life—you simply learn to adjust your sail.

Proverbs 3:6 says, "In all your ways acknowledge Him, and He shall direct your paths." Based on today's quote, we could certainly para-phrase it to say: In all your ways acknowledge him, and he will adjust your sails and make you a skilled sailor. We certainly can't direct the wind, but we can trust in God to direct us through rough waters and to adjust our sail!

God's blessings to you on this day! Have a blessed day!

**October 23—*Each day, as the sun rises, remind yourself that you are yet again given another chance to improve on yesterday.*—common expression**

As a youngster growing up, I often heard my dad use the phrase: "I'll sleep on it and decide in the morning." At the time I didn't know what he was talking about, but like many things in life when you find that you've turned into your parents, I now use that time-tested phrase often.

Today's quote contains an untold amount of truth and honesty. Each morning truly does bring new strength, new thoughts, and another chance to improve on the day before. I always find it amazing that we can hit the bed totally exhausted, so tired that we are unable to focus, and after a few hours of sleep and rest we can hit the ground running, revved up, and ready to go with the chance to be a better person than the day before!

Another one of the beautiful aspects of life is that we don't have to wait for a new calendar, a new week, a new month, or a new year to start a brand-new beginning. We have that ability to start from any second, any minute, or any hour of any day we choose and start a brand-new beginning. We have that ability every morning to put on a positive attitude—to make the day and shape the day any way we want.

Remember, you can't go back and make a new start, but within you and with God's help, there is the ability to make a brand-spanking-new ending! The second your eyes open every morning, that present is waiting on you. Remember that every day is what we choose to make it. So, the choice is yours and totally yours—what kind of day will you make?

God's blessings to you on this day! Have a blessed day!

**October 24—***It only takes one person to change your life: You.* **—common expression**

We all cross paths with people daily who, for whatever reason, are looking for a confrontation or an argument. Some are chance encounters, others are at work or on social media, and oftentimes it's people we know. A fact that a lot of people don't know, or haven't learned yet, is that how we react to these people and how we handle those situations is entirely up to us.

I heard a speaker recently say that getting in an exchange with a person, particularly a person looking for an argument, is giving up your power to control your own attitude. Please read that previous sentence again and let it really register.

It took me a lot of years to learn that most times in that situation, no comment is the absolute best comment. As the saying goes, "Silence is a powerful voice." In fact, by not making a comment, you control both your attitude and the situation at the same time—and never utter a single word.

Or, as my late mother often told me, "God gave you a mouth that closes and two ears that don't . . . that should tell you something." Certainly knowledge is important, but wisdom is even more important! As today's gem states. it only takes one person to change your life: you. And always keep in mind that you are in charge of you!

God's blessings to you on this day! Have a blessed day!

**October 25—*Every day is a new beginning. Problems and mistakes from yesterday are just memories of lessons learned.*—anonymous**

It doesn't matter if it's trying to build or renew a relationship with God, trying to get a better job, lose weight, start college, get fit, be more positive, be more thankful, be kinder, or hundreds of other things—the very first step is to believe in yourself. There's a single sentence we've all heard often that holds much truth: "You don't have to be great to start . . . but you have to start to be great."

In other words, you have to believe in yourself enough to take a small, tiny step toward your goal and in a new direction. And when you muster the courage to take that small step, you have to rely on your faith to help you keep "stepping." The second sentence in today's quote refers to something inside you greater than any obstacle you will face. In my mind, that something inside you is the love, grace, mercy, and strength that come through knowing Jesus as Savior.

Philippians 4:13 says: "I can do all things through Christ who strengthens me." Please note that wonderful verse doesn't say we can do a "couple" of things, or a "few" things, but that emphasizes that we can do "all" things through Christ. So, if you're trying to start a new journey, take that first step armed with the truth of Philippians 4:13— and remember again that all means all—big and small.

God's blessings to you on this day! Have a blessed day!

**October 26—*Do not give your past the power to define your future.*
—common expression**

Every person at some point in their life gets knocked down. It's just a given . . . it's inevitable. But the true character of a person—what separates the victors from the victims—is measured by how we deal with our tests and problems and how we get back up and move forward.

Issues involving work, finances, relationships, family, and health are only a few of the ways that life can knock us down. One thing that is often overlooked in life is that the strongest people aren't always the ones who win, but the people who don't give up when they lose. And in most instances, these defeats are only a temporary condition. Giving up and becoming a victim is what makes them permanent.

We have to dig deep within ourselves sometimes and really trust in God, but we have the option every minute of every day to choose what direction life's tests and problems take us. I believe the single most important thing we can do when we're faced with these difficulties is to hand them to God and put our trust in him. Let go and let God, and in the end we will be victors and not victims.

The beauty of this quote comes in the last six words: "compared to what lies within us." Because what lies within us is the ability to do whatever we set our minds to do, to dream big, work hard, strive to be better every day, be a positive influence, reach for the stars, and choose the exact direction we want to take our lives.

God's blessings to you on this day! Have a blessed day!

**October 27—*No one ever injured their eyesight by looking on the bright side.*—common expression**

I read this quote and immediately thought about the numbers involved with counting blessings (or looking on the bright side), compared to adding up troubles. Everybody encounters a few troubles along the way; that's just part of life. But what if every time we started adding up the troubles we're dealing with, we immediately started counting our blessings and looking on the bright side? Regardless how many troubles you might be experiencing, there is always a bright side.

Let's look on the bright side today, come on . . . it won't hurt your eyes. You woke up this morning, blessing one; you opened your eyes and could see, blessing two; you placed your feet on the floor and stood up, blessing three . . . and your blessing list goes on and on from there. And keep in mind that I haven't even named some of the real good stuff yet, like caffeine, sunshine, Fridays, long weekends, and payday! The list of real blessings in our lives is infinite, and the opportunity to look on the bright side is unlimited.

There is always, always something to be thankful about. I recently ran across a quote that ties this particular offering up nicely: "Today be thankful and think how rich you are—your family is priceless, your time is gold, and your health is wealth." Based on that quote, the bright side is so bright that we should all wear sunglasses.

God's blessings to you on this day! Have a blessed day!

## October 28—*Your mind is a cupboard . . . and you stock the shelves.*—Thomas Monson

I'm a visual person, so being able to actually picture a person's mind as a cupboard really puts this quote in perspective for me. Every single day— in fact, every minute of every day—we have within us the ability to stock the shelves of our cupboard with what we want. We can stock positive, helpful, caring items, or we can stock seeds of negativity, divisiveness, distrust, and bitterness. It can be a cupboard that is neat and tidy, or it can be a cluttered mess. And the amazing thing is that the choice is ours every day. Every person with a pulse makes the decision every morning, when they open their eyes, of what they will place in their cupboard that day.

So, the question begs to be asked: What are you stocking the shelves of your cupboard with every morning? Do you begin with an attitude of gratitude, a thankful heart, optimism, and the goal of trying to be a better person than you were yesterday? Or, do you begin the day stocking the shelves with bitterness, getting even, negativity, doubt, and fear? Again, the choice of what goes in your cupboard—at any moment of any day—is yours, period.

At no extra cost I'm going to toss in a second quote that goes well with today's offering: "Your mind is a garden. Your thoughts are the seeds. You can grow flowers, or you can grow weeds."

Our prayer daily—no, wait, our hourly prayer—should be to ask God to help us, to check us, and to hold us accountable for what we place in our cupboard and for the seeds we plant in our garden.

God's blessings to you on this day! Have a blessed day!

## October 29—*Every day is a second chance.*—common expression

I love this quote because it's a great reminder that while each new day brings new challenges, it also brings a fresh slate, a new start, new opportunities, and a second chance to enjoy life and be a better person.

Enjoy this one-of-a-kind day, because tomorrow will be a different day. That means we get one shot to do this one right. So, smile often, be kind to others, dream big, laugh a lot (and at yourself), and count your blessings because they are many. Also, leave the baggage of yesterday and the past where it belongs—in the past!

We know that today is called the present, and rightfully so, because it's a present from God. It's a present that contains another chance, a new opportunity, and the hope to be a better person. The second your eyes open every morning, that present is waiting on you.

So, what are you waiting for? Embrace this wonderful day, this second chance we've been given to get it right

God's blessings to you on this day! Have a blessed day!

**October 30**—*Courage is resistance to fear, mastery of fear, not absence of fear.*—**Mark Twain**

Certainly, courage can be defined in a lot of different ways regarding a lot of different types of battles. But when I read this quote, my initial thought is that this one, small sentence defines perfectly those who fight the daily battles and struggles that life sometimes throw our way. I would like to add one more sentence to this quote: Courage is also defined by those who battled on, pushed forward, and refused to let past mistakes, missteps, and setbacks keep them down.

We've all witnessed people go through a difficult experience and then let that particular event define them and become their reason to frown and have a bitter, sour attitude about every aspect of life. On the other hand, we also see people who go through the same struggles and use a difficult experience for motivation to become stronger, better people, to help others, and to achieve their goals. In short, they turn obstacles into an opportunities.

I recently read a quote that speaks volumes on this subject: Your past has given you the strength, wisdom, and compassion that makes you the person you are today, so celebrate it. Remember, getting knocked down in life is a given . . . getting back up is a choice!

God's blessings to you on this day! Have a blessed day!

**October 31**—*You make a living by what you get; you make a life by what you give.*—**Winston Churchill**

A lot of folks will read today's offering and quickly state, "Well, I don't have anything to give anybody." My answer back to that group would be this: Sure, you do!

You see, I believe the word "give" in today's quote means much, much more than material possessions. There are so many things we can give daily; the list is never-ending. You can give a few minutes to call a friend going through a difficult time, maybe just to listen to that friend and be a sounding board. You can give a smile, a pat on the back, a hug, or even just a kind word. You can pay for the car behind you at the drive-up or buy someone lunch anonymously. And for those with a shred of imagination and innovation, the list of things we can all give is virtually endless.

Sometimes even the smallest gesture can change a person's entire outlook that day. And the amazing thing is, while you are helping somebody else, you are also helping yourself more than you will ever know. We all get so caught up trying to making a living, but my prayer today is that we all try to find a few minutes each day to make a life and give back. No act of kindness, no matter how small, is ever wasted.

God's blessings to you this day! Have a blessed day!

## November 1—*Don't focus on the dot.*—Jim Muir

I read a story recently about a college professor who gave her class a surprise test. She handed out the single page test face down, and after all the students had been given one she told them to turn the paper over. On the single piece of paper in the center of the page was a small black dot about the size of a BB. The test, she told students, was to write what they saw on the page. After the allotted time was up, she collected the papers and then read each student's paper aloud. Every single student, to a person, wrote about the black dot. Some wrote about its size, others about its placement on the page. She pointed out to students that not one single person wrote about the white on the page or how there was so much more white space than the small black dot.

She told the students that she was not going to give a grade on the test, but emphasized that their writings about the small dot on the page provided one of life's greatest lessons. She said the small dot represents the troubles and difficulties in our lives, while the vast white area that goes unnoticed is the good things, the blessings we fail to sometimes see.

I love this story and the lesson involved, but the reaction of these college students is not all that different from most people, me included. We all have a tendency to zero in and focus on the dot (the problem) while totally missing the good things. We talk about the dot, we write about the dot, we worry ourselves sick about the dot, we fix our attention on the dot, and we obsess about the dot, while countless blessings from God—blessings that are staring us right in the face—are ignored.

After I read the story about the college professor, I wrote down the five words that make up today's quote. It's just five simple, little words, but they provide a powerful message that we all need to remember. Break the habit . . . don't focus on the dot. Instead, look closely at the rest of the white sheet of paper (the blessings in your life) and focus your attention and an attitude of gratitude there.

Let me say it one more time: Don't focus on the dot!

God's blessings to you on this day! Have a blessed day!

## November 2—*In God's garden of grace, even a broken tree can bear fruit.*—anonymous

The first word that came to my mind when I read this quote was "beautiful"—what a simply amazing and beautiful one sentence nugget of gold. In only twelve words, the unknown author has shined a bright light on the beauty of Christianity, the greatest love story ever told!

In one way or another we are all like the broken tree mentioned in today's quote. We've all made mistakes, we've all gotten off course, we all pack some baggage, we all carry some guilt, we all deal with shame from our past, and we all have a few life-related scars.

But it's God's forgiving grace that determines our direction in life. God's grace is more than a second chance, or a third chance, or any number of countless chances. It's an unfailing, unwavering love for us regardless who we are or what we've done. I recently read another quote that provides the exclamation mark on today offering, by another unknown author: "Shame says that because I am flawed I am unacceptable. Grace says that even though I am flawed I am cherished."

God's blessings to you on this day! Have a blessed day!

**November 3**—*Life is too short to argue and fight with your past. Count your blessings, value your loved ones, and move on with your head held high.*—**anonymous**

The first sentence of today's quote speaks volumes. There truly are many, many people who argue and fight every single day about their past. And the fact that the first sentence is spot-on accurate makes the second sentence an impossibility for many people. In short, there are a lot of people who simply can't move past the past because it's where they live.

Today's offering points out and identifies that many people lose their happiness by looking in the rearview mirror, wrestling with their past; in the process they ignore their blessings, their loved ones, and the goodness around them. Living in the past, or rehashing, rereading, or reliving yesterday will not change or alter one thing that happened. Instead, it drains today of its strength and gratitude. Simply stated, living a life where we continually look back and live in the past is a surefire way to make you feel inadequate and like a failure.

For those who battle the past, the surefire remedy is to take up permanent residence in the present. Remind yourself hourly if necessary that each day is a present from God. It's a present that contains another chance, a new opportunity, and the hope to be a better person. The second your eyes open every morning, your present is waiting on you as your gift to enjoy. We all hold the power to make this day anything we want it to be. We can't change the past, we can't predict the future, and we cannot measure our life against others. But we have in front of us a blank sheet every morning; we hold the pen and can write any story we want that day. My prayer is that we learn to stop arguing and fighting with the past and learn to be thankful for our present—today.

God's blessings to you on this day! Have a blessed day!

**November 4—***Giving up on your dream because of one setback is like slashing your other three tires because you have a flat.***—anonymous**

Take a good look around at the people in your life, even those who are just casual acquaintances. The common denominator in every single life is that we have all tasted failure at one time or another—and some more than others. You will notice that I wrote "we" because I certainly include myself in the list of those who have failed. Also, I added in those five additional words to the previous sentence—"and some more than others"—with myself also in mind.

The key point in today's offering is that we are all going to fail; again, the word "inevitable" comes to mind when talking about failures in life. But it's what we do with those failures, how we react to them, and how we move on that determines how our life story plays out.

I recently read a quote by an unknown author that stated, "Failing at things in life is inevitable. It is impossible to live life without failing at something unless you live so cautiously that you might as well have not lived at all—in which case you failed by default."

Some people miss the point completely, but there is glory in failure. The glory comes every time we fail and then stand up, dust ourselves off, square our shoulders, set our jaw with determination, and find the grit and strength from within and through our trust in God to move on and fight another day! My prayer today is that we never, ever let failure become the final chapter of our book.

God's blessings to you on this day! Have a blessed day!

**November 5—***Happiness comes when we stop complaining about the troubles we have and offer thanks for the troubles we don't have.***—Glen Rambharack**

When I first read today's quote, I was struck immediately by the fact that this one-sentence beauty brought up a point that I had never, ever considered—to offer thanks for the troubles I don't have. What a unique concept!

It's easy to sometimes form our own little one-person pity party and then whine and complain about all the troubles we have. I have organized a few of these parties myself so I know firsthand how petty we can be in our complaints. "I don't have this, and I don't have that—wah, wah, wah!"

But what if we approached every single day looking at the troubles we don't have?

Here's a great example: On most weekdays I make my way to a local gym where I live. On my drive there I pass by a building that almost always has a parking lot jam-packed with cars. It doesn't matter if it's 6 am or 3 pm, there's always a lot of people there. One day it dawned on me that it was a building where people get kidney dialysis, and the thought crossed my mind about how thankful I should be that I am starting my day at a gym compared to the way others are starting their day. It certainly gave me pause to consider how blessed I am. Or, as today's quote says, "Happiness comes when we stop complaining about the troubles we have and offer thanks for the troubles we don't have." Certainly, that is a thought that we need to keep close to our minds every single day!

God's blessings to you on this day! Have a blessed day!

## November 6—*If we all threw our problems in a pile and we saw everyone else's, we'd grab ours back.*—anonymous

Perhaps the best thing I can add to today's one-sentence gem is to tell you to read it again and again, and then start adding up all the blessings in your life that do not have a price tag attached.

First and most importantly, remember that your faith guarantees you eternal life and was purchased for you with amazing grace on an old rugged cross. Then add in your family and friends, they're priceless; your time is gold, and your health is wealth. Interestingly, all the things on that list—which, by the way, are the most important elements of life—cannot be purchased.

Without question, there is always something to be thankful about—always! What are you thankful and grateful for today? You might want to grab a pen and notebook, because if you answer honestly about all the little things we all take for granted and then add in family, friends, freedom, beauty, wonders, excitement, and the physical and mental ability that make up your life, it will take you a while. If we all wrapped our minds around gratitude, to help us see what is there, we could all probably spend the rest of the day compiling our "thankful list."

I'm going to ask for some audience participation today. It's easy sometimes to look around and feel as though you've come up short, that you're not exactly where you should be or want to be. I want you to take a moment, stop what you are doing, clear your mind, and take inventory of your life and the wonderful, marvelous, beautiful things that God has given you—things that cannot be bought. If you're like me, when you start adding up those things that money can't buy, it won't take long to determine that you are a rich person!

God's blessings to you on this day! Have a blessed day!

## November 7—*Don't let someone dim your light simply because it's shining in their eyes.*—common expression

When I ran across this quote—just thirteen little words—I loved it immediately. You see, it took some time but I've learned that there are people who I believe roll out of bed with the intention of trying to dim somebody's light that day. You know the type of person I'm talking about—they're the ones walking around with the black cloud over their heads, searching for a place to rain on a sunny day. These are the folks who completely overlook the countless blessings in life. They're the ones with a problem for every solution. If you show them a beautiful rose, they will point out the thorns.

But the key thing—something it also took me a long time to learn—is that these people cannot dim your light, they cannot dull your sparkle, and they cannot rain on your parade without your consent.

In short, never, ever let yourself be defined by somebody's comment, opinion or—let me go ahead and say it—by their ignorance. Remember, your value doesn't decrease based on somebody's inability to see the good and the worth in you.

So get out there today, get your sparkle on, and let your light shine brightly!

God's blessings to you on this day! Have a blessed day!

**November 8—***Always pray to have eyes that see the best, a heart that forgives the worst, a mind that forgets the bad, and a soul that never loses faith.***—anonymous**

In only one remarkable sentence, the unknown writer has covered the gamut of what we should strive for every single day. As a writer you should always try to say more in fewer words. The impact and importance of today's offering based on that premise is comparable to not just hitting a home run but knocking one completely out of the ballpark! Yes, it's just that good!

Consider this: What kind of world would we live in if we all started each day with this prayer, and the desire to conquer these four important areas of our lives? Just think about it and really focus on what this sentence is saying: eyes to see the best . . . a heart that forgives the worst . . . a mind that forgets the bad . . . and a soul that never loses faith.

Those four examples provide us with a template, a measuring stick of what we should pray daily, and what we should strive and work to be as Christians and as human beings. Perhaps the greatest thing I can add to today's offering is to encourage you to read this single sentence again and again, memorize it, and etch it in your mind. These are truly words to live by and words to cherish!

God's blessings to you on this day! Have a blessed day!

**November 9—*I am not what I ought to be. I am not what I wish to be. But, by the grace of God, I am not what I used to be.*—anonymous**

When I first read through today's quote, my first reaction was that this is a person who "gets it."

I believe many people, me included, have lived these three sentences and understand what it takes to be a better person and a better example of how God can change lives. Combining the first two sentences, many, many people live with the realization that we are not what we ought to be and not what we wish to be. These folks fail daily, struggle occasionally, but fight the good fight and continue to strive to be better people today than they were yesterday.

The last sentence, of course, is the kicker to this quote. I love the fact that the writer inserted five very important words in the last sentence—five words that make all the difference in the world. What if this quote read: I am not what I ought to be. I am not what I wish to be. I am not what I used to be. Ho-hum, it's kind of boring, right? But it's those five words—"But, by the grace of God"—that make the difference in this quote. And it's also those five words that make a difference in our lives.

It's the beautiful grace of God that makes us understand that we are not who we ought to be or wish to be. But it's also that same grace that sustains us on those days when life piles on. I recently read a quote by Jerry Bridges that fits in well right here: "Your worst days are never so bad that you are beyond the reach of God's grace. And your best days are never so good that you are beyond the need of God's grace."

Remember, when you run alone it's called a "race," and when God runs with you it's called "grace."

God's blessings (and grace) to you on this day! Have a blessed day!

## November 10—*Failure is a bruise, not a tattoo.*—common expression

I'm a visual person, so let's paint a picture with today's clever quote: Imagine that you walk up to a person who has a black eye—a shiner that looks rough and maybe even has some swelling. While it's a nasty-looking mark on their face, you know that in a week or two it will be healed up and you will never know it was there. On the other hand, imagine you walk up to a person who has a tattoo completely covering all the skin around their eye—the same location as the black eye. Anybody that looks at this tattoo realizes that the ink stains and the marks left behind will be there forever and ever. It's a permanent mark that people will talk about and point at; it's a mark that person will always carry.

Sadly, many people go through this exact thing when they fail. They feel like any failure—marriage, financial, relationships, or work-related—is a tattoo they must wear the rest of their lives. They've set up residence in the past, while the present rolls by them day after day. And certainly, nobody can start a new chapter in their lives if they keep rereading the last ones.

Remember, you are not defined by your past and you don't reside there. Your past was only a bruise and it's healed. Instead, you are prepared by your past—prepared to keep your eyes on that big windshield in front of you, to plan your future with purpose and to frame your life with faith in God. We all have a blank 365-page book in front of us, and today is the first chapter. The key thing is that you are the author of that book and you can write the story anyway you choose. And remember, don't look back . . . you're not going that direction!

God's blessings to you on this day! Have a blessed day!

**November 11—***No one can make you feel inferior without your consent.***—Eleanor Roosevelt**

When I read this, I thought of a story I read recently that said that the best way to improve your self-worth is to stop giving other people the calculator. There are people who roll out of bed every morning with the intention of raining on somebody's parade. Their goal every day is to plant a negative seed anywhere they see something positive. And then once that negative seed is planted, that little voice that lives between our ears takes over and tries to convince you that you're not good enough, smart enough, talented enough—fill in the word in front of "enough"—to reach your goals and accomplish your dreams. This is the same voice that keeps people in dead-end jobs, harmful relationships, and dozens of other life-traps.

As today's offering points out, nobody can make you feel inferior without your consent, so this is why you can never, ever give your self-worth calculator to somebody else. Keep it in your hand, always. Then be strong; don't listen to the enemy between your ears, and don't let a negative comment from the naysayers and the black cloud-doomsday crowd dampen your enthusiasm or crush your spirit.

The key thing is that the detractors can't defeat you without your consent. In short, never, ever let yourself be defined by somebody's comment, opinion, or ignorance. Remember, your value doesn't decrease based on somebody's inability to see the good and the worth in you!

God's blessings to you on this day! Have a blessed day!

**November 12**—*One moment of patience might ward off a great disaster. One moment of impatience might ruin a life.*—**Chinese proverb**

Read today's quote again and really let it sink in. Chances are you probably know somebody who has lived one of these two contrasting sentences. Maybe that somebody is you!

Now, consider this—can you imagine how much different life would be for everybody, how many bad situations would have been averted, how many hearts would not have been broken, how many dreams wouldn't have been shattered, if we all just exercised that one moment of patience?

I've learned that I don't have to reply to everything that is said or done to me. In fact, I've found that sometimes the very best response is no response at all and that the loudest answer is silence. Just think about the amount of negative energy exerted by some people daily in an attempt to get even, make somebody look bad, or simply cause trouble. What if those same people used their energy and imagination in a positive way? How much better would the world be? Many people have the belief that you can reply in anger and get even with another person. I've learned that it's much, much better in life to try and get even with those who helped you, and to happily ignore those that harmed you. My prayer today is that we all remember this two-sentence gem and exercise that moment of patience—it might ward off a great disaster!

God's blessings (and patience) to you on this day! Have a blessed day!

**November 13** —*Today I will do my best. If I have a good day, I will be proud of myself and thank God. If I have a bad day, I will not dwell on it and I will thank God again. I will forgive myself, I will put the bad day behind me, and I will move forward.*—**anonymous**

While every short sentence in today's quote is meaningful, the very first sentence is the most important. Today will never, ever come again, so it's imperative that we all do our absolute best. We get one chance at it on this day—just one chance, that's it. And the plain fact that today will never come again puts even more importance and significance on doing our very best.

The key to today's offering can be found in the sentence that deals with a good day versus a bad day. Certainly, we need to follow this sound advice. If we have a good day, enjoy it, thank God for it, and then put it to rest. On the flip side, if we have a bad day, remember it was a bad day and not a bad life, thank God for another day, and put it to rest.

One of the most harmful things we can do is to drag a bad day to the next day. If you get into this bad habit, before long you'll be dragging a trunkful of bad days behind you. Perhaps the best two words in today's quote are the last two words: move forward. Regardless if it's a good day, a bad day, or an in-between mundane day, we must move forward. Remember, life is like riding a bicycle—in order to keep our balance, we must keep moving forward.

God's blessing to you on this day—a day that will not come again. Have a blessed day!

**November 14**—*Don't allow yourself to wake up with yesterday's issues and problems troubling your mind. See every day as a new chapter.* —**anonymous**

I love this quote because it's a great reminder that, while each new day brings new challenges, it also brings a fresh slate, a new start, and new opportunities to enjoy life and to be a better person.

Enjoy this one-of-a-kind day because tomorrow will be a different day—and that means we get one shot to do this one right. So, smile often, be kind to others, dream big, laugh a lot (and at yourself), and count your blessings because they are many. The key point in today's offering is that we must, in order to see every day as a new chapter, move on from yesterday's issues and problems.

We know that today is called the present—and rightfully so, because it's a present from God, a new chapter. It's a present that contains another chance, a new opportunity, and the hope to be a better person. The second your eyes open every morning, that new chapter is waiting on you. This a new chapter the Lord has made for me, and for you. We are doing a great disservice to our Creator if we do not rejoice and be glad and thankful for this day—this wonderful present—that we have been given.

So, what are you waiting for? Embrace your new chapter and make it a good one!

God's blessings to you on this day! Have a blessed day!

**November 15**—*You have three choices in life—give up, give in, or give it all you've got!*—**Zig Ziglar**

While today's offering says that we all have three choices in life, growing up with my parents I would have bet that there was only one choice— give it all you've got. My parents were hard-working, determined people who spiced up their vocabulary and life lessons with old-fashioned sayings. They seemed to have one for any situation.

And speaking of give it all you've got, I've heard my dad say countless times, "You've got to pull yourself up by your bootstraps"; "You've got to put your shoulder to the wheel"; or, "Get knocked down seven times . . . you get up eight." You get the picture. Regardless of the situation, you always give it all you've got, period. That was a mindset learned early in life because it was repeated often. Looking back, I'm thankful for that because it has served me well. A give-it-all-you've-got mindset, coupled with the grace of God, can sustain a person and carry you through difficult and trying times.

My prayer today is that regardless of your situation—good, bad, happy, sad, or anywhere in between—you give it all you've got. In many, many instances in life, it's the only option we have.

God's blessings to you on this day! Have a blessed day!

**November 16**—*The circumstances we ask God to change are often the circumstances God is using to change us.*—**Max Lucado**

It's been said that circumstances do not make the person—they simply reveal the person. As wonderful as life is, it is still filled with problems, trials, twists and turns, and difficulty. It's how we all handle those things that define us. I've learned through the years that sometimes those circumstances are completely out of your control and that the only way to handle them is to let go and let God.

Many people miss this point, but regardless how bad things appear, your present circumstances do not determine where you can go in life. Instead they only determine where you start! Instead of focusing on the circumstances you cannot change, throw all your positive energy into the circumstances you can change. We can change many circumstances in our life simply by changing our attitude. Remember, it's not about circumstances but what you're made of that matters most.

God's blessings to you on this day! Have a blessed day!

**November 17—*Life is too short to begin your day with the broken pieces of yesterday.*—common expression**

We've all had those days—some of us many consecutive days—when you feel you gave your best and at the end of the day still feel beat up, beat down, and worn out by life's difficulties.

One thing I've learned is that we have to put each day to rest and start fresh each morning with a renewed energy. Otherwise, it's easy to start dragging the broken pieces of one bad day to the next and then the next and the next, and soon we're dragging a trunkful of bad days with us everywhere we go. And that's a lot to pack around day after day after day.

Remember, every day is a new beginning, another chance. Every morning starts a new, bright, clean page in your life story. The beauty of this is that you are the author and you hold the pen in your hand. Let me say that again: You hold the pen in your hand. With God's help you have the ability and strength to write any story you want. Leave the broken pieces of a bad yesterday behind and write a great story today!

God's blessings to you on this day! Have a blessed day!

**November 18—*When you forgive, you in no way change the past—but you sure do change the future.*—Bernard Meltzer**

I have heard it said that forgiveness enlarges our future and that it's a gift we give to ourselves. I want to add one more thought to that: Forgiveness doesn't make you weak; instead, it sets you free.

Maybe the best illustration comes from a book where the entire premise is based on forgiveness. Matthew 6:14 says: "For if you forgive men their trespasses, your heavenly Father will also forgive you."

Some folks have held a grudge and been upset for so long that they can't even remember why. They just know they're mad, and by gosh, they are going to stay mad forever. These people might as well be locked away because they are already prisoners and don't even know it. Their lives are ruled by retaliation, getting even, and trying to get the upper hand. What a sad way to live your life!

An excellent quote by an unknown writer puts anger in perspective: "Anger doesn't solve anything. It builds nothing, but it can destroy everything."

Perhaps the very best point I can make about dealing with anger and being quick to forgive is found in Ephesians 4:32: "[B]e kind to one another, tenderhearted, forgiving one another, even as Christ forgave you."

Maybe it's time to enlarge your future, unlock the door, and set a prisoner free—yourself.

God's blessings to you on this day! Have a blessed day!

## November 19—*If you can't be content with what you've received in life, be thankful for what you've escaped.*—common expression

Perhaps it's an age thing, but I've thought often about the exact thing mentioned in this quote. Certainly, I am blessed and give thanks daily for those countless blessings in my life, but I also find myself occasionally thinking about those forks in the road where I had to make a choice—or in some instances had it made for me—about the direction I should go.

I believe that every step I've taken on that winding road, and the people I crossed paths with, was directed by God. And you know what? It doesn't matter if anybody else believes that, because I do. I would challenge you to do the same thing—take inventory not only of what you've received in life but also take a good hard look at what you've escaped. Certainly we all have much to be thankful for, the countless blessings that have come our way; but if you're like me you can also be extra-thankful for what you've escaped, those things that didn't come your way, those roads you didn't travel. Today's offering is worth repeating: "If you can't be content with what you've received in life, be thankful for what you've escaped."

Hindsight, as we're often told, is always 20/20, but I cringe when I think of some of the paths I was on and the direction my life could have gone. In short, we should all be very thankful for the many paths we've traveled in life, and in some instances should be even more thankful for the paths we didn't travel.

God's blessings to you on this day! Have a blessed day!

**November 20—*My scars tell a story. They remind me of a time when life tried to break me and failed.*—anonymous**

I don't know of any person who has gone through life and not picked up a few scars.

Scars—not the visible ones but those we get from going through the daily struggles of life—are evidence that we lived, made mistakes, healed, and hopefully learned. But those scars can also act as a roadmap, a guide for our lives.

You see, we have the option every day to choose what direction those scars will take us. The older I get, and the more I observe, I'm convinced that life's scars do one of two things: They either weaken us, or they strengthen us. How many times have you seen a person go through a bad experience—and again, we all have a few life scars—and then let that particular event define them and become their reason to frown and have a bitter, sour attitude about every aspect of life? On the other hand, we also see people who go through the same struggles and use their scars for motivation to become stronger, better people, to help others and to achieve their goals. In short, dealing with the scars of life really comes down to a choice: Do they become an obstacle, or an opportunity? My answer to that question is clearly "opportunity."

Scars only show us where we've been, the roads we've traveled, and the people we've dealt with—they absolutely do not define our future. While people like to remind us often of our mistakes and point out our scars, I am thankful beyond words that it's God, through his son Jesus

Christ, who is in control of forgiving those mistakes, erasing our scars, and wiping the slate clean.

God's blessings to you on this day! Have a blessed day!

**November 21—*A rainbow is a promise of sunshine after rain, calm after storms, joy after sadness, peace after pain, love after loss, morning after night, and a bright beginning after a painful ending.*—common expression**

Throughout life there are always going to be personal storms—and sometimes those storms are going to rage. For some people, these storms provide a reason to quit or give up. For others who know that God is in control and their rainbow is on the horizon, the storms of life will be used as nothing more than stepping stones to help them keep pushing on and moving forward. We're all going to battle life's storms. The key thing to remember, when we're trying to navigate those choppy waters, is that we have to go through the storm and rain in order to get to that bright rainbow—the promise.

Be sure to note how many times the word "after" is used in today's quote. Joy after sadness, peace after pain, love after loss, morning after night and a bright beginning after a painful ending. After . . . after you go through it!

It's been said that life is like a rainbow because both rain and sun are needed to make the colors show. Keep that in mind the next time you are in one of life's downpours. The sun will pop out soon, and so will your rainbow!

God's blessings to you on this day! Have a blessed day!

**November 22—*Why not celebrate Thanksgiving every day?*—Jim Muir**

I was still in bed this morning when this question crossed my mind. I love the fourth Thursday in November as much as anybody—the turkey, dressing, all the trimmings, the pumpkin pie, and getting together with family. I love the four-day weekend and leftovers and the feel of autumn in the air. While I thought about the question I use for my daily offering, I couldn't help but think of the fact that we choose one day a year to give thanks, or do a thirty-day countdown in the month of November. But, what about the other days on the calendar? Where is our thankful meter at on those days? Let me point out that I'm asking that question and challenging myself as much as I am anybody else.

There's a quote that I've used in the past that says, "What if you woke up today with only the things that you thanked God for yesterday?" That's a question that should cause all of us to do some soul-searching. And of course, that's a question we should ask ourselves every single day, especially in all the months that don't start with an "N."

Perhaps the best way to know the answer to that question is to give thanks to God every day for all things—make every day Thanksgiving. I recently read a story that pointed out that a grateful and thankful heart is one that finds the countless blessings in seemingly mundane, everyday life—not just in November but in the other eleven months also.

In all things, give thanks, every day—even on days when you don't have pumpkin pie with whipped cream! By doing that, we will all know the answer to today's question! Certainly, every day should be Thanksgiving Day!

God's blessings to you on this day! Have a blessed (and thankful) day!

**November 23**—*Sometimes you are delayed where you are because God knows there's a storm where you are headed. Be grateful.*—anonymous

As I get older, I can look at so many places in my life where I had thought I had the timing and the circumstances all figured out, only to end up going a totally different direction. Oftentimes when I'm asked to speak I talk about God directing my path—away from some things and toward others. Regardless of what anybody else thinks, I believe that God has directed my path, and that at this moment I'm right where I'm supposed to be.

But I have to admit that I didn't always go willingly. You see, I have a tendency to try and do God's work for him, based on my wants and my timing. I've learned, sometimes the hard way, that's not the way it works. God's direction and timing are always perfect.

I can't count the times in the past few years that I've made the comment: "Boy, God was sure looking out for me (or a member of my family) to keep us away from that situation." And many times, the situations I refer to happened decades ago. There's a Bible verse that explains this exactly and straight to the point: "A man's heart plans his way, but the LORD directs his steps" (Proverbs 16:9).

My prayer today for all of us is for an extra heaping-helping of patience as God directs, corrects, and protects us!

God's blessings to you on this day! Have a blessed day!

**November 24**—*Distance yourself from negative people.*—common expression

I don't know if there is anything more annoying than being in a great mood and then running into a Negative Nellie or a Naysayer Nelson (there are plenty of both), who immediately launches into a tirade about all the bad things happening to them in particular and the world in general.

This group, who eat razor blades for breakfast and wash it down with prune juice, are on the lookout daily trying to put a damper on any good mood that they encounter. These are the folks that you learn to never, ever ask how they are doing—that is, unless you have thirty minutes to kill listening to them describe every ache, pain, problem, and complaint they have had during the past decade

Today's offering, only four words, speaks volumes about the best remedy in dealing with negative people. The best solution is simple: Don't deal with them! Do not allow the negative energy of some people to affect you, and don't let negative people keep you from seeing all the positive around you.

Author Steve Maraboli offered a great quote on how to deal with Chicken Littles who walk around telling everyone the sky is falling: "Let go of the people who dull your shine, poison your spirit, and bring you drama. Cancel your subscription to their issues."

The key word in today's one-sentence offering is "distance"—learn to keep a healthy distance from negative people. They have a problem for every solution!

God's blessings to you on this day! Have a blessed day!

## November 25—*God's plan for your life far exceeds the circumstances of your day.*—anonymous

It's Monday, and I'm still tired after a busy weekend. It's Monday, and I have more work to do and more places to be than I can get done today. It's Monday, and I didn't sleep very well last night. It's Monday, and I have a little "catch" in my shoulder that's bugging me. It's Monday, and I feel like pulling the covers up over my head and staying in bed. It's Monday, and I'm not ready to start another work week. It's Monday . . . blah, blah, blah . . . it's Monday.

Those were a few of the thoughts that went through my mind before my feet ever hit the floor not only on Monday mornings but on other mornings also. Then, right in the middle of my pity-party, a special verse ran through my mind: "This is the day the LORD has made; we will rejoice and be glad in it" (Psalm 118:24).

As I pondered the beauty of that verse, my pity party gave way to an attitude of gratitude—gratitude for a "blessings list" too lengthy to list . . . but here's a few! I am thankful for my faith, family, friends, a job, places to go and people to see, and I am doubly thankful that my feet are able to hit the floor this morning to start this day that the Lord has made. I can say with certainty that at the top of my "blessings list" is the knowledge that all those blessings flowed through God, who is Christ Jesus. I did nothing to earn them, nor do I deserve them, yet the list of good things in my life is infinite; my blessings are countless and unlimited. As I have mentioned often, always remember that of all the attitudes we can acquire, an attitude of gratitude is the most important and the most life-changing.

So bring it on, Monday . . . or any other day! God created this day for me, and I am ready to take you on!

God's blessings to you on this day! Have a blessed day!

## November 26—*The shortest distance between a problem and a solution is the distance between your knees and the floor.*—**Charles Stanley**

As a young writer many years ago, I was often told by editors to "write tight." In other words, put as much punch as possible in as few words as possible. I thought of that when I read this single and powerful sentence. In only eighteen words, the writer delivered a perfect blueprint for any problem, regardless of size, that we might face.

The key between success and failure, I believe, can be found in today's simple offering. Hitting our knees and asking God's help in attacking those difficult, life-changing areas of our lives with prayer is the key to real change. Otherwise, we're just dragging problem-filled baggage from one year to the next.

And when practicing that short distance between your problem and a solution, let me remind you of one of my favorite verses that goes perfectly with this sentence. "I can do all things through Christ who strengthens me" (Philippians 4:13). Remember, that verse doesn't say, "I can do some things . . . or a few things." It says, "I can do *all* things."

My prayer today is that any time you're looking for a solution to a problem, you'll recall this perfectly worded sentence and also the verse that reminds us that *all* things are possible through Christ.

God's blessings to you on this day! Have a blessed day!

### November 27—*Don't let what you can't do stop you from doing what you can do.*—John Wooden

All of us have lived this quote at one time or another. We've faced a large project or mammoth task and became so overwhelmed that instead of at least making a dent in it, we didn't do anything at all. Have you ever looked at an overwhelming situation in your life and said, "I don't even know where to start to try and correct this"? And in many instances, inaction leads us to stay in the same rut. Or, as today's quote says, we let what we can't do stop us from doing what we can do.

When you think about it, this quote can really apply to every single aspect of your life, any goal you've set, any challenge in front of you, any attempt to improve yourself . . . again, every single aspect of your life. Remember, success is the sum of small efforts repeated day in and day out. We just have to be stronger than our excuses! As is often the case, this quote reminds me of another I used a while back: "It is better to do something imperfectly than to do nothing flawlessly."

If we cannot do great things, my prayer is that we will all have the strength and wisdom to do small things in a great way.

God's blessings to you on this day! Have a blessed day!

**November 28**—*Every day is a new beginning. Take a deep breath, smile, and start again!*—**common expression**

Let's break down today's quote into two separate thoughts and take a look at each.

Certainly we all know, as the first sentence points out, that every day is a new beginning, a new start, another chance. However, there are many people—people who are well aware that each morning represents a new start—who immediately latch on to the problems, troubles, issues, and obstacles from the previous day (or days) and bring them into a new day. These folks can forget the new beginning, scratch a new start, and mark off any possibility of another chance. Some people have never figured it out, but each day truly is a new beginning—so dragging yesterday's problems into today will not make tomorrow any better! Let me paraphrase the first sentence: "Put yesterday to rest. Every day is a new beginning."

The second sentence of today's offering caught my attention because I love deep cleansing breaths and smiles. In the middle of a stressful day, a stressful moment, there is nothing better than a deep breath. I recently read a story that talked about the therapeutic and health benefits of taking a deep breath and inhaling to the slow count of five (1001, 1002, etc.), and then holding it for the same count and then exhaling to the same count. I've tried it and it's a game-changer in the middle of a busy day. As far as smiles, many years ago I read a single sentence that has stayed with me: "A warm smile is the universal language of kindness."

So start each day fresh with no baggage, get those deep breaths in, and exercise the universal language of kindness by smiling often!

God's blessings to you on this day! Have a blessed day!

**November 29—***Morning is God's way of saying one more time, go make a difference, touch a heart, encourage a mind, inspire a soul, and enjoy the day.***—anonymous**

Today's quote caught my attention because I'm a morning person. I love to get up early and soak in the quiet and peaceful feeling that early morning brings. I recently read a brilliant but simple sentence about morning by an unknown writer, which I believe wholeheartedly: "Good morning is not just a word; it's an action, a belief to live the entire day well. Morning is the time to set the tone for the rest of the day. Set it right!"

I heard a minister talk a while back and she said something that really stuck with me, so much that it is part of my prayer list every single morning. It goes well with today's offering. She said we should begin every morning with the prayer and belief that "something good is going to happen through me that very day." Say that again and think about how powerful that statement is—"something good is going to happen through me."

What if we all, every single person, began each day with the belief that "through me," something good is going to happen—things like making a difference, touching a heart, encouraging a mind, or inspiring a soul? We all have the potential to be "through me" people every day. And because life is an endless echo, when you become a "through me" person your positive actions will reverberate over and over and over again. What you send out will certainly come back!

God's blessings to you on this day! Have a blessed day!

**November 30—***When you forgive you don't change the past, you change the future.***—Bernard Meltzer**

I would like to add a little to today's quote—not only does forgiveness change the future; it enlarges our future. One of the points that is almost always missed about forgiveness is that it is a gift you give to yourself. It doesn't make you weak; it sets you free.

Many people have carried anger, bitterness, and hatred around so long that they're not even sure what they're upset about. They just know they're mad and they plan to stay mad. Holding on to anger against another person is like drinking poison and expecting the other person to die

These people are prisoners, and their lives are ruled by resentment and retaliation. When I hear people say that they will never, ever forgive I think of a quote by Mark Twain: "Anger is an acid that can do more harm to the vessel in which it is stored than to anything on which it is poured."

Perhaps the very best point I can make in today's offering about forgiveness, and the template we should all use daily, is found in Ephesians 4:32: "[B]e kind to one another, tenderhearted, forgiving one another, even as Christ forgave you.'

How many times have you had to go to Jesus and ask forgiveness? If you're like me, the answer is: many. The four key words in Ephesians 4:32 is "as Christ forgave you." Keep that in mind when deciding whether or not you should forgive somebody. Maybe it's time to enlarge your future, unlock the door, and set a prisoner free—yourself.

God's blessings to you on this day! Have a blessed day!

## December 1—*Life is always a bumpy road; eventually you just learn how to drive on it.*—anonymous

Every person, and I mean every single person, has faced the proverbial "bumpy road." We've all been there; cruising along the straight highway of life, and then out of nowhere we hit a teeth-jarring pothole or sharp curve that's difficult and seemingly impossible to navigate. And many times when that happens, visibility gets poor, our judgment is altered, and our ability to even focus is hindered. It could involve family, a relationship, a financial situation, loss of employment, health issues, and the list goes on and on.

Always remember that it's not the times when we're cruising down the wide-open road with great visibility that defines us. Instead, it's those bumpy roads, sharp curves, and hairpin turns when the road is slippery and it's really difficult to see that shapes our character. Sometimes you have to slow down to a crawl to navigate these rough patches of life's highway, and sometimes you have to stop completely to get your bearings. Other times, when you can't stop and you have to keep moving, you have to turn loose of the steering wheel completely—let go and let God!

A great "bumpy road verse" states: "Trust in the LORD with all your heart, and lean not to your own understanding; in all your ways acknowledge Him, and He shall direct your paths" (Proverbs 3:5–6). That verse could be paraphrased to say: "In all your ways acknowledge him and he shall direct your paths . . . particularly when you're on a bumpy road!"

God's blessings to you on this day! Have a blessed day!

**December 2—*When something bad happens you have three choices. You can either let it defeat you, you can let it destroy you, or you can let it strengthen you.*—common expression**

I'm a believer that today's quote is spot-on accurate! How many times during your life have you seen a person go through a bad experience, and then let that particular event define and destroy them and become their reason to frown and have a bitter, sour attitude about every aspect of life?

On the other hand, we also see people who go through the same struggles and use a difficult experience for motivation to become stronger, better people, who help others and achieve their goals. These folks somehow muster up the inner strength to turn an obstacle into an opportunity, and become victors instead of victims. Many times failing or losing reveals much more about a person's character than winning. Nobody goes through life without some adversity—some seem to have more than their share—but to me, it's how you handle the adversity that reveals your character.

The key point in today's offering is that you cannot, under any circumstances, let life's problems and trials defeat or destroy you. Fight on, attack your problem with prayer, trust in God, and in the end you will be strengthened!

My prayer today is that you take any obstacle in your life and turn it into an opportunity to help yourself and others, and that you also use the struggles in your life to become a stronger person.

God's blessings to you on this day! Have a blessed day!

## December 3—*Each day is filled with thousands of opportunities to change the story of our lives.*—Michael Hyatt

Have you ever noticed how many people, on a daily basis, talk about how they feel stressed, hopeless, anxious, and irritable? I recently heard a speaker talk about this very thing. He said that many, many folks cling to a feeling and an emotion instead of stating our beliefs.

We say we are tired, weak, and have no willpower, instead of saying what we believe: "God is our refuge and strength, a very present help in trouble" (Psalm 46:1). We complain that we can't get this done or don't have the strength to finish a project, instead of loudly proclaiming what we believe: "I can do all things through Christ who strengthens me" (Philippians 4:13).

Instead of stating what we believe we latch on to a feeling, an emotion, and as the old saying goes, "the words we speak become the house we live in." And of course, the house we live in refers to what's within you . . . what's inside you . . . what you carry with you every step you take in life.

As today's offering points out, what you believe or don't believe will do one of two things in your life: create opportunities or create obstacles! And it's because of this that we must—let me say that again, we must—wrap ourselves daily in what we believe. And if daily is not enough, do it hourly or by the minute! Under no circumstances can we let emotions rule our lives. Hold on tightly to your beliefs, develop an attitude of gratitude, and protect the "house you live in."

God's blessings to you on this day! Have a blessed day!

## December 4—*Adversity introduces a man to himself.*—Albert Einstein

Today's quote, in only six words, speaks volumes and explains that it's through adversity, trials, and troubles that we learn what we're made of, who we are, and how we react.

Every person—young and old, rich and poor, and every description in between—at some point in life gets knocked down. It's just a given . . . it's inevitable. But the true character of a person—what separates the victors from the victims—is measured by how we deal with our tests and problems, and how we get back up and move forward.

Issues involving work, finances, relationships, family, and health are only a few of the ways that life can knock us down. One thing that is often overlooked in life is that the strongest people aren't always the ones who win, but the people who don't give up when they lose. And in most instances these defeats are only a temporary condition. Giving up and becoming a victim is what makes them permanent.

The key point in today's offering is that we have a choice; we have the option every minute of every day to choose what direction adversity takes us. I believe the single most important thing we can do when we're faced with the tests and problems of life is to hand them to God and put our trust in him. There is a familiar saying that states, "The shortest distance between a problem and a solution, is the exact same distance between your knees and the floor." Let go and let God, and in the end we will be the victors and not the victims.

God's blessings to you on this day! Have a blessed day!

## December 5—*There can be no positive results through a negative attitude. Think positive! Live positive! Stay positive!*—anonymous

I don't believe there is anything more important than a positive attitude, period. Stop just a moment and think about it: Our attitude has an impact on every single thing we do every day. I have often written and spoken about the importance of a good attitude; it's something that I pray about daily and work on daily. I am very aware of my attitude!

While a lot of folks worry about the clothes they put on each morning, many would be better off to concentrate more on the attitude they dress themselves in each day. A home, a business, a church, a work environment, and our relationship with every single person—attitude is the make-or-break difference in all of them.

I recently read a quote that stated, "There is little difference in people, but that little difference makes a big difference. You see, that little difference is attitude, and the big difference is whether it's positive or negative."

The interesting thing about developing a positive or a negative attitude is that the amount of work is the same. That last sentence might not be completely correct—because based on some of the negative people I've dealt with in my own life, it might take more work to be mad all the time. There are many, many things in life that we cannot control, but our attitude is one of the few things that we control daily.

So, this morning and every morning, when you sort through your closet looking for just the right clothes or accessories to wear to face the day, make the big difference the little difference and add a positive attitude to your daily wardrobe. As today's offering says, think positive, live positive, and stay positive!

God's blessings to you on this day! Have a blessed day!

### December 6—*Success occurs when your dreams get bigger than your excuses.*—anonymous

I recently heard a speaker talking about the many excuses that some people use to not get things accomplished. As I listened, I recalled people in my own life who seem to have a readily available list of excuses as to why they didn't get something done, didn't show up, didn't remember an important event. You get the picture—you've probably dealt with these same types of people.

One important thing I took away from the message is that excuses are not about *having* time; they are about *making* time. There is a huge difference between those two little words. You see, nobody has the time to cram everything into a day that is sometimes required, but when it is really, really important to you, you make the time, period. A second quote by Kenneth Blanchard that fits in well with today's offering states, "There is a difference between interest and commitment. When you're interested in doing something, you do it only when it's convenient. When you're committed to doing something, you accept no excuses; only results."

So, it really comes down to some simple choices. We either find a way or an excuse. We either make an effort or make an excuse. We either make the time or make an excuse. We either see results or see an excuse. The key point in this offering is that just like today's quote states, "Success occurs when your dreams get bigger than your excuses." Remember, excuses are the nails used to build the house of failure!

God's blessings to you on this day! Have a blessed day!

## December 7—*I cried because I have no shoes . . . until I saw a man with no feet. Life is full of blessings. Sometimes we have to look very closely to see them.*—common expression

Today's quote should make all of us take some self-inventory about the countless list of blessings in our life. The main focus of this offering is that we sometimes have to take a good hard look to see just how blessed we are each day.

I want to preface my comments by noting that I have had my share of bad days, and I have hosted many pity parties because life wasn't going the way I wanted it to go. Many of you are well acquainted with bad days and pity parties. Looking back, I find it interesting that all the while I was wallowing in pity I had a family, a job, a roof over my head, food to eat, clothes to wear, and good health. If you're honest, many of you have done the exact same thing!

A few years ago I heard a speaker talk about developing an attitude of gratitude, where you give thanks daily—for me, it was sometimes by the minute—for the countless blessings in your life. It was easy to give thanks for all the big blessings in my life, but I also thanked God for sore muscles, a job I didn't like, and my old red pickup truck. I literally gave thanks to God for everything . . . and I mean everything. It was not an overnight process, but gradually I started looking at the world through different eyes. As I've written and said often, an attitude of gratitude doesn't change the scenery; it just washes the glass clean so we can see the colors we've been missing.

Today I want to challenge you to develop an attitude of gratitude, and then look closely because your life is truly full of blessings!

God's blessings to you on this day! Have a blessed day!

**December 8—*Thank God for what you have, trust God for what you need.*—common expression**

I recently heard a story about trusting in God that is certainly worth repeating: There was a wealthy businessman who owned several successful companies. He had unlimited resources and homes in several locations around the country. Every year he invited several of his longtime employees with their spouses to his estate to spend the weekend. During the stay, the businessman and his wife would treat the employees to the best of everything, with no limit on expenses. One night the group was going out to eat at a ritzy restaurant and had to walk a short distance from the parking lot. As they were walking along, the businessman spotted something by the curb near a couple of discarded cigarette butts. He stopped, bent down, and picked up the object—a weathered looking penny. He looked at it and then put it in his pocket.

One of the wives of the employees was intrigued by what she had witnessed. She didn't say anything at that time, but as the night went on her curiosity got the best of her. Finally, late in the evening she mustered the courage to ask, "Why would a man, with all your wealth, bend down and pick up a dirty penny out of the dirt and put it in your pocket?"

His answer was immediate: "All my success and accomplishments happened because I trusted in God. Every time I see a penny on the ground, or anywhere else, I pick it up and look at it, because written on that penny are the words: 'In God We Trust.' It's a great reminder to me to always, regardless of the situation I'm in, to trust in God."

After I heard this story, I started seeing pennies in parking lots, on convenience store floors, and on busy sidewalks. It seems that every few days, I see a discarded penny. It is an immediate reminder for me to always keep my trust in God. It's been uncanny how on days I have something on my mind regarding a decision that I have to make that I will see, sometimes in odd places, a single penny lying on the ground. It happens so often that I now just say, "Thank you, Jesus," as I smile to myself.

The point of today's offering is simple: Thank God for what you have, trust God for what you need . . . and pick those pennies up, because they provide a great reminder for us all!

God's blessings to you on this day! Have a blessed day!

## December 9—*Blessed are those who see beautiful things in humble places where others see nothing.*—Camille Pissarro

There's an old and familiar saying that states, "One man's junk is another man's treasure." I believe the same can be said for seeing the beauty in life. Two people can look at the exact same thing and, as today's quote says, there are "those who are blessed to see beautiful things in humble places where others see nothing at all."

I suppose the conclusion from this is that much like beauty, God's blessings are in the eye of the beholder. For instance, there are those who completely miss what is happening around them because their idea of a blessing centers on material possessions—homes, cars, boats, and other toys—things that have a dollar amount and a price tag attached. There are other people who understand, through God's love and grace, that the true blessings in life can't be purchased.

In only one sentence, today's gem provides us with a bonanza of truth and a blueprint for what many people spend a lifetime searching for—the good life.

There's a quote I've used in the past that says, "A good life is when you assume nothing, do more, need less, smile often, dream big, cherish small joys, laugh a lot, and realize every single day how blessed you are for what you have." I find it interesting that in defining the good life there is no mention of wealth, status, fame, or fortune. In fact, if you read through this quote slowly, absorb every word, and really let it sink in, you notice that this simple list defining the good life is available to every person every day. Let me say that: every person, every day!

My prayer today is that we all learn to see all those marvelous, wonderful, beautiful things in humble places—God's daily blessings that are all around us!

God's blessings to you on this day! Have a blessed day!

**December 10—*The attitude you bring to the day is what the day will bring to you. Great attitude, great day.*—common expression**

This quote contains an immeasurable amount of truth about the way that each of us should face every single morning.

I am a believer that every single morning when we awaken, we each have a clean slate, a fresh start, and a new opportunity to make that particular day a good one. I am also a huge believer that within each of us we have the remarkable ability to set the tone for that particular day simply by the attitude we choose to embrace.

There is very little difference in people; however, that little difference is attitude and the big difference is whether it's positive or negative. So, as you go through your day, smile at people, be kind, strike up a conversation, ask somebody how they're doing—in short, throw a little sunshine out there today, and I guarantee it comes right back to you.

Many people spend a lot of time each morning choosing their clothes for that particular day, only to leave their home with a soured outlook on the day. These folks would be better served spending more time "dressing up" in a smile, a pleasant disposition, and a good attitude to meet the day. Remember, you're going to get back what you send out each day—great attitude, great day!

God's blessings to you on this day! Have a blessed day!

## December 11—*It's not happiness that brings us gratitude. It's gratitude that brings us happiness.*—anonymous

Sadly, most folks have these two sentences completely reversed. There are many people who believe that once they attain happiness, they will automatically develop a grateful heart.

Sorry, but it does not work that way!

In order to develop an attitude of gratitude we have to dress ourselves with the proper "wardrobe" every single morning. The wardrobe I'm referring to involves the thankful thoughts for our countless blessings that we place between our ears—that area where doubt, fear, discouragement, and anxiety often like to reside.

Developing an attitude of gratitude is really a simple process—we just start giving thanks daily, hourly, or by the minute, if necessary, for all the good things in our lives. And I mean everything—even contrary and negative people who show us daily who we do not want to be like. As I have stated often, an attitude of gratitude does not erase all the negative in our lives, but it does wash clean the window we look through daily, so that we can see all the blessings we sometimes miss.

It's worth repeating: It's not happiness that brings gratitude. Instead, it's gratitude that brings us happiness.

God's blessings to you on this day! Have a blessed day!

## December 12—*Attitudes are contagious . . . make yours worth catching.*—common expression

I am a big believer that one person in a leadership position can set the tone regarding attitude for a family, a church, an office, or an organization. So certainly I am in total agreement that, yes, attitudes really are contagious.

When I read today's offering I was reminded of a quote I've used in the past about lighting candles: "A candle loses nothing by lighting another candle."

When I revisited this quote, my first thought was about weddings I've attended where one candle is used to sometimes light dozens of other candles. But can't the same be said about a human life and our attitudes?

Think about the number of people you reach in person or by social media each day, each month, each year. Then, think about that number in terms of the attitude we have on display daily. Just like lighting candle after candle from one small flame, how many lives could be impacted by our positive attitude if we all took just a moment to offer a smile, a handshake, a small act of kindness, a pat on the back, a sympathetic ear, or an encouraging word?

Think about the impact and good will that would generate if every person started each day with the goal of lighting a single candle that particular day. And just like that one solitary candle, we would lose nothing by providing our light to others. As you go about your daily routine today, try to light a few candles along the way and make your attitude contagious.

Just like a cold or the flu gets passed around a family or an office, my prayer today is that our positive attitude becomes contagious, and that everybody we come in contact with catches it!

God's blessings to you on this day! Have a blessed day!

## December 13—*Whether you think you can or think you can't, you're right!*—Henry Ford

This one-sentence nugget holds an immeasurable amount of truth about the power that the mind and our attitude have in the daily decisions, big and small, that we make. I am a big believer that virtually everything we do in life comes down to a single word: attitude.

We have the choice every single morning, when our feet hit the floor, to choose our attitude, words, and actions for that particular day. We are in control of our attitude from the moment our eyes open; it's our decision alone and we are the only ones who can decide. And certainly, the decisions we make about the attitude we embrace and the words we speak will have a major impact on the "think you can" or "think you can't" question.

Sometimes it's not what's said but who says it that packs the biggest punch. Today's quote was from a gentleman who was a pioneer and a driving force in the creation of the auto industry. He was a man who knew more than just a little about success. Ford also said: "Begin with the determination to succeed and the work is half-done already."

I want to leave you with a great quote that I believe ties this all together quite well: "There is little difference in people, but that little difference makes a big difference. The little difference is attitude, and the big difference is whether it's positive or negative." I believe there is little difference between "can" and "can't" sometimes, and that the deciding factor in that difference is our attitude.

God's blessings to you on this day! Have a blessed day!

**December 14—*A positive attitude gives you power over your circumstances instead of your circumstances having power over you.*—common expression**

Every single morning when our feet hit the floor, we have the option of how the day will go—and this option is based solely on our attitude. Isn't that remarkable that we can wipe the slate clean every day, no matter what happened yesterday, last week, last month, or last year and try again? Certainly we will face struggles and problems almost every day, but again we have the option, with God's help, in how we handle them.

All of us, every single person, have days when we swing and miss and strike out—sometimes multiple times in one day. But the beauty of life is that the very next day, we have another chance to step up to the plate (of life), dig back in, and swing for the fence. We are in charge of our attitude. So, if you're trying to drive down the freeway of life with a flat tire . . . change it! It's the only way you'll get to your destination.

Remember, disappointments, struggles, and problems are inevitable, but letting them defeat you is optional. So this morning and every morning, when you get spiffed up to face the day, add a positive attitude to your daily wardrobe. Having a positive attitude is asking how something *can* be done, rather than saying it *can't* be done!

God's blessings to you on this day! Have a blessed day!

## December 15—*Where there is no struggle there is no strength.*— common expression

I'm convinced that life's struggles do one of two things; they either defeat us or strengthen us. How many times have you seen a person go through a bad experience —and we all go through bad experiences — and then let that particular event defeat them and become their reason to frown and have a bitter, sour attitude about every aspect of life?

On the other hand, we also see people who go through the same struggles and use a difficult experience for motivation to become a stronger, better person, to help others and to achieve their goals. They turn an obstacle into an opportunity and they become the victor instead of the victim. Many times failing or losing reveals much more character about a person than winning. Nobody goes through life without some adversity —some seem to have more than their share —but to me it's how you handle the adversity that reveals your character. It's how you handle the struggle that determines your strength. Some people simply hunker down and quit and others say 'watch this' and then pull themselves back up and fight on.

When I hear the word "strength" mentioned the first word that comes to my mind is "persistence." I'm convinced that any strength developed in life, both physical and mental, comes from persistence. I've learned through the years, while traveling down a few bumpy roads, that persistence is a wonderful and much needed quality.

Persistence, in a nutshell, means you never, ever give in and you never, ever give up regardless what you're facing. Persistence means if you get knocked down seven times . . . you persistently get up eight. I believe with God's help persistence is one of the greatest virtues any person can have or develop. I'm convinced that persistence is a key component of strength and overcoming life's struggles.

My prayer today is that you take any obstacle in your life and turn it into an opportunity to help yourself and others and that you use the struggles in your life to become a stronger person.

God's blessings to you on this day! Have a blessed day!

**December 16—***To achieve great things or to accomplish small things the formula is the exact same—start where you are, use what you have, and do all you can.***—Arthur Ashe**

Everything we do in life has to have a first step involved. And of course, that first step is always going to be the hardest one. Even when we're at the end of that thousand-mile journey, the last step will not be as hard or as difficult as that first one. But while that first step is the hardest one, there is also joy, freedom, and excitement in moving a new direction.

I love this quote because it's in the present—start where you are, use what you have, and do all you can. That means right now! There's no procrastination, no putting it off, no waiting for a first-of-the-year resolution. Not tomorrow, not next week or next month . . . right now!

My prayer for all of us is that regardless of whether we are trying to achieve great things or accomplish small things, with God's help and grace, we will have the strength, stamina, and determination to take that difficult first step . . . and then keep on stepping.

God's blessings to you on this day! Have a blessed start-where-you-are, use-what you-have, and do-all-you-can day!

## December 17—*Worry is a misuse of imagination.*—Dan Zadra

Almost every day I remember little things that my mom and dad said about a variety of subjects, particularly life. And of course, as other baby boomers like me have learned, I also now repeat many things my parents said—things that annoyed me when I was younger but that I now see as small nuggets of gold and the gospel. Yes, you're right—I've turned into my parents!

This past week I recalled a day many years ago when I said something to my mom about being worried, and she gave me advice that I still remember.

"You can worry until you make yourself sick, and it will not change one thing that is going to happen," she told me. Then she added this gem: "Worrying will rob you of your happiness. You need to always remember that 99.9 percent of what you worry about will never happen." When I read this quote about "using your imagination to create something you don't want," I thought of her wise words from decades past.

I heard a speaker recently talk about worry. His comment is certainly worth tucking away: "Worrying about every little thing that could happen is like walking around with an umbrella on a sunny day . . . waiting for it to rain." So maybe the moral of today's offering is to put your "worry-umbrella" away for good, and quit using your imagination to create something you don't want!

God's blessings to you on this day! Have a blessed day!

## December 18—*Tough times never last, but tough people do.*—Robert Schuller

Just to put it bluntly, sometimes we have to be tougher than the problems we're facing. In fact, a good dose of stubbornness, perseverance, and a strong backbone will carry you a long way when dealing with some of the struggles life throws our way.

It's amazing how a single sentence or phrase can catch our attention and stay with us for decades. When I was in high school I recall a coach/teacher using a phrase I have thought of countless times throughout my life: "When the going gets tough, the tough get going." I can't tell you the times in my life when things were not going well that I recalled those simple words. And it would never fail that when I did think of that phrase, there was always something that welled up inside of me and made me square my shoulders, work harder, become more determined, get tougher, and get going. I learned many years ago that today's offering is 100 percent accurate—tough times never last but tough people do!

Many people experience a failure (or failures) in life and then use that as a standby excuse to never try again. Do not become that person! It's been said that hardships and failure often prepare ordinary people for an extraordinary destiny. I truly believe that, because it seems that a constant rule for people who have enjoyed success is that they simply refuse to give up.

Somehow these people use setbacks, failures, obstacles, the doubts and negativity of others, and the word "no" as motivation to reach their goals. These folks learn that it's not a failure to get knocked down—failure comes when we refuse to get back up. Let me hit you with a double-whammy as a final thought today: Tough times never last, but tough people do, and when the going gets tough the tough get going! Now, toughen up, and get going!

God's blessings to you on this day! Have a blessed day!

**December 19**—*Every new beginning comes from some other beginning's end.*—**anonymous**

As we roll through the final days of the year, there are many people already looking ahead to January 1 with a long and growing list of resolutions. For many folks a new year represents a clean slate, and so people make resolutions to improve and be better at this and that. But one of the beautiful aspects of life is that we don't have to wait for a new calendar, a new week, a new month, or a new year. We have the ability to start from any second, any minute, or any hour of any day we choose and start a brand-new beginning.

The main point in today's offering is that we have that ability every single morning to put on a positive attitude, to make the day and shape the day any way we want. Remember, you can't go back and make a new start, but within you and with God's grace and help, there is the ability to make a brand-spanking-new ending! Today is called the present, and rightfully so, because it's a present from God. It's a present that contains another chance, a new opportunity, and the hope to be a better person. The second your eyes open every morning, that present is waiting on you. And just as today's gem points out, new beginnings are often disguised as painful endings. We just have to have the courage and strength to take that first step.

So, the choice is yours and totally yours—what will your new beginning be?

God's blessings to you this day! Have a blessed day!

## December 20—*There is no education like adversity.*—common expression

Many people are graduates of the "school of hard knocks"—the imaginary school folks often mention where they have gained an education about the difficulties that life can deal us. As for me, I hold a doctorate degree from that infamous institution.

Seriously, when I read today's one-sentence quote I thought about the people, including me, who have used this reference often. Certainly, as today's offering points out, there is no education like adversity.

We would all like to have bright, sunny days when there's not a cloud in the sky and everything is moving along like a well-oiled machine. But we all know, in reality, that's not life at all. Life is a wonderful gift every day—but some days life is not easy. In fact, saying it's not easy is an understatement because some days it's just downright hard. That's what makes this quote so accurate. If you've lived through some adversity, you get it; you understand exactly what I'm talking about. And if you've lived a sheltered life with zero adversity, there is no need for me to try and explain. Either you get it or you don't!

Adversity helps develop character, compassion for others, honesty with ourselves, perseverance, patience, and empathy. There are even days when adversity provides a great lesson in humility, because we get to eat a large slice of humble pie without a Diet Coke to wash it down.

I'm a firm believer that every obstacle in life provides us with a great opportunity, with God's help, to grow as people, learn from mistakes, and most importantly help others who might be trying to navigate troubled waters or find themselves perched on a wobbly branch in the tree of life.

Remember, adversity does not build character—it reveals it!

God's blessings to you this day! Have a blessed day!

### December 21—*Obstacles do not block the path; they are the path.*—anonymous

On our way to trying to achieve our goals or start a new chapter in our lives, we often encounter obstacles in our path. It doesn't just happen to you; it happens to everybody with a dream or a goal or a desire to change.

When we come to these life obstacles that are squarely in our path, we have three choices— just three. We can find a way to get over or around the proverbial brick wall that's in our way, run through it, or beat our heads against it and give up. Obviously, the last choice is the least preferable.

Being a person who has faced more than my share of obstacles in my path, I can honestly say that these walls actually serve two very important purposes. First, I believe some walls are placed in our paths to see just how much we really want the goal or the change we are striving to accomplish. Secondly, if you find a path that does not contain a few obstacles along the way, you're probably on a road that doesn't lead anywhere.

I love the quote by Christopher Reeve, "A hero is an ordinary individual who finds the strength to persevere and endure in spite of overwhelming obstacles."

My advice on obstacles is simple: Be a hero and find your strength; trust in God; conquer anything in your path; and finally, never, ever give up.

God's blessings to you on this day! Have a blessed day!

**December 22—***It's not the critic who counts, or the man who points out how the strong man stumbles or where somebody could have done better. The credit belongs to the man in the arena whose face is marred by dust and sweat and blood.***—Teddy Roosevelt**

While the sideline is a safe place, I want to be the man in the arena who is mentioned in today's quote. Even if it means dust and sweat and getting bloodied once in a while, in the game of life I have absolutely no desire to be a sideline guy.

Clearly, today's offering is an excellent analogy of life—you're either on the sidelines pointing out those who stumble or the faults of others, or you are in the arena fighting the fight daily. That fight could be raising children, dealing with an illness, a difficult job, or an insane schedule. It could be working two or three jobs trying to make ends meet, trying to rebound and rebuild from a broken relationship, or trying to recover from an addiction. There are countless life battles that place us every day in the arena of life, working and scratching our way along.

The message in today's offering is simple: Regardless what type of battle you are dealing with today, with God's help stay in the arena and fight with all you have in you. My prayer today is that God will give you strength, courage, wisdom, and a double heaping-helping of hope.

God's blessings to you on this day! Have a blessed day!

**December 23**—*Be somebody who makes everybody feel like somebody.*—**common expression**

It takes a rare and exceptional person to be able to pull off what today's offering talks about—the ability to make everybody feel like somebody. Certainly, that should be one of our goals, and our prayer daily should be to connect with all people in a positive way.

Our daily interaction with people is so important, in ways that we might not even realize. Somethings as simple and as casual as saying "hi" or "good morning" to a stranger might very well be the only interaction that person has all day with another person. What might seem like nothing to one person could mean the world to somebody else.

We should begin every day with the prayer and belief that something good is going to happen through us that very day. Say that again, and think about how powerful that statement is—something good is going to happen through us. What if we all, every single person, began each day with the belief that through us, something good is going to happen? Maybe it's just a smile, a kind word to a stranger, a pat on the back, a call to an old friend, or any number of countless things, but we all have the potential to be a "through me" person every day.

It's been said often that a person's true character is most accurately measured by how you treat those who can do nothing for you. And keep in mind, a smile, a kind word, or a pleasant attitude can make two people feel good—the other person and you!

God's blessings to you on this day! Have a blessed day!

**December 24**—*The best of all gifts around any Christmas tree is the presence of a happy family all wrapped up in each other.*—**Burton Hillis**

Every day of the week has a distinct and different feel to it, something about that particular day that sets it apart from the others. Every holiday also has its own special feel. Give that some thought and you can conjure up in your mind what a scorching hot Fourth of July is supposed to feel like, or memories of a cold, crisp Thanksgiving Day.

But in my estimation, there is no holiday that has the special feel, the excitement, enthusiasm, and joy that is found on Christmas Eve. My best memories of Christmas—kids, grandkids, and loved ones seem to always drift back to "the night before Christmas."

Enjoy the holiday, enjoy your family, reach out to at least one old friend, give a gift to somebody you don't know, try to help somebody in need, and keep it planted firmly in your mind what we're celebrating—the birth of our Savior!

God's blessings to you on this day! Have a wonderful Christmas Eve and a blessed day!

**December 25—*Want to keep Christ in Christmas? Feed the hungry, clothe the naked, forgive the guilty, welcome the unwanted, care for the ill, love your enemies, and do unto others as you would have them do to you.*—Steve Maraboli**

The common theme in this book has been to take a quote and then add a few paragraphs of my own as a daily offering. However, when I read today's quote through a couple of times I realized that there is nothing for me to add to this . . . nothing . . . because it's perfect!

So, from my little corner of the world to yours . . . Merry Christmas! And if you want to really remember the reason for the season, just read through this quote one more time.

God's blessings to you on this day! Have a merry Christmas and a blessed day!

**December 26—*In short, the Christmas spirit is the Christ spirit that makes our hearts glow in brotherly love and friendship and prompts us to kind deeds of service.*—anonymous**

This quote is perfect for the point I hope to make today—December 26. Almost everybody loves the weeks and days leading up to Christmas. Certainly, it's hectic and stressful, but there is this feeling that overtakes people, including me. We're more thoughtful, less easily angered, and more caring and concerned about needy children and the homeless. We reach out to people in our lives we haven't talked to in months to offer season's greetings, and we gear up for family gatherings trying to make them perfect in every way.

Everything builds toward this gigantic climax on December 25, when all rejoice and everything seems right with the world. Then on December 26, almost like a switch has been flipped, we trudge ahead, business as usual—until we are overtaken once again next year by that wonderful thing called "Christmas spirit."

But why does it have to be that way? Read the quote again: "the Christmas spirit is the Christ spirit that makes our hearts glow in brotherly love and friendship and prompts us to kind deeds of service." Here's the key point in today's offering: How much better would the world be if we all carried just a little of the Christ spirit with us from December into January, February, March, and all of the coming year? I believe we all know the answer to that question! Just a little something for you to think about on this, the day after Christmas!

God's blessings to you on this day! Have a blessed day!

### December 27—*Be sure to taste your words before you spit them out.*—anonymous

There are two things in life that can't be taken back, can't be recalled—time and words. While time is extremely important, I believe it pales in comparison to words. I see every day the power that words have, both good and bad, positive and negative.

Say a kind and caring word to somebody and you can make their day; make a hateful, angry and mean-spirited comment and you can ruin their day. Words are powerful and everlasting. Words can heal and unite, or damage and divide.

Again, today's quote is one that I wish I had learned (and practiced) years ago. But better late than never, I suppose. Choose your words wisely, chew on your words if necessary, roll them around in your mind, or bite your tongue until it bleeds . . . but don't speak in anger. We've all heard the phrase, "You can't un-ring the bell." Well, the same holds true with what you say. You can't "un-say" words. Once those angry, hurtful words are said, just like time you can't recall them; you can't bring them back.

Today's offering is worth repeating: "Be sure to taste your words before you spit them out."

God's blessings to you on this day! Have a blessed day!

## December 28—*Savor this day, because it will never come again.* —anonymous

I read today's quote and I thought it would be interesting to look up the definition of the word "savor," just so we will know exactly how the unknown writer wanted us to handle this day, a day that will never come again. According to dictionary.com, the word "savor" means "the power to excite; breathe in; to give oneself the enjoyment of; to breathe in."

Read through that definition again and let it sink in slowly. Then consider how you will approach today—a day that will never, ever come again. We get one chance at it on this day—just one chance, that's it. And the plain fact that today will never come again puts even more importance and significance on that definition.

Think about the many people you will come in contact with today, and then apply that definition. Think about the many different situations you will encounter today and then, again, apply the definition of "savor." Something as simple as reaching out to an old friend, saying a pleasant "good morning" to a stranger, or holding a door for somebody you don't know might be the only positive interaction that person has on this day—a day that will never come again.

Remember, it was Mother Teresa who said, "Kind words can be easy to speak but their echoes are truly endless."

God's blessing to you on this day—a day you should "savor" that will not come again. Have a blessed day!

**December 29—***If the only prayer you ever say is "thank you," that will be enough.***—common expression**

Each day when I thank God for my many blessings, I always quickly add that I am also thankful for the knowledge and understanding that those blessings flow through God. I have done nothing to earn them and I've done nothing to deserve them, and I feel blessed to totally understand that.

We've all heard the question asked, "What if you woke up this morning with only the things you thanked God for yesterday?" Ponder that question and give it some deep thought before you answer.

If you're like me, that's a sobering thought. We are all guilty from time to time of taking our countless blessings for granted. We all get caught up on the hustle and bustle of life and neglect giving thanks daily—or perhaps even hourly—for the countless, unlimited, infinite blessings in our lives. And when you look at the beauty and the gifts we enjoy such as family, friends, and health, and then add in the tiny miracles that take place in our lives daily from the time we open our eyes each morning until we close them at night, using words like "countless," "unlimited," and "infinite" to describe our blessings is spot-on accurate.

Perhaps the best way to answer the question I posed earlier is to give thanks to God every day for all things—make every day Thanksgiving. I recently read a story that pointed out that a grateful and thankful heart is one that can find the countless blessings in seemingly mundane, everyday life. And once you find and recognize those countless blessings, be sure to say "Thank you!"

God's blessing to you this day! Have a blessed and thankful day!

## December 30—*Gratitude turns what we have into enough.*
## —Melody Beattie

Most of us have heard and recognize this quote about attitude. But today, I want to dig a little deeper about a word I write about often: attitude.

Every time I read a quote about attitude, I think of a great passage written by Dr. Charles Swindoll. It is one of the greatest and most truthful passages I've ever read and it spells out exactly the importance of our daily attitude. I have used it several times when I've been asked to speak and I have it typed out and taped to a shelf above my desk. You will recognize an oft-used sentence near the end (I used it in an earlier devotional, in fact). Here it is:

> The longer I live, the more I realize the importance of choosing the right attitude in life. Attitude is more important than facts. It is more important than your past; more important than your education or your financial situation; more important than your circumstances, your successes, or your failures; more important than what other people think or say or do.
>
> It is more important than your appearance, your giftedness, or your skills. It will make or break a company . . . a church . . . a . . . home.
>
> You have a choice each day regarding the attitude you will embrace. . . . You cannot change the years that have passed, nor can you change the daily tick of the clock. . . . You cannot change the decisions or reactions of other people. And you certainly cannot change the inevitable. . . . What you *can* do is play on the one string that remains—your attitude.
>
> I am convinced that life is 10 percent what happens to me and 90 percent how I react to it. The same is true for you.[4]

---

[4] Swindoll, "Attitudes."

As we prepare to flip the calendar over to a brand-new year and a brand-new set of challenges, my prayer today is that we tuck this gem away. And when that 10 percent of life happens to us, we can all recall these wonderful words and use our 90 percent to react in a positive, Christlike way. Remember, "Gratitude turns what we have into enough"!

God's blessings to you on this day! Have a blessed day!

### December 31—*Tomorrow is the first blank page of a 365-page book. Write a good one.*—Brad Paisley

As we come to the end of another year, most all of us will pause and reflect on the year just passed and the brand-new one that lies before us. Many of us will also resolve to make improvements in our life in a variety of different ways.

I love today's quote simply because it's a great reminder that each of us has within us the ability and strength to make the coming year what we want it to be. If I could hang a title on that 365-page book that has all blank pages I would call it "Opportunity." Because you see, you hold the pen in your hand. You are the author and what is written—or isn't written—on all those blank pages is determined by you and you alone.

I want to emphasize this, because what will fill those blank pages for all of us really boils down to two things: We either accept conditions as they exist in our life, or we accept the responsibility to change them. Will the pages of next year's book be filled with optimism, kindness, purpose, an attitude of gratitude, positive thoughts, and understanding? Or will those pages be filled with pessimism, negativity, doubt, fear, resentment, excuses, and blame?

Again, you are the writer. You are the author and regardless what happens in your life, the words that fill those pages will be determined by you. Let me repeat and emphasize that one more time: What is written will be determined by you and you alone. My prayer today is that we can all look back one year from today and be happy, satisfied, and proud of the way we filled those blank pages. It's up to you and you alone—write a good one.

God's blessings to you on this day! From my little corner of the world to yours . . . Happy New Year!

Printed in the United States
by Baker & Taylor Publisher Services

Every person, regardless of who they are or where they live, goes through difficult times. But it's what we do with those difficult times that shows our character and resolve and determines the roads we choose in life. *Offerings* is a yearlong guide to help deal with the inevitable adversity in life.

Signs of struggle are all around us, and negativity is not hard to come by. Everyone needs hope, and *Offerings* provides that hope, one day at a time, all year long. It only takes a few minutes to read each offering, and there is one for each day of the year, allowing the reader to start each new day with a positive outlook on life.

Jim Muir is a graduate of Rend Lake College and has work history in coal mining, newspaper, radio, and public service that spans more than 45 years. He was elected in 2016 as Franklin County Circuit Clerk. Jim and his wife, Lisa Kay, reside in Sesser, IL. They have six children and eleven grandchildren.

**$14.99**
SEL021000 SELF-HELP /
Motivational & Inspirational

ISBN 978-1-632694-92-8